ANSWERED BY FIRE

CORRIE TEN BOOM PREPARED ME FOR NOW

SHARON JACKSON

This Book Published By:

RainDancing101.com
5260 78th Avenue North #1773 Pinellas Park, Fl. 33781
SharonJackson@Iwrotefire@yahoo.com

All rights reserved. No part of this book may be reproduced or transmitted in any form or by any means, electronic, or mechanical, including photocopying, recording or by any information storage and retrieval system without written permission from the author, except for the use of brief quotation in a review.

Copyright © 2014 By Sharon Jackson
Revised 2019

First Printing 2014

Library of Congress Catalogue

Table of Contents

Dedication

This book is dedicated to everyone everywhere
who has discovered goodness.
Who know that all goodness emanates
from the heart of a loving Father.
And in the deepest, darkest pit of sorrow, rejection and despair, it is most often the loving heart of a true believer who is there to reach down and pick up someone like me.

Introduction

Answered By FIRE
Corrie ten Boom Prepared Me For Now

You are invited on a journey. One that will lead you into the life of an ordinary woman and her own lifelong search for wholeness. The story here is not for everyone. It begins at graveside, with the shocking finality of death and the end of a traumatic relationship. She then traces that relationship to its stormy beginning.

Slowly, you will see purpose and meaning being woven into Sharon's empty life, much like a tapestry, only to see her fall again. And again. What circumstances intervene to bring her back to her search for truth? Nothing short of a miracle. Just one of many. Once a little boy clung to his mother's side, always asking 'why, why, why'. When he became a teenager, he no longer asked her 'why' - he *had* all the answers! But when he became an adult, he'd learned what *a few of life's questions are!* Like him, Sharon feels she's learned what a few of life's more important questions are. Journey with her and find reason to hope and to be encouraged. It is my hope that you do. Sharon Jackson.

Don't only practice your art
but force your way into its secrets.
For it and knowledge can, raise men to the divine.
Ludwig van Beethoven

Foreword

Sharon knows what it is to be helpless, hopeless, broken-hearted and alone. Yet, hers has become a life full of amazing events and fascinating people, entire chapters devoted to many of them. Some are celebrities... like Corrie ten Boom, whose life story was portrayed in the book and movie *The Hiding Place*, with whom Sharon's family was privileged to spend time.

Since that epic week that was spent in private meetings, dinners, hotel rooms, banquets and concluded at the convention center, Sharon has come to realize how much Corrie influenced her life. A longer association followed, detailed inside this book. More recently, Sharon realized that Corrie's influence indeed trained her for the present era. You will find much of that preparation shared here. Sharon had many mentors, but none like Corrie.

Sharon Jackson (@Iam_4ewe) just *tells her story* of miracles, chock full of shocking truth.

Come grow with her as you read along. Due to the fact Sharon lived with a Muslim, faced tough decisions regarding abortion, and many moral decisions about her own life - this book is controversial by its need to reveal the truths Sharon found, and the wholeness that came to her.

However the media will call her book 'controversial' because her story intrudes on many of society's *sacred cows*! Yet, Sharon expects to harness those winds of controversy in order to win those who are hurting and *hungry* for the same truth she found - in a world that's filled with myths and half-truths. Read her story. Then give this book to someone you Love.

He drew a circle and shut me out;
Heretic, rebel, a thing to flout.
But Love and I had the wit to win;
We made a circle and drew him in.
Edwin Markham

PART I

The Siege

"Only 20% of us came out alive. And when I was free I knew I had work to do. Betsie would say to me, "Corrie, we must go over the world because we have a message from experience that the LIGHT of Jesus Christ is STRONGER than the DEEPEST DARKNESS!"

Corrie ten Boom

Is there a single ingredient that could positively impact you, or our negative world? *Yes! Information.* No weapon is so powerful as 'information'. I want to kindle brushfires in people's minds and hearts for *their own new beginning*! To inspire them to realize their own value, in our culture, and in their own arena of life. *Author.*

1

A Final Rejection

I stood motionless and alone, watching the vault slowly lowered into the ground. There was no tent or pretty green carpet, nor baskets of flowers to lessen the pain. The sun sat to our left, leaving a chill in the air.

I shuddered.

Only my daughter Rhonda and her daughter Krista, age 8, stood there with me.

Most mourners are spared such finality. But not here. Not today.

It was fitting however that other mourners had gone, including a huge family of siblings. I stood there with her to see her come to her final rest on earth.

Not lonely. *Alone.*

A friend named Pat remained, who stood at a distance so as not to intrude. I appreciated her presence, and her consideration of this moment. The imprint from the vault seemed to blaze up at me with such finality as it was slowly lowered in the grave – Ovah S. Williams, 1922-1992.

Suddenly, the greatest emptiness I'd ever known overwhelmed me. *"My mother's dead!"* my mind screamed. Gone from my life forever. I watched as the backhoe began to drop cold dirt onto that shiny nameplate, covering it completely. That great emptiness now turned into an even greater sorrow.

Yet, the hurt would not end at that graveside.

Friends and loved ones had packed the funeral home and then trailed to the cemetery for final services, only to be met with her final irony -the wrong plot was dug.

Like an enigma, her life puzzled me. At her death, I was aware of a kinder woman than I'd ever known in my lifetime. One I'd somehow never known. That gentler side was most evident from the warm circle of friends who'd crowded the mortuary, and brought in food. Mostly strangers to me, I now felt moved by their genuine caring. I'd known Mom only as distant - and sometimes hard - capable of emotion yet never toward me.

Who *was* this woman, who took to her grave the secret of who my father was? My blood type had revealed her secret past, just fifteen months before she died. I wrote of my hurt and anger, yet she never mentioned or acknowledged the letter. Our relationship improved after that letter, however, and I'd felt we'd at last resolved our differences during my long stay with her the month before she died.

Now it no longer mattered. She'd reached from the grave to hurt again.

The bag of personal items from the hospital lay on a garage shelf. Musing through it, I picked up the last book she would read as an avid reader of romance novels. It was titled "Amethyst Meadows." Appropriately, it was a story of a woman who had traveled to a distant city attempting to settle a tangled inheritance.

Yet, time would reveal that my own inheritance was not as entangled as I'd thought. Mom had taken great pains, it seemed, to leave my half-brother a fortune in cars, life insurance and investments plus the house she'd lived in 30 years. And she'd left only household possessions to me - *to transport 1200 miles home.*

Even of those, anything of value was mysteriously missing upon my arrival only hours following her death. I'd paid this woman honor - though unmerited - as long as she'd lived. And I'd cherished whatever crumbs of favor came my way.

Too late, I hated her.

These chains, these chains, so hard to break!
Not even for my loved ones' sake!
A mother's love, unreconciled.
A daughter's loss, who felt reviled;
Hardness left in word and deed.
But at the end, she planted seed...

2

High Deception

Harsh noises and loud voices from the army camp were a far cry from the serenity of plowed fields and grazing cattle on the gentle hills of Kentucky. Ovie (as she preferred to be called) missed the peaceful valleys of the Appalachian foothills where she grew up.

***These* were sounds of war.** Foreign sounds and a foreign place, far away from anything familiar. Nothing seemed *peaceful* here.

Ovie had accompanied her husband James to Fort Carson near Colorado Springs just months after the World War II began. Like many young men then, he'd enlisted in the army right after Pearl Harbor.

Life had taken an ominous turn for all Americans that December 7, 1941, at the bombing of Pearl Harbor. It forced our government to join the war enveloping Europe then, and now the entire world.

Ovie watched through the window as soldiers marched by the house where they lived on base, each one in step to orders barked by a drill sergeant accompanying them -LEFT, LEFT, LEFT, RIGHT, LEFT. Nearby, jeeps and tanks rolled noisily down the street, headed to the railroad down the mountain. She was homesick and miserable.

Newlyweds when they arrived, Ovie and James had married just a few days following Pearl Harbor. James trained as a gunner, but he was stationed there long term due to his experience with horses. He trained horses and pack mules for shipment to North Africa and also to Europe. The mountain region on Pike's Peak prepared them for rough terrain where vehicles had difficulty traveling overseas. James could lead a horse even without a halter.

Like countless others of her generation, Ovie had been part of the mass gravitation from rural communities to the big money found in northern cities, in factory work. This move became known as the *Great Industrial Revolution*. It, and the war, revolutionized life in America. Paychecks that had only been a dream during the Great Depression were now a reality. And after the war began, working in those factories became more than just a job. It was an act of patriotism and a concerted effort to win the war. The tanks, guns, planes, and bombs needed for war required laborers to produce them.

War is big business.

Since most able bodied men went to war, women soon took their places on the assembly line. Perhaps no event so changed the face of the American family. Women have worked outside the home ever since. Instead of growing their food in gardens, they now bought them at the corner market. Instead of making their own clothes, they now shopped for them. And instead of rearing their own children – someone else did. First it was family, then babysitters, then *anyone*.

It was easy for Ovie to move to the city. Sis, her older sister, had already married and lived in the north. Soon Ovie was able to find work in a textile factory, known as a cotton mill.

It was there that she met a tall - yes - dark and handsome half-Cherokee Indian. Soft spoken, he would steal her heart for a lifetime. She liked his dark complexion, and high cheek bones. She'd never met a man like him. He always spoke her name as "Ovah", like honey rolling from his lips. She swooned.

But, here in Colorado Springs, not even the splendor of the snow-capped Rocky Mountains, nor her love for James could dull her longing for something - anything - familiar in this frightening new world. She marveled at how 'war' had changed her own life, taking her far from home, family and friends. But not just her life - everyone she knew.

Growing up on the family farm during the Great Depression had not been easy. In those days, people lived strictly from what they were able to grow on the farm. There was no other option in the country. They grew large gardens and tended orchards in summer, and canned in the autumn for the long winter ahead. When fruit ripened, they buried it deep in the ground, where year round temperature remains 54 degrees. They raised poultry for eggs and meat, especially on Sundays. Cattle were regarded as too valuable to slaughter, so chicken was the mainstay at the dinner table. But after a good frost, an occasional hog was killed, salted down and hung in the smokehouse to cure; kept and eaten until hot weather arrived.

The only purchases necessary in those days were corn meal and flour for baking needs. Money from the sale of eggs usually paid for those, plus any extras like baking powder. Ovie had seven siblings then. She and her brother Max were the oldest next to Sis, who was always frail. She liked to work inside the house and tend the smaller children. That left the farm work to them. It was also their duty to walk the long journey to the closest store to buy meal and flour. They walked barefooted, preserving their only pair of shoes for school.

The corn meal and flour sacks became heavy on that long walk home. But Ovie didn't mind. She got to choose the colorful patterns that would soon become school dresses for herself and her sisters. Her Mom, Sally made one for each of the six girls. Egg money also permitted Sally to order dress patterns from the Sears catalog.

On school nights, each girl would hand wash their dress, and iron it in the morning in front of the huge iron, wood burning cook stove that stood in the middle of the kitchen. Sally always said, *'Being poor was no excuse for being dirty!'* This was long before electricity or inside plumbing came to the countryside where Ovie lived. Cumberland Dam providing power wasn't built for another twenty years.

Ovie and Max chopped the firewood, milked the cows, and worked in the fields. It was hard work, but Ovie was strong and competitive. Quite the tomboy, she loved beating the boys in the community riding horseback. No one owned tractors back then either.

She and Max used those horses to put in the crops, plowing the fields and raking the hay.

Hay and corn had to be stored in the barns in order to get the horses and cattle through long winter months. Ovie would rather be free outside than doing inside. That was for *sissies.*

Sally, who was full Irish, also tended the beautiful flowers in the yard. Husband Mack, took care of the heavy duty farm work like snaking logs from the woods for firewood and taking the cows to be bred. He built horse-drawn wagons for other farmers in the area.

A space heater in the living room kept one end of the farmhouse tolerable on wintry days. Sally's cook stove made the other end bearable. Winter nights, the children took a warm brick upstairs to their feather beds, and crawled underneath a mountain of handmade quilts to keep warm. Only a tin roof separated them from the elements –and a warm brick. But the space heater downstairs stayed warm most of the night, the heat rising to their bedroom. Mack rose early to light the fire again. Times were hard growing up then. But they were hard everywhere! City folks stood in soup lines in cities across America just to survive the Depression.

At least, Ovie's family always had plenty of wonderful food!

Sally and Mack both worked six days, which meant everyone else did too. But Sundays were a day of rest and fun. After church, Sally's colorful yard would fill with friends and neighbors. *Dinner on the lawn* was her custom before it ever became fashionable. Everyone was welcome to enjoy her twelve course meal (seriously!), in the midst of blooming flowers. Between cooking, quilting, sewing and canning, she always had time for her flowers!

Laughter on the weekends made up for the hard work week. Though demanding, life seemed simple and uncomplicated then.

Eventually, the younger children became old enough to take on some of Ovie's tasks. So she began thinking of a better life. The big city life was calling her by name.

At that time, higher education seemed reserved for the ultra-rich. School of any kind was not a priority among rural folks. Some didn't finish elementary school. *Survival* had been the main priority far too long. (I was in high school before Mom got her high school diploma through her work). But Ovie was confident that life would be better *somewhere else,* and she'd wanted one of those big paychecks others came back and told her about.

When she first went to stay with Sis, Mom told me she got a job at a local dime store, making $4 a week. This was 1941. Now in the highest mountains of Colorado at Fort Carson, Ovie had watched regiment after regiment of soldiers train at the army base, and then leave for their assignments. It seemed an endless procession piled upon endless days.

An elderly neighbor couple befriended Ovie and James. He was never home much, it seemed. She appreciated their kindness. Ovie worked part time in a little town nearby to pass the time. But she *still* had too much of it.

Word had come from home that Max too had joined the war. She feared for her brother, knowing he was sent to Europe.

Several of James' buddies had been killed and two of her childhood friends. Another was missing.

With James gone so much, Ovie was lonely.

War - and preparation for war - was frightening to her, especially when she was alone. James also felt those stresses. A gnawing gut feeling told him that he too would go to the front lines soon. Somehow, he and his friends sensed this war was unlike any other. London was being bombed, with no end in sight. Terrifying rumors of Hitler's death camps had surfaced, yet no one really talked about it. *It couldn't be true.* This was the 20th century for God's sake! It was just too barbaric to be true. Ovie knew that much of the time James spent away from home was *not working.* James began to spend more time with his buddies. Only they seemed to understand. Drinking dulled the throb of that fear in his gut when he faced reality, and the news of buddies lost.

Thanksgiving came. Now, Ovie could hardly bear the thought of another holiday season away from home. From the other room, she heard strains of "My Old Kentucky Home" playing on the radio. For a moment, she allowed herself to imagine waking up in Sally's house again....

The familiar smell of her huge flakey warm biscuits wafting in the air, she knew there would be eggs, sausages, bacon, homemade jams, freshly churned butter, honey and apple butter on the table. Just when she thought she might hear Sally call for breakfast, she snapped back to reality.

WAR.

She knew it wouldn't happen. Besides, she feared for James. She loved him dearly, and wouldn't leave him alone, especially during holidays. Her dreams of going home would have to wait.

That sweet old couple then dropped by again to invite both Ovie and James to Thanksgiving dinner at their home. Gratefully, Ovie thanked them, and said 'Yes.' But James was called on duty that day. She ate alone.

Those lonely days would soon be forgotten as James was ordered to Italy the next April. Ovie boarded a train to return to her sister's in the Midwest, and take up her old job at the cotton mill. She could visit Sally weekends.

Ovie was unaware that the high altitude of the Rocky Mountains can affect a woman's menstrual cycle. When she got home, she discovered that she was already five months pregnant with *me*. She was also unaware that Thanksgiving weekend would resurface to haunt her in stunned amazement over four decades later...

3

Walker Was A Dog

I was born a War-Baby - that always seemed appropriate to me. As a child, if I wasn't in a war, I was causing one. I was born August 16, 1944. This was just prior to Baby-Boomers who were born after the war ended. Dad was in Italy when I was born. He would be overseas another year when the war ended. Italy was where some of the bloodiest battles occurred. The horses he trained played a big role there due to the mountainous terrain.

Mom stayed with Sis for a while when she got back. She never seemed to feel close to her, except for ties of blood, but she did feel compelled to compete with her all her life. Sis's marriage, life, and children were always 'perfect' you see, and Mom always had trouble *measuring up* to Sis's image of her.

She never did, but she quit trying near the end of her life.

Effie was a childhood friend from Kentucky, and had married Max before he went off to war. She and Mom were close all their lives. After returning from Fort Carson, Mom confided to Effie she didn't feel cut out to be a mother. Even though back alley abortions were performed then, they were illegal. So there was really nothing that could be done at this point because Mom was too far along in pregnancy with me to safely abort.

I was a Wednesday child, said to mean 'full of woe'. Mom tried to please the family and play the part of a happy mother, especially to Sis - who even named me - which I learned only after Mom died. I don't know why she felt the need to compete with Sis, but she did. Pressure, I presume.

But Mom resented her role as a mother, and soon sought her old job back. It was her patriotic duty, she felt. At first she paid Effie, then a sister, then *anyone* to care for me in her absence.

Many times, she said in my presence, "I should never have become a mother."

When Dad came home, they used his veteran's program to buy a house down the street from both Sis and Effie and Max who lived across the street from one another. Max had returned home safely too, but not whole, a man who drank himself to death over decdes. Both he and Dad spent evenings at the local tavern until late. They spoke occasionally of the carnage they'd witnessed in war. Misery loves company, so they *commiserated* together. Mom attempted to 'fix' this by hiring a weekly sitter for me. That way, she could be with Dad at the bar when he went out. Otherwise, she was home (after work) and alone.

Except for *me*.

That didn't help matters with Dad, though. The drinking grew worse, and quarrels more frequent and violent. One time, when I was about three years old - one of my first memories - Mom threw a huge glass ashtray at Dad and broke two ribs. Another time, Dad kicked my favorite doll thirty feet or so through the house into my lap, shattering it to pieces. (Dolls were china then).

While Mom and Dad visited Sally and Mack one evening, when I was about 3 years old, I fell down their stairs severely cutting my chin. Drunk, Dad picked me up and spanked me for playing on the stairs, blood spewing over both him and me and the floor. I still bear the scar.

Alcoholism. It weighs its heaviest cost on children.

Finally, Mom could no longer pretend that things were right with her and Dad. Nor could she bear the stress of caring for me, working a job, and trying to salvage her marriage. She desperately loved Dad, and feared losing him. *I had to go.*

One cold winter weekend, she gathered me and a few things and bought a bus ticket to Sally's. The Greyhound bus stop was a long mile's walk from home, on a lonely country road. She walked in bitter cold, her hands so tightly clutched around me, that Sally couldn't get her fingers undone. Ovie told her mother that she was afraid for my safety due to Dad's drinking. She asked her to care for me a few weeks, until she could get things worked out. She told her mother she would pay her.

What could an old woman say who'd raised eight children already, and who was caring for her aged father? She'd told her other children 'no' to keeping their children, but thankfully she said 'yes' to Mom.

The youngest child, a boy named Ray was yet a teenager, born to Sally late in life.

Two of the youngest girls were still home, but looking for work in the north. Weeks turned into months, and months turned into years. Except for two weeks in the summer, I lived there eight years until I was eleven.

I was three when I arrived to live with Sally. Born with a club foot, I still couldn't walk well. Some family said it was from constantly standing in a crib, usually in dirty diapers. I was extremely tiny then. Sally called it 'puny.'

In the months just before Bonnie and Mary Lou left home, they took on the task of trying to teach me to walk. Summer came, and they took me out into the yard, and tried to help me by walking me between the two of them. But I always fell down. Nothing worked.

Then one day, both girls realized how much I delighted in a big black and white American Shepherd dog that was Grandpa Mack's pet. So they tried placing a scruff of his long fur in my hand and told me not to turn loose. I followed him by the hour around the yard. In a few weeks, I was walking normally.

Ironically, his name was *Walker.*

The girls both left home, but Walker stayed. We became fast friends. I soon learned he would obey my every command. Naturally, I took delight in that. One day, Sally came to the front screen door to see what all the furious barking was about. I'd succeeded in encouraging Walker to completely chew the bark from one of her newest trees she'd planted in the front yard. (about 3" around). It died. We both were punished.

Walker and I had a habit of lying in the shade underneath the old pear tree that shaded the house on one side, my head on his back. Like other children everywhere, I lazily dreamed and mused at the cloud formations, guessing at images I saw. Life was lonely on the farm. I loved it when Ray was home but he worked at the lumber mill when he wasn't in school . We had no close neighbors, but I had Walker. So all was well.

Things had not changed much then from when Ovie was home. Electricity didn't arrive in that rural area until I was age eight, in l952. This was the late 40's, so we listened to the big battery radio in evenings in the living room at night. Or Sally read to me Zane Grey and Black Stallion novels by an oil lamp. I loved horses and so I loved these times.

I was too young to do chores. Sally's dad who'd come to live with Sally, chopped stovewood for cooking. His name was Arch. Mack now used coal to heat the space heater in the living room. But Sally didn't like the suet that fell from it onto everything outdoors.

Mom wrote to say she was divorcing Dad. I remember loving him. Sally would often say how gently he called my name. She liked that.

Then one day, when I was five years old Mack came from town looking strained. I could hear him and my grandmother talking in solemn voices I couldn't overhear. I had no idea how their hushed words would affect me.

It was 1949, and we lived in a very rural community, the nearest town miles away.

At that time, nothing was more feared than a rabies outbreak. And it could spread furiously through both wild and domestic animals. Plus one of our dogs was a hunting dog that roamed the woods, thus tending to mingle with other dogs and wild animals. A couple of dogs and one cow had already gone rabid in a community near ours.

There was no vaccine then. Only *fear*.

I watched through the kitchen window as Grandpa Mack walked down the long lane to the barn, leading Walker and our other dog. He opened the barn door and walked in with them. I wondered why. Moments later, two shots rang out. I can still hear them.

My best friend was dead.

4

Mack Sims Road

Grandpa Mack was a dog lover too. He usually kept two dogs. One was for a pet, but the other for the business of rounding up the cattle twice a day. Grandpa believed it ruined a working dog to make a pet of it, so I wasn't permitted to ever play with that particular dog. Ray liked hunting dogs.

Our dogs often had interesting names such as Walker, Rusty or Bugle. Ray had some interesting names too! Two Walker hounds he owned, a brother and a sister, were named Blood and Guts! Guts was the female, marked the prettiest to me, and had just gotten grown when she got bitten by a copperhead snake. She died. Hunting in the woods posed that problem. We even had poisonous snakes in Sally's huge garden and yard.

I had two face to face encounters with copperheads about four years of age. One on a stump outside the milking barn, and one in an aunt's house on an iron bed rail. Both times, their heads were only inches from my face. I don't care for snakes, or people who like them.

Our farm sat on the top of a knoll. The top was always planted in crops, so that meant pasture for the cattle spread in a circle around that knoll, with a pond on two sides of the knoll. The workhorses usually grazed nearby.

The phrase 'til the cows come home' always amused me. *Because they never do!*

Morning and night, they were usually on the opposite side of the farm for milking. So, a twice daily task was to go get the cows. That meant finding the lead cow who wore a bell, i.e. the 'boss cow.'

The working dog was helpful - once the cows were found - but that dog couldn't ever seem to find them *alone*! Go figure. That meant two trips a day to round up the cows, and then the dog would nip the heels of the boss cow, and the rest of them would just follow her to the milking barn.

Grandpa Mack was good with both dogs and horses. He kept two or three horses at a time to plow and work the farm. That gave one a break from the team during plowing or harvest time. A few neighboring farmers were now looking at tractors, but Mack believed in the old way of doing things.

I liked the fact that the horses he kept were not huge draft horses, but a mixture with the small hot blooded horses. That made them lighter on their feet and much easier for me to ride! His best plow horses always knew not to step on the seedlings as they turned the corners of each row. I often followed him barefoot in the freshly plowed dirt.

Grandpa trained the horses that way.

One high spirited gelding he owned for years was named Prince. He could get pretty feisty for a gelding at times. That usually frustrated Mack, especially after a long day in the field.

I was often in the kitchen where Sally prepared dinner (supper to them), and Grandpa Mack would drive the horses down the lane that stretched to the barn where he would unharness the horses. But he always stopped the team at the house for him to get a cool drink of water first.. A gate separated the barnyard from our yard.

If Prince acted up while he got a drink, restless for their own relief and a roll in the sandlot, Sally and I would hear

Mack snap at him, "I'll knock you *down*!" We'd both chuckle to ourselves at that amusing statement, since Mack didn't weigh 140 pounds sopping wet! Mack was six feet tall, and very lean. His bib overalls and the long sleeve shirt he always wore hid his slender frame, except for Sunday church. He always wore long sleeves due to always being in the hot sun. Plus he was terribly modest. I only saw him once without a shirt, and I thought he would have a stroke getting it back on quickly.

It became apparent that Prince had not sufficiently learned to respect Mack. (*Nor had we!)* I guess he didn't think he had to, since he weighed over 1200 pounds!

One day, Mack was on his way to the barn with the horses after a long day's work when Prince acted up once too often. Grandpa yelled at him.

When he returned to the team, Prince stomped and jerked impatiently, pulling against the harness that held him, neighing loudly.

The next thing we knew, Grandpa had slapped that horse on the side of the neck. The blow apparently so stunned Prince that he fell to his front knees, with only the other horse's harness holding him up!

Neither Sally nor I chuckled after that. *Prince behaved better too.*

Grandpa Mack was a man of few words, and he tried to make them count. Prince and I both respected that. *We all did.* If we said anything about other people in his presence, or that he disapproved of, we were immediately corrected. He didn't like it. I didn't know it then, but he used Biblical phrases to correct us, like "Hold your peace" meaning *shut up* now*!*

In addition, Mack had a particularly queasy stomach. He couldn't tolerate discussion of anything at the dinner table that might make him nauseous. We always watched our words, and if he ever made a noise that sounded like "Hoo-up", we knew to hush right then. He might urp at the table's edge!

Summer afternoons found Grandpa Mack and his favorite dog under the shade tree for a nap. Of course, when you get up at 4am to begin the day hand milking cows, you're probably due for a nap by then. After milking, he spent the day in the fields until it became too hot. After napping, he went back to finish the day then milking again. Grandma helped with the milking as they sold cream then, used for making butter, cottage cheese, etc.

Mack went to bed with the chickens, we always said. It was wasteful in his mind to stay up after dark. As a child, I thought his routine was immensely b-o-r-i-n-g.

Visitors were always ushered on a tour of the farm - like it or not. They entered through the front door, and the next thing Sally knew, out the back they went with Mack to see the new calves or tobacco crop or latest changes. Mack loved his farm but this practice annoyed Sally no end.

Every neighbor for miles around knew they could borrow anything they wanted from Mack. He would never ask them to return it. He didn't believe in it. And some *didn't.* Sally felt it was weakness on his part, and that he should make them return items, or else not loan again to them. No matter If they asked, it was theirs.

Each evening before bedtime, Mack always wanted to listen to the news. The Korean War had flared by this time, and was of great interest to him. A lot of neighbor boys who'd worked crops for him had gone to fight there.

Grandpa Mack was not an educated man. He couldn't even sign his name. But that fact did not discount that he was a mathematical genius. It was impossible to cheat him in money! Or math concepts. Or checkers, because he always won! A favorite sport in the family was to try to trick him in any numbers game.

After Walker died, Grandpa Mack took special mercy on me. Until Mack died our relationship was unique, and one his own children resented, because he did things for me he never did for them in growing up, except for Ray. If he went to town, he always brought home corn candy for me. And he brought me a blanket once.

Many of his children resented Mack; some hated him. *They had their reasons.* But he'd mellowed a lot when I came along. And he also attended church without fail then, something he wouldn't discuss with Sally. (They always attended separate churches in the community.)

Mack also knew of my love of horses. So he sometimes allowed me to help harness and care for them, or ride one of them to the fields - under the watchful eye of Sally, from her kitchen door. At evening, I ran to the field to wait for a ride on one of them to the barn.

At that time, it was too difficult for me to see these as good times. All I knew was that I desperately loved my mother, and this was not my real home. "Home" was with her. And I lived for the day when I was confident she would take me home to live with her, like she'd promised.

Mom's visits became less and less frequent. No doubt that was my own fault. Her visits were increasingly traumatic for me, as I would cling to her as she was leaving. Sally would tear me first from her arms, then her legs, then her clothes, as I begged her to take me with her. (I was about five then.)

Afterwards, I cried for hours, even all day. I didn't eat for days. Neither bribes nor punishment worked. I was still seriously underweight then.

Now however, I view my time spent with these wonderful people as a rich heritage. I was well into adulthood before I could fully appreciate their strength of character, tremendous integrity whose word was sure, and the genuine human valor of both Sally and Mack.

Mack died only after I was married with children.

As was his custom on wintry days, he came inside to lie down for his nap in the living room.

Sally worked in the kitchen two rooms away, as was also her custom. "Sally?" Mack called out to her as he sometimes did. "What, Mack?" she answered. "Is Sharon in there...?"

A few minutes later, he called again. "What is it, Mack?" She asked.

"Is Sharon in there?" he asked once more. "No Mack, Sharon isn't here." Quiet.

Then he said, "I thought I heard her singing"

Moments later, he had the stroke that would take his life.

I'm convinced the singing he heard were those of angels. My children noted birds sang happily at his funeral.

The road where he tended his farm for six decades is now named in his honor. A fitting tribute.

5

The Matriarch That Mattered

Webster's dictionary defines 'matriarchy' as a "social system ruled by mothers and women.' I never knew Sally's mother as she died long before I was born, but from all I've heard and observed, this system was established in our family by Sally herself. Born Sarah Elizabeth in 1898, Grandma Sally bore six daughters (seven but one twin died at birth), and two sons. They learned this system well.

Sally had her strong **reasons**. One was her father. The other was her husband, and compounded more by the desperate times in which she lived.

Known by all in the community as an upright woman, Sally was deeply respected. Even more so than Mack. Sally stood 5'9", but her very erect posture made her seem taller to me, until later years when she became stooped. Her eyes were clear crystal blue. Sally never wore pants, even to work in the garden or outside. Unless dressed up, she always wore a long apron with huge pockets that hung over her knees. It kept her dress clean from all her baking.

In the garden, where she spent a great deal of time, she wore a big brimmed bonnet to ward off the hot sun, the long hair she'd worn all her life spun into a bun underneath. She'd never cut her hair until I was twelve years old.

When the two of us worked in the garden, she sometimes carried a salt shaker, and a small paring knife. Then at break time, she'd find a cool watermelon underneath a shade tree, and slice it for the two of us.

A tremendously proud woman, all of Sally's children were born at home -a couple without even the aid of a midwife, much less a doctor. Her strength reminded me of the pioneers who settled the West. Hers was an adventuring spirit, such as the time we discovered an underground spring one day while walking the farm. She dug it out with her hands using a pointed rock. She pretended like I'd helped. When we walked by there from then on, we were able to get a cool drink of water. As others did so as well.

Born in Virginia, Sally had four brothers and sisters. Some were highly educated and held lofty positions, one in Boy Scouts of America. She always longed to go 'home' to see the mountain laurel she said grows wild on the mountains there. She never did. She nursed her ailing mother many years while raising her own children. While she carried her fifth child, her mother died. Strangely, that child bore a close resemblance of Sally's mother, down to the blue eyes. Other children had Mack's brown eyes.

Sally didn't believe in 'airing your dirty linens.' That she felt it was ill manners. And while this is good policy overall, perhaps it contributed to why our family never talked openly to one another. I observed however, that this didn't keep them from talking *about* each other. I never liked that and felt it was a lack of loyalty.

This later caused me to shun family members.

Much of what I learned about family history came from whispers I overheard among Sally's daughters, who gossiped.

But this convinced me that the social system in our family began during the Depression, after Mack had disappeared for two whole years. I never could determine exactly 'why' he was gone. Some said a breakdown occurred or hospitalization, but others said it was another woman. Others said he just left. I didn't trust them though, because some of them hated Grandpa Mack.

Wherever he was, it meant Sally was left alone during the Great Depression with the children, to survive. And whatever the reason, it was shameful in Sally's mind. And worse in her mind, *a sign of weakness.*

I thought perhaps Sally didn't want anyone to know there was mental illness in the family, so no one spoke of it. People kept such things quiet back then. Other times, I didn't think she'd believed he'd been sick during that time because of the way she treated him, often with contempt. I don't know if she was ever able to fully forgive him in his lifetime. Perhaps after.

One of the few times she ever mentioned this dark period in my presence, she told of harnessing one of the horses one winter day, then driving it deep into the woods.

She went alone as it was too dangerous for the children. She tied the horse, sawed a tree down, trimmed the limbs - all of this with a handsaw - and tied the tree to a chain attached to the horse's harness. Then she slowly drove the horse home, 'snaking' (as it's called) it through the woods avoiding other trees while exiting.

Once home, she permitted the children to chop the wood up for the space heater and wood cookstove so it could be taken into the house to burn, watching out for snakes on the logs. This process required knowing what kind of timber burns best in those woods.

Sally also raised and canned a TWO acre garden then. And helped milk the cows, the children churning their own butter.

All this made Sally bitter towards Mack over the years. She disdained his weakness, however it manifested. Or the fact she had to be *strong* for him!

I had my own theory about what happened upon Mack's return from his mysterious absence. Divorce was out of the question in the mid 30's, so I believed their relationship became like so many today - a *tradeoff*. He could come back - but she would run the show. Though a far cry from a milque-toast personality, his love of his farm caused him to surrender.

His children would have never said he came back because he loved them. Perhaps it was the only life he knew. Or the farm he'd cleared with his own hands.

Then there was Sally's father, "Arch". Webster's define the word as an adjective for 1) chief, pre-imminent (his view of himself) and 2) sly, roguish (our view of him). Arch was full Irish and walked with a cane. He had a huge ulcer inside his right hand about the size of a golf ball - I'm not sure why he never had it taken off.

As a young man, Arch had been a sheriff in Virginia about the turn of the 20th century.

His tales, as he liked to spin them, convinced me he was a mean man. He told of killing people during that time. (Of course it was legal; he was the sheriff!).

He frightened me. He had sparkling blue eyes that batted, and he called me and my cousins who visited, "lads and lassies".

Sally's other siblings came to visit, but Arch was never welcome to go home with them. But they loved Sally's cooking and came regularly. In his latter years, he grew senile and referred to Sally as 'that old woman' whose name or relationship he couldn't recall. He *was* certain however, that she was a thief and was taking his money from him. So he slept with his wallet under his pillow to keep it safe.

I felt he was too mean for his other children to tolerate, all of whom he promptly warned about Sally as soon as they arrived.

When he was still able, he chopped wood for the kitchen cooking stove. He seemed to enjoy that, though it pained me to see him with anything as threatening as an axe! He remained very strong until the end, especially in upper torso body strength.

My cousins and I were aware of that strength first hand, because our farmhouse was circled with three porches, where he sat in a rocking chair in the daytime. When we played outdoors, we always remembered to run in wide circles from the porch where he sat.

That's because he would reach out with his cane, grabbing us to pull us to him. If he caught us there was no getting away. We never knew what he wanted, but if no one was around, he offered *me* money to *feel me up*.

There was one time I took the money and then ran like heck. I figured he deserved it!

The next day after school, I bought a plug of tobacco, like Sally chewed, at the general store. I accidentally swallowed some and got drunker than a dog!

Truth was, I was a little devil then, of sorts. My cousins Billy Joe and Donnie came from Indy to visit us one weekend. They were about my age, but I regarded them as 'city- slickers' who knew nothing about the country. I'd been in the city since I'd stayed in the city each summer.

We were playing in the orchard once and one of the boys looked over behind the smokehouse where Sally kept her bees. So I asked them if they wanted some honey, and told them they could get all they wanted if they just lifted those lids to see inside. They *did*. Of course, I stood back from them.

I did get two stings out of it all. But Billy Joe must have gotten a hundred and was only saved when Ray grabbed him and ran and jumped in the pond with him. Donnie got a few stings, but Billy Joe could easily have died then.

Arch wasn't amused because bees didn't sting him, ever. I figured they had enough sense to fear *Beelzebub.*

Arch always thought I was the smartest of the cousins because I could spell 'gnat'. When I was about seven or eight years old, it was my custom to accompany Sally and Mack to do the milking. One early morning, it was rainy and cold. Sally left me sleeping on the couch, going to milk without me.

Suddenly awakened by something, I realized Arch was standing directly over me, peering strangely as me. I had never seen anything like this scene in my entire life, and his naked body was right in front of me.

He hovered over me, trying to straddle me. I was terrified!

His inability to move fast aided my escape. In complete panic, I squirmed my little frame off the end of the couch and fled to the barn. Sally immediately noticed I'd come without a coat and it was very cold. She busied herself getting me a jacket from the storage room.

The only thing that terrified me more than what I'd just experienced, was telling Sally what had happened. I worked up the courage and tried to tell her. She was certain it didn't happen the way I remembered it. Perhaps I was dreaming, after all, I *was* sleeping.

I noticed however, that from then on, she always made a point of taking me with her to do the milking, no matter how early or how late.

Sometime later, a neighbor came to visit. Though I knew her from the general store, I'd never seen her come to our house before. I overheard a terse conversation between her and Sally, standing at the edge of the yard. Speaking in a low voice, the neighbor said that Arch had offered her two teenage daughters money for something I couldn't understand (I don't think I knew what the term *sex* was then).

And she wasn't going to have it!

Arch never left the farm after that. Sally made certain of it. At least she'd believed somebody, I thought.

Apparently personal hardship, abandonment issues and her rogue of a father convinced Sally of her philosophy that "Sex was a task, and *man* was the taskmaster." And since the male species tended to roam (much as a rogue), they need to be *controlled* by women who had more sense and certainly self-control.

Despite these negatives, which were never made public, Sally was a wonderful woman and everyone knew it. There was something regal about her to me, the way she carried herself. Neighbors often came to get her counsel on matters, if they had a problem. She was wise, and her counsel was just. I know because I often listened in. The positive impact of her life far outweighed the negative. Hers was an immeasurable and wonderful impact upon me, lasting a lifetime. Furthermore, she was the only person in my young life who ever really cared anything about me, or invested time in me.

It grieves me to add, that for all the areas I most admired Sally - in my opinion - that greatness seemed to bypass her own children. Yes, my mother included. They seemed to major in minors, finding excuses for failure and their poor choices.

Perhaps, Sally was so involved in matters of survival that she herself had no time to discuss virtue and character in raising them. When I came along, she had *more time* for me, talking to me as we did our chores, trying to answer all my endless questions.

Though family may not choose to believe it, I can only say this is *my* story! Mom kept her secrets well hidden, not wanting Sis to be privy to any of her problems, and she was never close to any of her siblings with the exception of Ray.

I made the decision early on to think and live positively. I couldn't deal with their problems - and mine too - and all the drama associated with the results of poor choices they'd made. I couldn't find any encouragement there. Or examples to emulate either! Abraham left his home and family, and went out *not knowing*. I did also.

But in the end, we are little different from Sally. Our own life philosophy is woven out of life experience *unless we've found a higher criteria than mere human experience.*

Something *higher.*

As a high school senior, I was there at Sally's when we took Arch to the hospital the day he died. That evening, Sally was in the cafeteria getting a drink. Ray and I were alone in the hospital room with Arch as he lay comatose. Ray stood at the side of his bed, and I stood at the foot.

Suddenly, Arch awakened and looked toward the ceiling as though peering at something. Something horrifying. Just as suddenly, he sat straight up in bed still peering at the ceiling, only to be thrown back down onto the bed like a limp rag; as though stung in the chest by a giant bee. He was dead. *I wasn't sorry.*

6

Charles The First

In 1952 when I was eight years old, our remote community changed a great deal. The Tennessee Valley Authority was finally able to string poles and electricity to our area off the major highway. That translated to a host of changes in our household. We not only had electricity, it also meant having a refrigerator. A water pump brought water into the house for indoor plumbing. I no longer had to draw water at the well outside the kitchen. We also had hot water, plus a new bathroom.

Progress had arrived at the flip of a switch but it was the switch on the television that had everyone's attention. I'd seen television on my summer visits to my Mom's. One time, Grandma Sally and I walked to a neighbor's to join a group who watched a Billy Graham Crusade there.

It was after that time that Ray talked Grandpa Mack into buying a tractor. He'd never driven anything but horses and wagons. Over time, Ray taught him how to drive it. He always kept a horse or two anyway. Some of this 'progress' became regrettable to me. Gone were the evenings when Sally read to me by the oil lamp. And gone were the times when, after Mack retired, we'd listened to the battery radio to serial episodes of "Amos and Andy" and "Fibber McGee."

Another change came about that time for me. My first two years of school had been a one room schoolhouse in our Parlor Grove Community, called the Okay Schoolhouse. It was about a third of a mile to walk from home. But educational standards were changing, and some parents thought the bus should come take us all to the new elementary school in town. But the Okay School house was okay with me.

Mrs. Elsie Faulkner was a superb teacher, even with six grades crowded together. She and her husband owned the motel out on the main highway. There at school, she taught us music, like "Swing Low, Sweet Chariot" and others. She'd taken up for me when other kids teased me. I had trouble with hand-eye coordination, so I couldn't skip rope, play jacks, or roller skate, which were all the recess activities. I started out early in life being an outcast.

And lonely.

One particular girl named Norma Jean gave me lots of heartache. I liked her and she was popular, but I felt she was jealous of the one thing my mother did for me, which was send me pretty dresses to wear. I did have one friend, and Mrs. Faulkner always paid special notice to me, so I felt safe there in spite of Norma Jean.

I was tiny, but an older distant cousin who lived over the hill from us, named Alpha Mae, had taken me under her wing on the long walks to school. That was good because the journey was frightening. The biggest danger was snakes, some of them poisonous.

Woods covered the side of the road, so getting around them was very scary to a six or seven year old.

Alpha means "The First" and today I view her friendship as being indicative of the great wealth of wonderful friends I gained later on in life.

One time when I got into sight of our house, I decided to take a short cut. Since Grandma Sally could see me from the house and was watching for me, I bent down to crawl through the barbed wire fence. My clothes got caught in the wire, and there I was, bent over and snared. Alpha had moved on down the road but looked back and saw my dilemma. She rescued me. The old schoolhouse was torn down that summer.

Living with Sally, I had many daily chores. Carrying in the stovewood for her cookstove, working in the garden, helping with the picking, cooking and canning the vegetables. And most of all, the eternal dishes. Three meals a day on the farm, starting with early morning (6am) breakfast added up to a lot of dirty dishes!

In fact, meal preparation at our house was all consuming. Sally rose at 5am to prepare her wonderful country breakfasts. It annoyed her immensely if anyone in the house - like visitors - dared sleep past one of them, so everybody else had to be up by 6am. If they weren't, that translated to her a serious character flaw!..

If they dared "*lay up*" in bed all day, it meant they were lazy and generally worthless. I could never figure out this term. How does one *lay up* in bed?

Maybe because they were upstairs, laying.

After morning dishes, a break would come. *Yeah, right. Not at Sally's house!* We headed to the garden in the shade, before the day got too hot. There we picked beans, tomatoes, lettuce, carrots, peas, cantaloupe, dug potatoes, shucked corn, etc. Then we washed them, made dinner (lunch to me) by 11am, which was the main meal. If we had farm laborers, they had to eat as well as Mack, served promptly at 11am. Then the dishes.

Afternoons brought a break. *Not!* We headed to the garden, again, for hoeing, planting or to make canning preparations - depending on what was 'in' - like green beans, or beets, or cucumbers. If they were in season, we picked gooseberries, blackberries or grapes to make jams, jellies and pies. Do you have *any* idea how many pans it takes to make jelly?

Or to *can*?

Each summer, I would eventually ask Sally what she planned to give me for my birthday in August. Her answer never varied. "Well" she would say, "The grapes oughta be ripe 'bout then." She knew I liked burnt grape jam, and she always saved some on the bottom that she could scorch for me. Thankfully though, she kidded about the birthday.

Thankfully too, the evening meal was leftovers, for dishes. No microwaves then, so we heated some things up on the stove for supper. Doing the dishes wasn't altogether lost on me, however. It was then Sally and I had our serious talks. One of us would wash, and the other dry. Sally would do her best to answer all my questions about life. I had a lot!

Once, I felt particularly troubled about the biggest topic of the day, one that was on everyone's mind - the *bomb*. It hadn't been that long since our nation bombed Japan to end WWII. I wondered why I should want to grow up and have a family in a world where a threat of total annihilation now existed. The future seemed gloomy to my little mind. Sometimes, frustration with my endless questions leaked through. I washed and she dried. She stopped drying her plate, and looked down at me. Her response became printed indelibly upon my heart. I forgot it at times in life, but it has resurfaced countless other times.

"Sharon" she said, "Sometimes when we don't understand something, we just have to learn to trust the Lord." I didn't know much about God, but her answer somehow sufficed. I did know that Sally believed in the Bible, because I sometimes saw her reading it. And on Sundays, we attended the local Baptist church.

Our outings to church however, meant little to me, except that *I'd better be good* there. The one thing I remember learning was, that one look from Sally, and I knew I was *dead* when I got home!

When Ray was home, he would chase and play with me, often scaring me with frogs. Sometimes he and I had long talks, where I learned what dreams are, when he shared his with me. Later on, like so many, he seemed to give up on those dreams.

If I could've just gotten Grandma Sally to give up her *cure-all* for every ailment, life could've actually been good there. But due to my erratic eating habits, she worried about my health. So her therapy for it - and everything else - was *castor oil.* Without the fear that I acquired for that remedy, I might've successfully starved!

However I found that, life for me had become tolerable living there. Maybe because I'd learned what to expect. I knew Sally had already raised her own children, and now deserved a rest in life. Plus she cared for her father. The result was, I couldn't help but feel like an appendix. Unneeded. But I knew she loved me.

A letter from Mom arrived, telling us that she was coming down to visit. I was happy - until I heard she was bringing her new husband! I didn't know she had one. A letter was how I'd learned she'd divorced Dad. Never saw him again as a child. Now this! Though that had been two years, I still hadn't adjusted to the first news.

This said to me that men were dispensable, at the whim of the wife and mother.

Sort of like *cars* that became outdated, I thought?

Mom always promised me that, if she could get things worked out, she'd take me home with her. Perhaps this was it! I allowed my heart to hope.

Mom and Charles arrived in the dead of night due to the long drive from the big city, and each had to work all day that Friday. We were already sleeping, but we didn't mind and were happy to see them.

As usual, Sally drew out a full meal in leftovers, along with fruit, etc. We all sat around her huge dining table that had hosted countless others.

Charles was very polite (now, I call it *smooth*) He seemed very kind to Mom. He was very handsome...until he took off his hat. He was totally bald, except around the sides. Full German but with no accent, He didn't look like anyone I'd ever met. His eyes were ice blue, and cold. He was strangely different, yet I found I liked him. I soon realized he was very stern, and that matched the way he always pronounced my name, "SHERN."

I recalled the sweet way my name rolled off Dad's tongue.

In spite of my reservations (fears) about Charles, I tried to win his favor. He acted pleasant to me. Yes, they would take me home.

Can I tell you weekend can be a very *long time?*

On Sunday morning after breakfast, Mom and Charles invited me to take a long walk with them on the path that wound around the top of the farm's knoll. It was shaded and pleasant. I skipped along happily, dreaming of riding in the car with them, home. But they told me after talking it over, they now felt it would be best for *me* if I finished the school year at Sally's. Maybe in the fall.

I knew it wouldn't happen then either. I felt like an ugly plot of betrayal had unfolded against me, though I was a mere seven years old. *Disappointment* was to become my bitter best friend.

After that weekend, I decided that Charles was not a nice man. Yet that would not keep me from continuing to try to win his favor. The following summer, they did buy me off by permitting me to spend several weeks with them. Mom hired a country girl to come stay with me. But Charles' mother volunteered to come stay with me instead.

She turned out to be a kind women who slept in my bed (we had a two bedroom home), and said her rosary nightly, being Catholic. I liked her. She had other sons who visited that I also liked. But Charles seemed mean to me.

That summer, Charles' mother aided Mom with housework and cooking. She also *did the dishes!* There was a catch however. I learned you'd better be finished eating by the time she was, else you would take a bite and the plate was whisked from beneath you between bites!

She was super tidy!

About two years later, Mom wrote (about the only way we ever heard because we didn't see them much then plus Sally didn't have a phone until much later) that she was going to have a baby. Imagine my surprise! Was this the same woman who ranted that she should have never had *me?* Or she should never have been a mother? How was this going to affect *me?*. (If I'd only *known*!) I despaired then of ever having a personal mother.

When I was nine, on Easter Sunday, Mom and Charles had a baby boy named David. I didn't know whether to be glad or feel in competition. This event was to become both my dream come true, and my worst nightmare.

I didn't think Charles liked me, but that was only half-true. He died saying *he'd always hated me and always would.*

7

Welcome To The Brewery

The neighborhood where Mom and Dad lived after the war was starting to go downhill. Mom and Charles had chosen to stay in that house when they married. Five years after, the old homes had deteriorated, industry had moved in, the complexion of the neighborhood had changed. It all began to look tired and old. Effie and Max had moved closer to his work, and Sis had sold her house too. A bottling company across the street made the street noisy, and a local bar two doors away was loud. Mom said only riffraff went there anyway. There was always fighting, even an occasional stabbing.

I figured she ought to know, so I guessed that only *good riffraff* attended the bars she and Charles went to in the other block. I did know that Sally said that no bar was any place to look for a husband because good men didn't hang out there. I didn't think I knew any good men, so I wondered how Sally would know that too. I was confused. But Mom always seemed to find her love interests in bars. I supposed she was comfortable there.

I was eleven, and just finishing up sixth grade. Big changes had come for me. A year earlier, Mom suddenly got the wonderful idea to bring me home at last. I was to learn a lot about *that.* Home. Four walls do not a home make. I had left the serenity of farm life far behind for big city streets! But I'd spent enough time in the city during summers that I already knew those streets were filled with danger.

Mom's work schedule now posed problems for her concerning the care of David. She took him weekly to a sitter on Sunday nights and then picked him up on Friday evenings. But Charles wanted David home weekdays too. Unbelievably, it was then that Mom realized she had a daughter who was babysitting age, who might even be able to cook and clean too.

So-.*Welcome Home Sharon*! I had no idea living between two taverns plus all the beer flowing via Charles and all his drinking buddies inside the house, made this domicile seem - and often smell - more like a *brewery.*

Moving home turned out *not to be* what I had in mind. It was my job to have meals ready when Mom got home. I could go to friends if I had my housework done after school. And if there was a family outing planned on weekends, such as a movie or the mall? I wasn't invited. They were sure I had homework, or something to do. Or housekeeping. The only place I was invited was to accompany Charles on his daily fishing trips to nearby lakes.

Then, I had to *clean and gut* and *cook* the fish he caught. I usually stayed home to rest up for all that!

I didn't think of Cinderella then, only years later.

Though I continued my attempts to win Charles' favor, I knew that he only tolerated me. But David was his whole life. He seemed to worship him. David *was* very cute! He had long lashes that made people mistake him for a girl, and big blue eyes. Though I babysat David, I was not permitted to make him obey; only watch him to keep him from getting hurt. Try doing *that!*

During the school year, Mom still took David to the old sitter.

All was not well on the home front. Somehow, I'd learned Mom was Charles' fourth wife. The first had died; another ran a bar in town. No one among the family knew that all though. He had a grown daughter with kids.

The first time I realized all this was when Mom came into my room in the middle of the night and woke me up to take me with her in the car to look for Charles. She scouted several bars for his car, making me lie on the back floorboard while she went in. It wasn't long before I knew he would usually be at his ex-wife's particular bar. Sometimes I waited, in fear, on that floorboard for a very long time. If I didn't wait in fear on the floorboard, I hid behind the long thick drapes in the living room while they bar-hopped. No, sheer *terror*!

Though Charles did drink, he never missed work, no matter what time he got in. He was responsible. His boss depended on him, as a plumbing foreman on construction jobs.

Mom's brother Max spent time at our house, drinking with Charles, many nights a week. Max enjoyed any drunk. First Dad, then Charles, then anyone. Max too was a functioning alcoholic with a good paying job.

One night, Max lingered. Mom wanted to retire. I walked with her as she escorted him to his car. He was so drunk he didn't know which car was his! Then, he couldn't unlock his own door. But he drove 27 blocks home! That night Mom warned him (she didn't drink much but also had some common sense!) "Max, one day you're going to kill someone!"

Max's response was the typical slur of any drunk every lawmen hears, "I'll be *alright*." (They've never had more than 'a couple beers'). And he *was* alright. *That* night. But **a night**, years later he drove south on the interstate to visit his mother during a rainstorm. Effie sat beside him. A volunteer flagman at an existing accident never went home again.

Max spent many years and much wealth fighting lawsuits and charges, trying to avoid prison for reckless homicide and lawsuits for damages. He ended up losing his driver's license for life. A very small price to pay for another human life. He paid in other ways though.

Nevertheless, Max still drank himself to death, but not before going blind, confined to wheelchair from diabetes, experiencing amputations.

I witnessed all of this firsthand - that merry-go-round of codependency that Alanon and AA talk about. I often rode to Kentucky on weekends with Max and Effie to visit Grandma Sally. (Mom and Charles saw it as a free weekend without me). But I watched as Effie sat in the middle and I on the passenger side. Max would harangue her to hand him his bottle in the glove compartment. She always gave in. Co-dependent people ENABLE alcoholics... Why would anyone, I pondered, jeopardize her safety (and MINE) by giving him that bottle? Codependency! It is a disease equally as *sick and serious* as alcoholism!

Help for the alcoholic doesn't usually come until the one who is in that relationship of codependency chooses to step off that merry-go-round and further, learns to allow the alcoholic to face his own consequences from his behavior! Stop providing his excuses! Stop the lies! No more *calling in* for him *for anything!*

There's no need for anyone to feel isolated, which is common. You're not! Many have pioneered the way for you. Go to the library. Find an Alanon group. There is help. Reach for it. When you get sick and tired *of being sick and tired*, you'll do something about! Hopefully *before* disaster occurs...

It became more and more evident to me that I was not a welcome addition to the 'family'. In fact, I wasn't even regarded as a member of it.

I could *live* there, but only as a *maid.*

I missed Sally terribly, but Mom didn't even want to hear it. But she let me hitch rides with people who lived back home.

These people worked in the big city, but often drove home on weekends to tend farm. This included relatives. That proved to have a price tag. The ride was free, but a couple of these men tried to molest me if I fell asleep. I tried to always ride in the back or never go to sleep!

Some of those men drank as well. Getting DUI's then was not nearly as serious or costly as it is now. But the results were just as deadly.

By this time, I had little respect for the men in my life. Grandpa Mack would only be appreciated later. Fortunately, I learned to stay one step ahead of those who preyed on me, mainly because I trusted none of them. I soon arrived at the same philosophy Grandma Sally had.

Circumstances became more heated at home when Mom's jealousy began to surface more. She and Charles fought often. Sometimes he hit her when she kept nagging him. One time he hit her so hard, his hand went through the back door window pane. Then, he wouldn't permit me to put a wet cloth on her head.

But that violence ended just after that! Mom told me why. She'd warned Charles that if he ever hit her again he would never have a good night's sleep in that house again! Because she would scald his privates! Only she used the slang he understood. *He also understood she meant it...*

On the flip side though, this caused me to have little respect for the women in my life as well. I certainly didn't want to be like any of them! Especially Mom. She'd wasted her life, in my mind, on some man who didn't even deserve her. How could she think so little of herself, I wondered? She seemed to feel she needed a man in her life to be whole. (There'd been others I learned, a series of men who'd 'rented a room' from her between Dad and when she married Charles. Yeah, *right*).

I felt Mom was intelligent except when it came to men. Yet my motto became 'to be walked on, you have to lie down first'.

And I vowed, that would be *over my dead body.* The women in our family seemed frivolous to me, and disloyal even to one another, evidenced by their gossip. The men I'd known so far, were milque-toast and some beastial - in my mind.

Good news came when we heard Grandma Sally was going to make a rare visit to the city. She couldn't travel much due to caring for Arch. He was also making an even rarer visit to his other children. So we knew her visit would be brief, yet it was exciting news to everyone.

Mom was thrilled too. She wanted her Mom to see how pretty the house was. She always kept a nice home. We both cooked and cleaned, preparing for Sally's visit. David, now three, played happily around our feet. He enjoyed all the activity. I couldn't help but love David.

The joy of that day was short-lived. Mom wasn't even there when Sally arrived. The telephone had ended our happy scene, dramatically changing all our lives. Charles was on the line. He was calling from *jail.* Could Mom come and get him out? *Why,* she had asked? What happened?

She soon left with no explanation to me. I kept David.

Sally arrived just in time to watch the evening news with David and me. The television cameras told it all.

They focused on a rainy highway about sixty miles from home. A couple of wrecked cars were shown, including Charles'. Then the camera panned to a patrol car. Beside it in handcuffs and sopping wet in the rain, stood Charles. One of his drinking buddies stood with him. A sheriff's deputy came over and put both of them into the police car.

David pointed happily to his Daddy on the television screen. He couldn't comprehend that it wasn't a happy scene.

The reporter explained that Charles had attempted to cross a double yellow line on a hill, in a rainstorm, when he struck another car head on. He'd failed a sobriety test. A three year old was dead. And a five year old critical. Both parents were hospitalized with unknown injuries. Charles and his passenger appeared to be alright, only a little banged up.

The story centered on a new prosecutor in that county who was determined to make an example out of this case, and of Charles. He said he planned to throw the book at him, charging him with drunk driving and reckless homicide. He'd also charged him with involuntary manslaughter.

All I could think about was Mom, and what she must be feeling. I knew she was suffering.

Mom returned home that night without Charles. Within days, he was tried, convicted and sent to the state prison! She was decimated of course.

Sally didn't stay long.

Later newscasts said both the parents of the children in the accident had a broken pelvis and other injuries. The five year old girl had brain injuries.

Mom had bar friends who referred her to a shady attorney. She immediately mortgaged the house to pay to defend Charles.

I tried to help Mom in the long months Charles spent in state prison, by taking the strain off her when she was home as much as I could. I secretly hoped it might be an opportunity to build the relationship I'd never had with her. Charles always seemed to shield her from me, keeping her busy or occupied or out. But that hope was in vain.

The very opposite happened, as Mom became obsessed with the legalities of Charles' case. She worked overtime for extra money, and spent every waking hour with David. On weekends, she and David left on a four hour drive north to visit Charles in prison. I watched her drop thirty pounds. I'd never seen her look so bad, or so sad. And

I'd never felt so alone.

One weekend, I went with her just to spend time with her on the long drive. I had no interest whatever in seeing the man who'd caused her this much grief.

Once there, I had to go in.

A dreary rain accompanied our arrival to the prison. Driving along the outside, I'd never seen such a dreadful place. It was very old, several stories high and surrounded by factories everywhere. Everything was shrouded by a gray haze, the fog blending with the tops of the buildings and factories.

We went through the search and inspections area. Charles too had lost weight. He even seemed glad to see me. *Prison must be really bad,* I thought. I never went back.

After about eight months, the attorney Mom hired was able to get the sentence overturned on a technicality, based on the new county prosecutor's zeal and inexperience. The attorney requested a new trial, allowing Charles to be released until that time.

Out on appeal, Charles waited while a series of delays and postponements eventually allowed the case to be thrown out. I learned this is a tactic used by defense attorneys, knowing that after two years, the case is often thrown out of court a brief not filed, a witness not present, someone ill, etc. A learning curve to me on sleazy attorneys and a failed justice system.

Most defense attorneys are paid liars in my mind.

I can tell you having Charles back in the house after a long absence, especially jail, wasn't a highlight for me. Worse, Mom seemed even more distant to me. I felt as if I'd totally lost her.

The long distance from Sally made things worse for me. She was the only person who'd ever cared about me.

I was in junior high school by then, and a certain assistant high school principal, A K. Jones, Jr. had taken a particular interest in me. He and my home room teacher conspired to get me into counseling, Mrs. Mize sensing my unhappiness during this time. Mr. Jones set a meeting with the school psychologist. I went once. It was a waste of time, in my mind.

Also, during this time, a school friend's family had learned of our family's trials (literally!). I hadn't told others, but my friend Connie begged me to permit her to tell her parents. I relented.

This family invited me to share their home any time. They were good people.

I knew this family felt sorry for me, but I didn't even mind... *I did too*! Their home was friendly and welcoming. I began to stay there as often as I could, taking solace there. Mom didn't care. She didn't even seem to miss me, only if I failed to perform my duties.

Connie was the youngest of several children. I liked her siblings too. The most appealing thing I liked about their home was that it had something foreign to me. Laughter.

It drew me there more than anything else.

Almost anything.

Other chapters have been about people until this one. But I chose instead for this chapter, a *substance that affects people.* One that robs relationships and jobs, ruins futures, destroys lives and people. It breaks up homes, ruins marriages and takes children from parents, fathers and husbands from wives, and mothers from daughters and sons.

The cost of it is often measured in terms of financial loss, but its toll on humanity is insidious and immeasurable.

Stop it.

Stop it right now! AA, Alanon, Drugs Anonymous, other people and *the public library* are there to help YOU.

It can, it will, consume your life.

The devil will see to that. True.

8

Mr. Jones–Where Are You?

Rummaging through her cedar chest one day - where I was not allowed - I ran across it. I didn't even know Mom had one. I immediately thought I needed it! A German luger gun that Max had given Mom after the war. I checked the clip. It was full. I slipped it into the gun and placed the safety one. Guns were not foreign to me, as I'd grown up around guns and people who hunted. Ray had permitted me to shoot a rifle occasionally, under his watchful eye. But I'd never handled a pistol. I decided to carry it. I had a very definite reason!

I'd begun to spend more and more time away from home. It was always at friends, but there was a problem. Unlike me, they had bedtimes. So I had to leave pretending that I did also, and spend two or three hours until time for my mother to arrive home from the second shift, promptly at 12:30am.

Since Charles was unable to work steadily, she always worked nights for the extra money.

That meant that I had to spend time on the street at night. I was used to the streets, often walking them, day and night, even downtown. I loved to stroll by department store windows and see the moving Christmas decorations and lights. I spent a lot of time at different libraries and knew their hours by heart. The big one downtown stayed open later.

Twice in the past, I'd evaded a bunch of men who'd attempted to pull me into their car. It was little wonder since I spent so much time on the streets, literally defying the odds of something dangerous happening. There were close calls. Fortunately, I knew the streets and alleys better than my potentials captors did, and was able to flee. Sometimes down an unlit alley unfamiliar to them, or into a lighted restaurant.

The last two times had been the worst terror I'd ever known.

Yet, I viewed the streets as safer than going home to what I knew awaited me, if Mom wasn't home. *Charles.* But I also knew he wouldn't start anything with Mom coming home soon if I arrived about 12:15am or so.

Release from prison didn't make Charles happy. He returned home a shell of a man, and sick. He could hardly bear to look at David now. For all his faults, I knew he *did* love children (except *me*). He had taken the life of a child the same age as David, stolen their child. Their other child had serious brain damage, leaving it retarded. Guilt and remorse that found no release began to eat at him. Literally.

First it was emotional. Then physically. I learned that doctors called this *psychosomatic* illness. Real illnesses produced from unhealthy mindsets.

Charles returned to work, his boss glad to have him back. Soon however, he began to have stomach problems. Severe abdominal pain turned into bleeding ulcers. Then came surgeries removing portions of the stomach. After three surgeries, doctors said, and he would have to have a replacement of a goat's stomach next time. His diet became baby food and pills. He couldn't keep either of them down though.

Soon doctors wanted him to go through shock treatments for his depression (common then and a practice doctors are returning to). He was only able to work infrequently, at most two or three days a week. Mom worked overtime, double shifts and also picked up riders for extra money.

Medications made it difficult for Charles to drink but he still would schedule 'doctors appointments' late in the day, and have me babysit David, while he went out occasionally. That meant he wouldn't be home till midnight, just before Mom. I hated those nights.

Mom had done everything humanly possible to help Charles. He knew that, and he owed her for it all. We didn't own a dog to kick. So he chose a convenient target.

A rebellious teenager in the house would do just fine. *Me*

In my mind, all our family's suffering lay at this man's feet. His weakness. How dare he feel sorry for himself? This was a battlefield of his own making; we were the innocent parties. I was a teenager. I didn't like this man, and had zero respect for him. I had better sense than to say it.... he knew it anyway.

Though doctors who ran tests and examined Charles told Mom he was volatile and possibly dangerous, she didn't believe it for one minute! More, they said his mind could snap at any moment and he could kill us all!

She had no reason to believe it. He was *schizophrenic* and always on display for her.

Kind, courteous, thoughtful - she only saw a good side.

I knew though – and neighbors too – the other side that surfaced on the heels of her departure! Doors slamming, screaming, throwing things, slapping me to the floor, cursing and unjust punishments. And *lies.*

Truly, I think Charles tried to drive me crazy. We lived in a duplex, one stacked on the other. Harold Padgett and wife rented from Mom. Very nice people. I kept hoping they would say something to Mom. They never did. People said little back then about abuse they knew.

At first I agreed with Mom. His behavior seemed childish to me. But when Mom came in the door, the house was cleaned from his rampage, and if anything was unfixable, *I did it.* Worse than any of this - I expected this from *him* - was that Mom believed him. She believed his lies – too tired, too weary to even ask me my side.

Charles was aware I didn't bruise. He took full advantage of that so as not to leave a mark on me that I could show Mom. His favorite place for me was the kitchen floor (while David watched TV in the other room, or played outside). He was always *sweet to me* in Mom's presence - or David's - all this coyness made me look like the liar.

He was very slick. ***Evil.***

I frequently replayed his doctors' words in my mind during those times; that he was hostile – his mind could snap – that he could kill us all.

Sick or no, I realized Charles was very cunning and ruthless. I didn't know if I believed in God or not. I didn't think so. But I definitely *believed in demons* because I knew I was living with them!

Every child with an alcoholic in the house knows you don't invite friends over. *You never know what they're going to do.* But it's very likely that person will embarrass you in a moment's time. Often out of spite.

I spent the night at friends every time I could, since my duties didn't fall during those hours. Connie's parents didn't mind if it was a school night. They understood. If I didn't come home on a Tuesday night, on Saturday Mom might ask me, "Where were you on Tuesday night?"

In spite of my home difficulties I'd thrived at school until then. I was in a big marching band that performed at events like the Indy 500 Parade, on Student Council, the Honor Society and other things. When I invited Mom to attend an event, she'd always beg off by saying she was too tired and would hand me $20. So I had money most of the time even if my peers did not.

I carried the gun for some weeks, quickly removing it when arriving home so as not to be discovered. Then, an aunt who always feigned interest in me (but grilled me about Mom), discovered I carried it one day in the car. She told Mom. Mom then got rid of it.

Its discovery turned out to be a good thing though. Two weeks later I was arrested for shoplifting at J.C. Penney's. Pity if I'd been carrying that gun!

Sitting inside the jail cell, I heard the detective calling my mother at work. I cringed.

Nothing would upset her more than my being in jail, except being bothered at work! She had a perfect record, was never late, and had never missed a day in decades.

I wondered what she'd do. While I sat there in the cell, I rehearsed the litany she'd railed at me all my life. I knew it by heart. *"I wish I'd never had you. You were an accident from the beginning. All you've ever done is cause me trouble. If you don't straighten up, I'm sending you to reform school (juvenile hall). You'll never amount to anything anyway!"*

She had her chance now.

Mom avoided my gaze through the bars when she came in. Police were willing to let me go since it was my first offense. Penney's would not prosecute.

Would she take me and pay my bail and fines though?

Other factors worked in my favor that day. I'd forgotten how competitive Mom was with Sis, whose children were perfect, grossly gifted, and super-intelligent. She made certain *everyone* knew it too! Sis's conversation translated that everything she had, or did, was *bigger, better, best.*

I later learned it's the language of insecurity and 'envy'. Mom didn't dare let Sis know about this little matter.

Sis was driven by pride and a need to control others. Mom fell under that broad sweep too. (Anyone who would let her control them did - she never liked me though!) If Sis found out about this, everyone in the family would know about it before dark! And it would mean Mom had failed as a parent. Plus Sis had helped Mom a great deal. She would disappoint Sis.

Mom made it clear she couldn't understand why I would shoplift when she gave me so much money. I saw that it wasn't a matter of honor or whether stealing was right or wrong.

It was pride. It was paying your own way in life! Something seemed twisted about all this. I think I stole that day because I was bored.

It was during this period that I began to love darkness. When I came into the house at night, I was too afraid to turn on the light, so I sat in the dark. I welcomed it for it hid me from harm and abuse. (I think Druid and Celtic teens of today love that darkness for the same reasons.) It can make one feel powerful.

Without my permission, Connie told her family that Charles beat me. But I was secretly hoping she would anyway! I began to stay there 3 or 4 nights a week. It proved to be the only respite I had over the years when things were the worst for me. The only times I avoided Connie's was church times. I went with them occasionally. But I wasn't interested in a God who had demonstrated so little caring for me.

I didn't know what I'd done that life had handed me such a raw deal.

I must have been wearing my depression. That and my grades were slipping. The "battle axe of the third floor" - my homeroom teacher Mrs. Myrtle Mize - expressed her concern to me. She knew I could do better. She wanted to help. Her concern touched me- I waved it off.

One day about this time, the assistant principal of our large high school summoned me to his office. I was scared to death, unaware what I'd done.

A. K. Jones, Jr. was a gifted administrator and assistant principal who would move on to much higher positions and prestige in his career. He motioned to a chair, gesturing for me to sit down. Picking up papers that lay on his desk, he looked at me intently.

I thought he would never open his mouth.

"Sharon," he began, "We got your test scores and I wanted to talk to you personally about them." I gasped, not knowing what was coming next.

"It seems," he continued, "That you received an extremely high score and I wanted to commend you. In fact, your score on the English portion was so high, for every 100 students in the nation, you would rank in the top 3%."

You could've knocked me over with a feather. I was totally dumbfounded at his words.

I didn't know what to say. I sat frozen.

"Your homeroom teacher (Mrs. Mize again) and I were discussing your situation, and I wanted to inquire what your future plans are."

Plans??? Was he talking about *college*? If that's what he meant, I was too busy trying to survive *this week*! I had no plans beyond the semester I was in. No one had ever discussed 'goals' with me. (Except when my mother did to discourage me if I ever made any. *So true*!)

Whatever my response was to him, it was sufficient for him to realize that I had an extremely negative outlook. He then gave me some advice. Advice that, when I got around to following it, changed my entire destiny.

That took almost ten years.

"Sharon, I have a question for you." He went on, "If I had a glass sitting here on my desk that held half its capacity, how would you see it? Half full, or half empty?"

I glared at the glass. He already knew my answer was '*why bother with a half empty glass anyway?*'

"I want to recommend a book to you, Sharon. I read it recently myself, and its powerful and revealing. I believe it will help you. The title is "The Power of Positive Thinking," by Dr. Norman Vincent Peale.

"Read it, Sharon. It will help you."

I said I would, but I couldn't think of what I could learn from a doctor. I promptly forgot about it.

But after school that afternoon, I walked home with Connie. I couldn't wait to tell her what had happened that day in A. K. Jones' office - namely because she was one of the few people who would even care. I'd become emotionally dependent upon her and her family. Emotions that had found no target in a lifetime, now centered on them. I needed them desperately, and I couldn't figure why Connie seemed to need my affection too.

After all, she had everything that I didn't - a family who loved her! Perhaps she just felt sorry for me - *I knew I did*!

Later, I walked home on McCarty, the same street as I'd done dozens of times before.

I made decisions while walking there. One decision was that I was never going to be like my mother.

I had no respect left for her at all.

Another decision was about the kind of woman I wanted to be. One that others looked up to and respected. My mind's eye saw a teacher or professor -someone confident and poised.

No decision would affect me however, like the one I made concerning God that day.

Anger took up residence in me. College? *Was he crazy?*

A cruel desire to make someone else hurt as much as I did, festered. All I'd ever wanted was a family - someone to love! It seemed like a small thing to ask, yet others had it. Even an arm around the shoulder to say, "You can do it, Kid!" *I was so negative that I failed to see that a marvelous man had just wrapped his arms around my empty soul.*

So just in case there *was* a God, I *decided to hate him anyway.*

Where are the A.K. Jones, Jr's today? He was a man who cared, when few others had.

He was a man who intervened in a troubled child's life to make a *difference*. To inspire goals and raise the bar of achievement- not lower the grading curve!! He lifted a standard.

Who aspires to mediocrity today, and of *Common* Core? Answer. Today's substandard teachers and their teaching methods, powered by the NEA.

Former Florida Governor Jeb Bush is a big proponent of Common Core, the newest educational standards embraced by 45 states (then!). It purports not to teach but raise achievement standards. Very vocal critics say it is forcefeeding children political propaganda, such as the Holocaust was a hoax, and those critics add that the sexuality portion is prepared by Planned Parenthood starting at kindergarten. Youth already graduate without the ability to read, consigning them to lifelong mediocrity.

Common Core is just more *government* control over citizens.

Jeb Bush said at a conference in Boston in 2014, "I want to hear (critics') solutions for the hodgepodge of dumbed-down standards that's created group mediocrity in our schools." Quite an admission about today's public schools!" Hellooooooooo?

The group Jeb spoke of are now mostly graduated, having entered the marketplace, dumbed down, trained only to live by their 5 senses.

Their minds are yet *virgin soil,* unchallenged and unlearned.

Proof of this is every college in America has remedial classes to bring students up to speed for college level classes, these failed by **existing** standards!

Now Common Core; hence comes **MORE commonness**!

Ivy league schools that once gave copies of the Bill of Rights and Constitution upon orientation, now give condoms and an AIDS packet! Moreover, traditional values are now vilified and ridiculed as *evil.*

You cannot summon people to valor, integrity or honor when you abandon traditional values that emphasize the *source* of knowledge and wisdom.

Because the baser nature in man will always prevail!

Take a look: Cheating is thought to be okay today in colleges and in the military as well.

Abortion is treated as birth control - some having seven or eight of them. (I know a beautiful woman who just had her seventh abortion). Seventy percent of the prison population are fatherless boys, and much of today's adults don't even marry!

I also know some excellent teachers and I don't negate their gifts and endeavors. Yet their efforts are so diminished by a 'system' today. Yes! Years ago, I learned our national education system had dropped to some of the lowest in the world, yet many teachers were totally oblivious of that fact. We are in the mid 20's in the world rankings today. We used to be first and leading only decades ago!

Conversely, the students who excel most in the U.S. are often *foreign*.

Why does society accept or even tolerate mediocrity? And in the case of Common Core - endorse it?

Where is *Greatness?* Or *Passion? Nobility?* "He who is noble plans noble things, and on noble things he stands." Isaiah 32:8 We were born for more than common! We can't change the world and be *like it!*

Run for the front door of your child's public school and get them into private or charter schools where you have a say! Trying to improve today's educational system is a total exercise in futility. It's constrained by ignorance and regulations!

You *can find inspiration* online at K-12.org, however.

The fact is that the 'mundane' of homework and chores, etc. are what teach children self-discipline and responsibility. Today's video games so stimulate children, they're so hyped on dopamine that most of life bores them! So church youth leaders are defeated before they start, and feel they must also offer 'hype' to draw them. Video games teach murder and *death*! Stop it now!

Meantime, turn off the television and introduce your offspring to the library, where *they can learn to visualize.* Greatness is found there. That's where Cabinet member Ben Carson who's a world-known surgeon **did** find greatness, when his Mom shut off the TV!

While you're there, look for a copy of The Marva Collins Story, the true story of a *real* educator and hero who started Westside Prep in Chicago. Twice tapped to be on Cabinet level position, she never accepted because she knew her methods *worked!*

Her reward was death threats from petty and envious peers. She's now deceased. But, she set the bar the first day by teaching her students to memorize Tennyson. No student listened to contemporary music after they begun! Nor could they ever say 'I can't' again!

All her students went to college, even problem and emotionally disabled students. "*I've never lost a child...*" Marva Collins' own words. Brains Matter.™

9

A Shady "Character"

Dear Sharon:

So what if life seems to have double-crossed you? You still have powerful choices, and you don't have to do anything you don't want to do in life. Nothing so terrible has happened to you that you can't still be the captain of your own ship and master of your own destiny. It isn't like you are an invalid or anything. You are young and your whole life lies ahead.

You may not have met them yet, but there are a lot of decent people in the world, and you can be one of them. Not everyone is negative or petty. You can choose your own friends. You can be different.

Therefore, you can pledge yourself to living your life as a decent person. Do so now!

Signed, Me.

Though not exact, these were my thoughts at age fifteen or so. I didn't put them onto paper. I didn't have to. They were written in my heart.

Many circumstances led to this assertion, however.

Though young, I'd read books and so I'd unwittingly stumbled upon a principle that I wouldn't understand until much later. It was a powerful dynamic that propelled my life in a positive direction, though accidental.

I'd made a *decision* and that decision determined my *conduct,* and conduct determines *character.*

If we don't like something about our lives, we need only the courage to make a decision to change it. If we follow through, *positive change is set into motion.*

I've said for decades that, *if I can't learn anything, I can learn what not to do!* No circumstance is without benefit in our lives. Failure comes only when we don't learn from the experience. All truly great people will have more failure in their lives than the average person. Babe Ruth held the ***strikeout*** **record for decades**, though no one ever talks about *that* record. The number of *hits* he made are what made him famous!

He kept trying...

Connie's family was religious and I wanted nothing of that. God had never done anything for me. I was weary of deceiving them. As the ebb and flow of relationships occur - I gravitated away from them. And I'd made up my mind to be 'decent' too.

In high school then, I now had other friends who lived much nearer to me. Two of those friends were sisters, Lisa and Marie. Lisa was a classmate. Their mother was a terrific cook. She served us wonderful snacks after school where she worked, and she always included me. Their dad seemed understanding about my home situation. He knew Charles by sight, and didn't mind if I took meals at their house.

Lisa and Marie and I had great fun attending school dances and after school functions. During this time in my junior year, a school jock named Jay took an interest in me. No one was more surprised than I was about it! Every girl in the school had a crush on Jay. I was so amused that I returned the attention, though I didn't really know what to do in the relationship. But I liked his good looks and clean cut appearance. I was in seventh heaven.

Not because he liked me; *because I was the envy of every girl in school!* (Not a lot of substance, I know)

Two of my closest friends in school were homecoming queens in consecutive years. I realized I'd somehow found my way in the 'in' crowd. I wondered how I'd gotten there.

Perhaps life had begun to smile on me.

One step inside my front door jerked me back to reality, however. And I knew that not *enough* had changed! The worse Charles' health became, the more cruel he became to me. He managed to kill my pet bird I'd taught to talk. No joy allowed! He was getting worse.

Meantime, Mom often said *she didn't know what she was going to do with me* since I was so out of control,. Charles simply couldn't do anything with me because I was so rebellious.

What is it with parents who think their flesh and blood will just relent to a man friend she moves in? It fosters rebellion, because they know this man is a stranger!

With working so much, Mom had no time to deal with me or the problems I caused her, she said.

I'd never taken Jay home with me except once when I knew Charles wouldn't be there. We went to football games and movies, and he was a perfect gentleman. I liked that - he was the *first* one I'd spent much time with. We merely held hands, embraced and kissed, but I soon found myself frightened about where this relationship was headed, and I didn't know why.

One day, in a fit of depression over the condition of my home life, and the fact I felt so far from the 'norm', I broke up with Jay. Later I wished I hadn't. *Too late.*

During the times that my adopted (by me) families did normal things families do, like vacations or travel, it made life very hard for me. I had nowhere to go except city streets then. We didn't live on the side of town where city parks existed. Holidays were the worst, due to lots of family activities that rarely included me. I had nothing to do. And it was cold.

The streets seemed so lonely, especially at Christmas. It felt like everyone had somebody to love, to buy presents for. Except for me. As I watched busy shoppers stride by me with arms loaded with packages, it seemed so little to ask....someone to love.

An upscale department store had an upstairs lunch counter that overlooked a 'tea room' downstairs. The store was so pretty at holidays, I liked to spend time there. (Remember I always had money!) Well dressed folks dined downstairs where boutiques put on fashion shows. I liked to sit at that counter and watch the watchers (still a habit).

I sensed there was a huge vacuum between that world and the ugly one I knew. These people seemed to enjoy life -and each other. They didn't seem as stressed as I always felt. I enjoyed their laughter.

How to enter that world, I pondered?

One particular day, when I was about 14 or so, I strolled the sidewalk, with no particular destination, time on my hands. I walked by a nice restaurant and through the glass window, I observed a very pretty, dark-haired woman eating alone. She raised her napkin to her mouth, and when she did so, our eyes locked. I will never forget that moment. Or her look. Her eyes gazed deeply into my soul that day, and for an instant, she *felt my aloneness*. And I felt her kindness.

It was a spiritual encounter. It warmed my empty soul.

Something penetrated my life that day. A thought? Her prayer? Perhaps both. Whatever it was, I felt her *compassion* and I knew someone saw my hurt and cared . I purposely walked by that restaurant several times, about the same time of day. I never saw her again.

If you've been keeping count, you realize that I had about five abusers in my life by now, if you count the neglect, verbal scorn and emotional abuse of my mother, and Charles. But the worst one was to come.

The streets bore their problems to me, but staying at my friends' houses presented another set of problems as well.

Big problems.

It was after a few months that I started spending time with Lisa and Marie, that their Dad began to indicate that he felt I should 'pay my way', so to speak. At first, I wasn't certain what he meant! Though I supposed he was a good husband and father, he soon became way too touchy with me.

His wife worked a lot, so she was out of the house. I'm not sure what this man worked at, if anything. But one day, when he had the opportunity, he summoned me into a room to show me something. It was my first exposure to pornography. I can't tell you how shocked I was that people did these things, much less allowed themselves to be photographed while doing them!

Pornography of *any* kind, especially involving children, was seriously against the law then and carried stiff penalties, unlike now.

My reaction was to pretend naivet'e and that I didn't know what his objective was. I quickly left, acting like it had no effect on me. I said nothing. But sometime later, Mom showed me a small newspaper clipping, that this man had just been arrested for selling pornography.

It wasn't the first time, the article stated. So I guess it was no secret to his wife.

After this event, this man would feign fatherly affection in front of the family and teased me, sometimes tickling me and pulling me onto his lap. Once there, I 'felt' his affection was anything but fatherly.

He became my worst abuser.

Though he was never fully successful, it became needful for me to develop new skills at outwitting him.

I needed these people, for I now had nowhere else to escape Charles except their home. I'd grown accustomed to not having to resort to the streets with them in my life. Besides I genuinely liked his family! *They couldn't help he was a pervert!* So this circumstance forced me to learn to *use* people. Matters had so worsened at home that I felt in constant crisis and that Charles might actually kill me.

I began to take full advantage of their hospitality, but was very careful to evade this man's reach. Or, I would play along, then punch or kick him hard when others couldn't see it. I fought him with everything in me - ***He** wasn't going to tell anyone!*

This was abuse in reverse, I supposed. Sometimes these altercations got violent because I fought him. If I was doing dishes alone in the kitchen, he'd deliberately pass by me, too close, sometimes stroking my breast or touching me.

Like his pornography, he was vile to me.

It seemed that I always had to work to be one step ahead of the dirt bag men in my life. Charles never attempted to violate me sexually, probably because he knew that was the one thing Mom *would* kill him for. She could be vicious. Men were so base in my mind, that I wondered if any of them could ever be trusted alone.

Or, if any ever thought *above the waist?*

It was my mother who pointed out to me that it was men who held the money, power and prestige of the world... certainly true then. I found myself envying the man's role in society and I wanted it. *They* didn't deserve it. I felt I could be a better man than they were, and more responsible. Most were brutish in my mind.

At the corner drug store, Lisa and I often met guys over ice cream or shakes who attended a nearby barber college. Their dorm was down the street and their attention flattered us. After all, we were still in high school, as juniors. They would spin their tales about their dorm life where they rotated cooking evening meals and what all they served. Most were from out of town and seemed extra nice.

One evening, a new guy named Larry sat down next to me. He told me about himself, his hometown and his family. He impressed me with his immaculate grooming and coordinated dress. His shoes shined and his fingernails were manicured. Most guys around that neighborhood had grease under their fingernails from working on cars!

Larry was a different kind of guy, in my thinking.

Later, I learned when Larry arrived back at the dorm, he announced, *"I've found the girl I'm going to marry!"*

Two weeks later, I left for my scheduled summer visit to Grandma's, a welcome reprieve to get away from Charles. Mom took David to the weekly sitter during those periods. If Charles wasn't working, David stayed home.

While I was away, Larry wrote to me often. I was amused but rarely wrote back... I had already researched places I could run away to. Teen Challenge was a big organization I'd read about that took in teen runaways and helped them graduate high school. But they were new then and didn't have any local facilities then.

I didn't know what I would do.

While I was away at Grandma Sally's, Mom and Charles moved! No Joke. I never saw that house of misery again!

Returning, and before my first day of school, Charles informed me he wanted me home school the next day to babysit David. He had a Dr's appointment.

Right. Along summer without a night out with the boys! I didn't show up. But I had my *reasons*.

The room Mom had prepared for me in the new house was beautiful. Too bad it had to be where Charles lived, I mused. There was a new cherry bedroom set, and beautiful green curtains graced the picture window.

Mom hadn't been gone to work on evening shift very long that day, when I heard a loud crash. Since David was out, I knew it was Charles. I raced to the kitchen to see what had happened. Mom's favorite crystal pitcher lay on the floor, completely shattered.

She had several expensive glassware and dishes.

That night, I noted that Charles stayed up well past his bedtime. At first I thought nothing of it as he was only working a couple of days a week then. Then, it washed over me like cold water the *real* reason he was up.

His malice for me was wholly predictable at this point.

When I heard Mom's car pull into the drive, I cracked my door. Charles immediately told her I'd broken her pitcher, 'foolin' around *like I always did.*'

Did he break it for this?

I was accustomed to living with a pathological liar who was schizophrenic. But I'd never adjusted to Mom's acceptance of everything he said, never conferring with me to even hear my side of the story.

I closed my bedroom door and made a vow. *I would run away.* I didn't know where. I didn't care. Anywhere would do. I'd already tried to kill Charles once in the spring when he deliberately shoved my new transistor radio off the table with his elbow, causing it to shatter. (They were all plastic then). But Mom came into the room behind me just in time to grab my arm with the knife in my hand-ready to plunge it.

One of us was going to die, sooner or later.

I would run away as far as I could. Not because of Charles. I knew he was mental.

Because of Mom.

That's why I never made it home to babysit. I was busy planning my getaway.

When I arrived home that night, Charles was asleep, no doubt tired from being up the previous night to spin his web of lies to her. I was relieved.

I laid the note I'd prepared for Mom on the kitchen counter telling her I needed book money the next day at school. That was true, but I wasn't going to use the money for that! I knew she would leave it. She was always proud of 'paying her way' in life. Working a double shift that week, she'd be out the door by 5:30am to pick up her riders.

Then I went to my room to pack. I was too afraid to turn on the light, so I opened the drapes wide at the picture window.

I packed by moonlight and silently slid the drawers open. I stuffed my suitcase into the closet.

Totally exhausted, I sank into bed. I slept deeply.

The next thing I knew, I awakened to a face glaring at mine only inches away. Morning light streamed through the window. It was Charles. His eyes were bulging and wide with rage. Having dental work done then, he had several front teeth missing. The remaining ones seemed like long horse teeth. I'd never been so close to evil...

"You think you're pretty smart, don't you?" He screamed, spit spraying into my face. "*If you ever do that again,* (defy him by not showing up for his night out) *I'll kill you, so help me God.*"

Then he proceeded to beat me with his fists, first about the head and face. Then, he took several direct blows to the stomach but they were softened somewhat by the bounce of the bed.

But he'd become so out of control, I feared he might kill me *then.*

However, he suddenly turned and walked out, slamming my door. Mom had obviously left for work.

I knew what I had to do.

I got up and looked at my face in the mirror. Blood trickled down my cheek from a cut beneath my eye. His ring... My lower teeth felt loose. My ribs hurt. I hurried and dressed.

A morbid fear came over me when I realized *I couldn't leave without getting the money from the kitchen counter.* He might attack me again.

But I had to have that money to leave.

Suddenly the phone rang. I knew it had to be the driver. Since Charles didn't have a driver's license anymore as part of his penalty for the accident he'd caused, he had a driver, an apprentice plumber he trained, whose job it was also to always drive him to and from work. *This was my chance.*

I entered the room as Charles scowled at me, still trembling. He was telling the apprentice that 'he didn't know if he could work that day since "Shern" had already ruined his day.' He was very upset.

What else was new, I thought sourly? I'm the source of all that went wrong in his life! Gratefully, he acted uninterested in what I was doing. I saw the money! I picked it up, resisting the urge to run.

Back in my room, I knew I had to leave with my suitcase now, before the apprentice arrived to pick Charles up - if he caught me, he would kill me.

Quietly, I held my breath and slipped out the front door while he was still on the phone. I was glad the kitchen was in the rear, yet I still had to walk to the corner in full view of the front picture window, lugging that big suitcase (the only one I had). I had about 300 feet or so to go.

At the bus stop, I stashed my suitcase behind some bushes while I waited for the bus. Good thing, for shortly, I saw the apprentice drive by. I hoped Charles wouldn't notice me when they drove back by. He didn't.

Ruefully, I thought, *I wish I'd done the world a favor and killed him when I had the chance!* Then I thought, No... he wasn't worth it. Running away was my only option, because it had come down to him or me.

One of us was going to die.

I waited thirty minutes on the bus. I vowed that day I would never go back. My birthday had just passed. I felt much older than my 17 years.

But the abuse was finally over that day. From Charles. From Mom. From Arch. From Lisa's dad and any other.

"As the fear of God is the beginning of wisdom,
so the denial of God is the height of foolishness."
R.C. Sproul

PART II

The Metamorphosis

- -

**Worry does not empty tomorrow of its sorrow.
It empties today of its strength.**

—Corrie ten Boom

10

In Hot Pursuit

Taking out my compact from my purse, I looked at my face in the mirror. The cut on my check stung, and my lower lip was blue and swollen. My ribs felt bruised. My teeth were loose. *The one time he left marks on me and I can't even show them to Mom,* I thought wryly.

The whirring of the bus motor made me drowsy. I laid my head back against the seat, closing my eyes, reviewing recent events.

I felt I was left with no other recourse than to show up at Sally's unannounced, and explain what had happened. If she didn't believe me, or tried to make me return, then I'd run away again and look for a city where a Teen Challenge existed. Sally had aged a lot since I'd been there when I was eleven and gone to live with Mom. And she still had Arch in her care.

Up until now, no family members had quite believed my stories about Charles' treatment of me. Mom was too skilled in running interference for him, explaining away behavior that might seem strange. Besides, she kept everything secret about Charles, like how many wives he'd had, except that he was very ill. That proved useful when she needed excuses.

The bus driver let me off at the highway, the same place Mom had gotten off with me in her arms fourteen years earlier. I then called and asked for a ride to Sally's.

Mack was getting older and didn't farm much now. Ray and his wife ran the farm.

When Grandma saw my face, she knew something had happened. She came through for me. I enrolled in the new high school up on the highway. Everyone there welcomed me warmly. They treated me somewhat like a celebrity, being a big city girl and all. The first week, they nominated me to a committee position. Though the lower classes were larger, there were only forty-two seniors in our class. That was a big change from the high school I'd left with hundreds of senior class members.

An odd thing occurred. People called me 'Susan' at first. Then I learned I had a look-a-like in that school. It was remarkable. People often mistook us for each other, but her folks had money. Big money. I didn't relate.

Only days after arriving, I received a letter from Larry. He knew the address from the summer and had hoped I was there. I'd left so quickly, he didn't even know where I was. He just guessed. I welcomed his letter.

For two whole weeks, we heard absolutely nothing from Mom or anyone up north.

What must she be thinking? She probably figured I'd have come back by now, I thought. But how was she explaining my absence to Sis? I didn't see family there very often, even if Mom did, but sooner or later it seemed like it would come up that I was no longer there.

Finally, Effie called Sally. Mom probably confided to her that I was gone, hoping she wouldn't tell Sis, and also hoping she would check to see if I was at Sally's for her.

"Sally," she asked, "Is Sharon down there?"

Grandma liked Effie and had always treated her as one of her girls.

But when she told her that I was there, it was with a firm voice. I wouldn't be going back.

Had it taken two weeks for Mom to care? I speculated that the dishes had piled up enough for her to miss me. Sally also told Effie of my condition upon arrival. Effie didn't comment.

I wondered how Mom could explain it all to Sis. But I didn't care. I made a decision very early that Sis might control everyone else in the family, and Mom too, but she wouldn't control me. She always acted gun-shy around me, as though aware of that..

The stream of letters from Larry continued. He'd bought a car. He was coming to visit at Thanksgiving.

A build-up of high school credits permitted me to graduate in only one semester, but I'd have to wait until May to get my diploma. That was alright, because I needed to get a job to pay for senior pictures and other graduating expenses. I couldn't put that on Sally.

I didn't fully appreciate them then, but the teaching staff at this high school were superb. They did all the paperwork for me to enroll and attend Eastern Kentucky state college nearby. I would go.

Larry came and visited, and then at Christmas he took me to meet his family. I liked them, particularly his Dad. He was a little loud when he got excited, and boisterous at times, (I wasn't used to that) but I found it fun he was a great conversationalist. We hit it off immediately. Larry was the oldest of three; a brother and sister. His brother seemed a little aimless; just graduating high school. . And his sister was a little coarse, I thought. (*Who was I to make that assertion?*)

Something about Sally's philosophy of not 'airing your dirty linen' That observation also proved true.

His Mom kept a warm and comfortable home, though unpretentious, and was the best cook ever. Best were the extended family I met at holiday dinners. One was an executive with Kroger. I knew that if I did ever marry Larry, I'd be marrying 'up'. After all, I knew what my beginnings were! I was a street urchin but I aimed to change that image.

In January, I went north to Ohio where my favorite aunt lived and I could stay with her family to find a job. I was too young, still 17, to work without a work permit (required then).

I surely wasn't going to ask Mom for it!

Soon I took a job babysitting for a woman with seven children. All but one attended school next door. He was the baby, about two years old. The mother failed to tell me he sometimes had epileptic convulsions! Somehow I made it through the first seizure, when she told me on the phone to put him in the tub, with cold water, if I recall that correctly. Her checks bounced on me about every other week! I had no choice than to wait on her to make them good. I stayed with my friend Alpha some of that time, as she lived in Cincinnati near the babysitting job.

Larry still wrote to me daily, though I rarely did. It was comical to me that this man had now followed me over three states. *He could be serious,* I mused. I liked Larry. He was enjoyable. We laughed a lot and had the same interests. We both liked horses and the same music. I felt relaxed with him.

It was during this time that I developed a new admiration for Larry. Never once over three years did he ever attempt to take advantage of me. Quite the contrary. He said he loved me too much. He'd resolved to wait until marriage, in the hope that I would marry him.

His decision flies in the face of modern philosophy that says youth have no control over their own bodies or minds. *Just little animals* who will do what they will do, without any ability to think, or have control over themselves.

Pass the condoms please!

Larry honored that decision until our wedding night.

The first time I saw Mom was nine months later at graduation. She tried to pretend that everything was normal. It was awkward. She didn't stay long. *Charles was sick*; he might need her. By now, I was used to men who always took precedence over *me.*

Larry came to my graduation. Mom ignored him. I didn't bother to introduce her to him.

Labor Day weekend found me at Sally's packing to go to college.

I once heard a football coach say that in every game, *there are four or five plays that determine the outcome of every game.* I think that is true of life too. We must never underestimate the power of the choices we make.

There's some that will determine our outcome too!

Larry called me to once again plead with me to come back to Indiana where he now worked the city I'd fled. He had a good job. I *didn't even* want *to do that.* I later felt that he feared I would go off to college and he would lose me to another dude.

You can get an apartment, he said. I vacillated. The thought of college was a little frightening to me, and like most teens, I was eager to start earning money regularly - with little foresight the minimal paychecks following.

This is what *parents* are for -guidance at times like these.

As suddenly as I'd left, I returned. I would live to regret that decision many times.

Though I went to college later in life, sometimes we must seize an opportunity. I let down those educators who'd spent time - and money- to get me registered as a student.

I found a job quickly typing abstracts, (abstracts preceded title insurance) and a nice two room apartment a block away from where Larry lived. He lived next door to Effie and Max.

I rode the bus to work, but later on, Mom gave in to guilt and signed for me to buy my first car, a modified 1957 Chevy Bel Air, candy apple red. I loved that car - so did everybody else! I don't think I ever really thanked Mom for that, I was so bitter at that time.

Life seemed pretty good then, *but soon the ache of loneliness returned. Something was missing!*

Dating Larry became 'old hat' and predictable to me. B.o.r.i.n.g. I started seeing another guy on the sly. Ted regularly picked me up from work for a brown bag lunch at the park. And occasionally I saw him other times when I could evade Larry's control of my time.

One day in the new car Ted drove (typical girl, I was impressed!), I observed a long scar down his inner forearm. I asked him about it. He said he got angry with his mom once, running his arm through the front picture window. Then taking me back to work, he'd playfully tried to run over a cat in the road on purpose.

I didn't have to write Dear Abby for counsel on *that* matter! I closed the door on that relationship when I shut the door to the car. I decided then, that Larry was 'safe'.

During Christmas holidays, Larry and I had a serious argument. I don't even recall why. We broke up.

My upstairs neighbor then started inviting me to attend parties after that. I went and was surprised she was so 'wild' - in my mind. Of course I was underage, but these parties bored me too. I just couldn't get excited about, or find the fun in, falling down, then vomiting your brains out at a porcelain altar! Not to mention the hangover. I'd gotten drunk once in Ohio and I vowed not to do it ever again. I wanted to be have control.

About seven months or so after we broke up, I got into my car and deliberately drove down Larry's street. I knew he was seeing a girl because Effie had told me. He was standing outside with her. Seeing me, he walked over to my car. She disappeared.

Though it'd been several months since I'd seen him, I still felt I was on pretty solid ground. And I had nothing to lose in my mind.

After exchanging pleasantries (which I'm not good at) I blurted out, *"I thought maybe we could get married."*

He didn't know what to say. I thought I saw his heart skip a beat, but then reservation swept over his face at the thought I could be joking.

No, *I wasn't joking.*

Three months later, we were married on a rainy day, October 19, 1963. We chose a huge old Methodist church I'd been attending. Yes, I'd resolved to be 'decent' and decent folks go to church I thought. I'd go but with as little involvement as possible.

Shortly after the news got out to the family, the aunt who always grilled me for info about Mom - who'd discovered my gun - stopped by my apartment to ask when the baby was due, since we were getting married so quickly.

Larry was standing beside me, and I could feel his blood pressure rising! This was the first time she'd ever visited me.

With family like this, who needs enemies?

Oh well. I would accept their gifts anyway. And I couldn't help if she judged me by *her* standards! Or lack of them.

Mom was so excited that, after everything, I'd turned out so normal. Guess she thought she'd be visiting me in jail. I'm certain she thought it would please Sis, but I did appreciate what she did anyway. She contacted the church and paid for an elaborate reception there. It was more beautiful than I would ever have imagined! It all fell together perfectly and my wedding dress – from a Montgomery Ward catalog – was beautiful.

It poured down rain that day. Everyone worried that I'd be late, as I routinely was then.

My aunt Mary Lou's husband gave me away, Howard. He was a good man, the only one in the family I really respected. I'd stayed with them some while working in Ohio. He'd mildly ruined me though. As an executive with General Electric, I felt for some years that decent men always wore suits... until I realized pedophiles do too!

Mary Lou was the only person I'd ever met who could quote scripture *ver batim.* It didn't seem to help her life though. She eventually divorced Howard for Jack Daniels. This was a grievous experience for me personally, and I'm sure her boys too, though one became a preacher! And was a terrible witness. What can I say but the truth here? All the religious people in my family were phony to me. Hypocrites.

Raindrops poured on the outside, and tears poured on the inside. I guess no one thought this would ever happen! Even I sobbed so hard I couldn't get Larry's ring on. But I was busy wondering if I was *doing the right thing and said so to Howard walking down the aisle!* The chapel was pretty full, between Mom's siblings and Larry's extended family.

The reception - where we received four toasters - was the closest to normal I'd ever felt. It soon wore off.

Only after we got the photos back did I see that the two candlelabras on each side behind us were never lit for the ceremony. *There never was any fire in that long term marriage!*

Then I discovered that our wedding certificate wasn't stamped either. But the license was filed, so it was legal. Turned out the preacher who married us was phony too...he became a well- known Methodist bishop but wrote profusely on why the *deity of Christ was untrue.*

Larry and I soon followed the American ritual of going into debt. First a car, then a horse. No misspelling here. H-O-R-S-E, not HOUSE. Both of us were horse lovers, and on impulse one Sunday evening, we bought a fifteen month old purebred Arabian stallion named Abu Razeyd for $1500. (That's about $4500 now) We called him 'Buddy'. (Abu means 'son of') We didn't even have a place to keep him, but the owner kept him for us until we located a boarding stable.

This was the beginning of a love affair; a virtual odyssey that I haven't recovered from.

Nor has Larry. We had that stallion all his life, 27 years. He was wonderful and spirited, yet so gentle with children, ours and many others, even though we used him for stud many years and made money with him that way. This gentleness was unusual - even for Arabians.

We showed him in the show ring, halter and under English saddle. We used a professional trainer to do so. This we did for a couple of years, then I became pregnant. When I was about six months along, the trainer showed him on a muddy track and he'd pulled tendons on his front legs. So those last four months of pregnancy had me on my hands and knees under his belly wrapping his front legs.

Naturally my daughter Rhonda came out an avid horsewoman! I have a picture of her on his back at about two months old, with my hand hidden behind her as she sat on his back.

Craig too loved to be around horses, the smell of leather and feed and that marvelous horse smell that is so addictive. We were definitely a 'horsey' family! Attending horse shows, and horse people always dropping by. And sleeping in the loft of the State Fairgrounds as a family and meeting friends there yearly.

No matter the future trials our family ever faced, we had Arabians through thick and verrrrrry thin. You'll see.

Thirty months after our wedding, Rhonda was born in a brand new, sparkling hospital in Bloomington, Indiana. It was so clean it shone, and had been open only one week. We lived where Larry's Mom and Dad lived then. I always went where Larry found the work, so I gave up the job I'd held as a receptionist for a major life insurance company for almost 3 years. It seemed the right thing.

The hyper-clean environment where Rhonda was born was such a stark contrast to me, given my perception of the ugly reality outside its doors.

I could not bear taking an infant into that ugly world.

In the delivery room, the staff rolled me over onto my stomach and placed Rhonda (named for actress Rhonda

Fleming) face upwards to mine on the corner of the gurney. I had no labor with her, (babies just dropped out of me) so she was totally awake. Her little eyes riveted upon me like little black balls, glistening.

Real love entered my empty heart that day.

The doctor informed me that Rhonda's right foot was turned completely up against the shin bone due to how I'd carried her. *(Too much time under a horse's belly?)* She'd probably need therapy and corrective shoes. That never happened. It was completely normal in a day or two.

At checkout, the nurse wheeled me to the exit in a wheelchair, Rhonda wrapped snugly in my arms. I held her tightly looking at the blue sky as we passed through the exit into the sunlight and into that evil world I'd experienced.

Fear gripped me. I'd never even been around an infant. I didn't know how to care for her! *Much less protect her from evil. Would she grow up like me?* I hoped not! (Obviously my perception was skewed due to the fact I was still so negative and only expected the worst, yet this *did* succeed in bringing me to the end of my self.)

I was oblivious to Larry walking beside me. Suddenly, I felt terribly inadequate to the task of raising this innocent child. I'd forgotten what 'innocence' was, if I'd ever even known it! But I knew she was helpless and wholly dependent upon me for her very life.

I'd married Larry under no false pretenses. He knew I didn't love him, because I would not deceive him. But he'd told me he had enough love for the both of us. I would learn to love him, he said.

I'd succeeded in living my whole life without giving my heart to anyone in love. Life seemed safer that way. In a flash, it had all changed. No longer could I live my life on a dare, in reckless disregard for my own well-being.

Now, someone needed *me*. And I knew I needed something beyond myself! My heart cried out, *God, I don't know if you are real, but if you are then* **become real** *to me...*

"Prayer does change things, all kinds of things. But the most important thing it changes is us. As we engage in this communion with God more deeply and come to know the One with whom we are speaking more intimately, that growing knowledge of God reveals to us all the more brilliantly who we are and our need to change in conformity to Him.

Prayer changes us profoundly." R.C. Sproul

"I think the greatest weakness in the church today is that almost no one believes that God invests His power in the Bible. Everyone is looking for power in a program, in a methodology, in a technique, in anything and everything but that in which God has placed it—His Word. He alone has the power to change lives for eternity, and that power is focused on the Scriptures." R. C. Sproul

11

Peales of Laughter

In my first book by this name that I'm now revising, I titled this chapter, *The Final Zinger*. The name fit, but I think you'll find that this title is more appropriate.

Larry and I soon found out that having a baby dried up funds we'd used to show a horse. Even boarding him was now a drain on the budget. When Larry got a new job back in the big city, we moved to a suburban place with a barn where we could have our horse without paying board. We enjoyed having him at home. More, we began to rent the extra stalls and found it lucrative. We also began to use our stallion at stud because half-Arabians were becoming very popular then, and that brought in several hundred dollars a month sometimes.

The house was a bungalow with an attached garage, and adequate, but small. There was a huge weeping willow in the front yard. It was magnificent, though it never stopped 'weeping'- branches everywhere.

The barn however, was state of the art with power, running water, and telephone. That became Larry's new home over the next five years. He only *slept* in the house. Me? I had two small babies, so I was confined to the house! We did however, have an arrangement where, after being put to bed, that we could hear them at the barn if they awakened.

Over those five years though, the roof on the house developed a troublesome leak. Larry worked on it, but his efforts were often unsuccessful. The owners planned to sell the acreage, so they didn't care.

I tried to talk Larry into buying the place ourselves, but he didn't want to. I was to learn that Larry liked to 'play it safe' and was not a risk taker of any sort. If we'd purchased that home, we could've recovered our money fivefold when it sold to a huge shopping center across the road. This became a sore spot to me as I realized he was governed by his fears.

He had his reasons.

Because I feared that Rhonda would ever be as lonely as I was as a child, I wanted to have another child soon. That way, if Larry and I ever split, they would have each other. But I wasn't quite prepared to have one as soon as I did -15 months after Rhonda meant two babies in diapers!

During pregnancy with Craig, my doctor had questioned me about my medical history and parents blood types due to an excessively high liver bilirubin test that said I would have problems on delivery. He feared the baby would need to have transfusions upon birth. (This was before a vaccine was developed that prevented this problem; *blue-babies.*)

I told the doctor that both my parents had O positive blood. (I knew Dad's blood type because I'd had his dog tags and kept them, even wearing them at times. I took them from Mom's cedar chest. They always had the soldier's blood type on them).

The doctor looked at me then, and mumbled something about how that was impossible if I had rh negative blood. One parent had to be negative too. I dismissed his remark as some misunderstanding, mine or his. Then completely forgot it.

I was eight months pregnant and like every other woman then, I just wanted him to "DO something to *hurry this up,* Doctor!"

Craig came out perfect, but lost weight the first six weeks. Doctors finally tested my milk, finding that the antibodies that were supposed to affect him at birth were now coming out through nursing! Painful weekly blood tests on him were made to monitor his dangerously high bilirubin levels. He also seemed prone to colds and flu.

While I'd initiated this love affair with horses, parenthood had dulled my interest somewhat. Not Larry. It became an obsession. I had spent many hours studying Arabian horse backgrounds and bloodlines, but with Larry, it had seemed to take on a life of its own.

He carried Arabian Horse breeders magazines like they were a *Bible or something*. Studying them always.

If I wanted Larry, I had to call him on the phone (cell phones were a long time coming). It was too difficult to watch small children around huge horses.

Holidays were the only time I saw much of Larry. That was because we always went to his parents' house. His sister and brother both had girls when we did, then we each had boys. All six were so cute then, like stair steps. It was fun watching them play and grow up together. His Dad had horses too, so Larry took his horse magazines to talk about while there.

I had now become an avid reader too, but not about horses. Mostly philosophy and poetry. Ralph Waldo Emerson was my favorite. One day, I read a quotation out loud to Larry from Emerson. It was, "A man is what he thinks about all day long."

"Hmmmm ..." Larry replied, "Then I'm a horse."

Yes, I thought, *and I'm married to a horse's rear end!* Yet I found his answer comical. Larry made a job change and the money turned out to be much less than promised.

With Craig's endless trips to the hospital for tests, to the doctor for treatment, and my not working too, our first real money crunch occurred.

Birth control pills were relatively new then, but against my better judgment I went on them. Family couldn't wait until we had two children when Craig was born, but were now worried we would have *too many*. They felt we had our hands full.

I agreed with them, that my hands were full, at least.

I learned of a new local costume jewelry company that was experiencing phenomenal growth. I checked into it and the woman who started it had become a self-made millionaire. She sounded quite remarkable, and their office wasn't far from where we lived. While I'd never really tried to sell anything before, I thought I'd try it. I surprised myself with great success conducting home parties. Women began to snap up my items.

After working this job for only a few months, the company threw a banquet and invited the reps to attend. I'd met the owner by then, at the shop when I went to refill my supplies. But I hadn't had an opportunity to talk with her. At this dinner, I found myself sitting next to her. She looked very glamorous and wore her beautiful jewelry well.

Of course, her success was impressive to me. I'd never met a real millionaire, personally. Or anyone quite like her. And she seemed to like *me*.

At one point in our conversation however, she stopped me in mid-sentence, and touched my arm. I could tell she wanted to interject a point.

"Sharon," she said, "You really ought to read this book called "The Power of Positive Thinking" by Dr. Norman Vincent Peal. It will help you."

Of course, her objective was only to help me become a better salesperson. But, I was quite shaken by this comment from her. Initially, she'd commended me for my success in selling her jewelry. On the other, she'd told me I needed further help!

False *pride* reared its ugly head, and I felt indignant. Yet her comment carried some weight with me.

Wasn't that book familiar, or something? Some doctor...

Later, I remembered that it was the same one A. K. Jones, Jr. had recommended to me ten years earlier.

Mom had taken some vacations days to help me with each new baby when I came home – like *she was any good with children*. But I appreciated her physical help around the house.

She seemed to be genuinely trying to make amends. I let her. But I always seemed to hold her at arm's length. There was just too much to forgive. I didn't understand why I did so; I just thought it was all the hurt I'd borne which I considered *her fault*.

Within ninety days of beginning birth control pills, I had a radical reaction to them. I went to the surgeon to be evaluated, told him my symptoms and that I couldn't stand up at all, and he asked me when I could be at the hospital. I was thinking *next week*. No, he *meant tonight or in the morning*! *Radical* reaction.

Twelve weeks following surgery, I asked my surgeon about my inability to even get well, or even stand up much. *Could it be the birth control pill?*

He assured me they'd been blamed for a little of everything, and he didn't think so (proving my philosophy that doctors are only licensed to practice medicine!)

Then, on my regular visit to my Ob/Gyn I asked him the same thing. His version was quite different. He told me he wished he'd known about this; he would've taken me off the pills then. And Yes, they were indeed the reason about 3% of all women do have radical reactions such as I had. But since the number is so small, doctors didn't make a practice (?) of telling women.

I thought, *That's fine - unless you're one of the 3%!*

While ill, I'd elected to go to real estate school, thanks largely to my success in selling jewelry. Since I couldn't work then, I thought I could be using the time for something productive. And I felt it would a good future career with children.

I will never forget what my mother said when I told her of my plans. She asked, "*Why* would you want to do that for?" Oh right Mom... we wouldn't want to try to improve ourselves in life, would we? Factory work suited her fine.

She was the biggest downer in my lifetime, for certain. Now if I'd told her I was going to take a factory job and work it for 30 years like her, it would have been a different matter.

Finances were further complicated now with income taxes. The new job Larry had taken required he do his own withholding. We hadn't, barely surviving. Now we owed IRS. April 15 came and went. A slow panic began to build. Not in Larry. We still had medical bills to pay, and I'd added to the burden by paying for real estate school besides.

I went for the real estate exam the end of January. *I failed.* This was a terrible blow to me. My one hope had been to begin to help with the bills. Depression loomed.

Meantime, a nasty leak refused to be fixed in the children's room. If the children needed shoes, we didn't have the money, Larry felt. However, he didn't hesitate to buy halters and bridles for the horses! Depression became full blown.

A nagging thought hounded me. In spite of finances, I was convinced Larry was a good man, and I didn't really deserve him. Maybe if I was a better wife... He deserved a wife who cherished him. I must be doing something wrong. Maybe everything was my fault; that I was jinxed or something. *I felt like it!*

And *why was I the 'rare' one who always had unusual problems and circumstances?*

After all, Larry had had a difficult childhood too. Guilty for not loving him in a romantic way, I knew I did love him in every other way. But he deserved better than me.

During this time, I had no one to talk to. Larry felt that we should be enough for each other as a married couple. That worked for him, because he had all his horsy friends, who when they visited, bypassed the house and went straight to the barn. Anyway, Larry didn't seem to need people like I did. I didn't want to need them – but I now realized I did.

Secretly though, I feared having any real friends. I didn't trust my emotions. Another nagging, persistent thought told me that one day, my precious children would look me in the face, and say *"Mom, you're gay aren't you?"* The final zinger. The very thought tormented me. Self pity now prevailed.. I didn't even know if I was gay, but I didn't love my husband that way, though I performed my conjugal responsibilities. But I was gay when I was young. Maybe that was what was wrong anyway.

Maybe *that* was why I always felt like the fifth wheel in life.

Slowly, I began to feel so inadequate as a mother I felt *anyone* would be a better mother than I could. It was April. Tax time and we now owed two years. I couldn't even look at our stack of bills. I just shoved them into the drawer. I'd planned to be working by now.

A plan began to unfold in my mind. If I failed the upcoming real estate exam, I thought, I'm going to end this misery. I made a plan to overdose in the car and I chose an isolated place so the children wouldn't find me. I'd mail a letter for Larry to find my body the next day.

A week before the state board, I went grocery shopping with the children at a different grocery. Consequently, l spent more time scanning the racks at the entry, filled with books on my right. My eyes fell onto a bright red cover on the very bottom shelf.

The sticker said "Best Seller". The title of the book was *The Power of Positive Thinking*, by Dr. Norman Vincent Peale.

Suddenly, I remembered both occasions where I'd been told to read this book! Both people had said "It will help you." *Maybe this isn't just coincidence,* I thought.

I certainly knew I needed help right then, too.

I bought the book and took it home. I put the children down for a nap, and sat down in the rocker and read the entire book in one sitting.

The writer told of ordinary people doing extraordinary things with their lives. I didn't recall ever meeting any. (Duh! I didn't think of the people who told me to read this very book!

Like so many, I was simply too *blinded* by my own negativity. (Deceived people don't know they are deceived, **because they're <u>deceived</u>!**)

More, he said that God was for me. That was news to me. I only knew preaching that said we needed to 'suffer for Jesus', (especially Sis - who proudly bore her cross. But that's not what it means!) Other teaching of hers was that if you're sick and miserable, that too glorifies Jesus. Sis always had a half dozen ailments but never got sick enough to die .... just annoy everyone *so they wished she would!...* I felt she would outlive us all!

(Note to those bothered by my candor here: I was a sinner then, doing what sinners do best - Sin! But on that subject, Jesus *named* sin and Paul, Peter and John *named* backsliders and trouble-makers and told us not to imitate them. Jesus himself called religious leaders of His day, 'sons of hell brood of vipers, whitewashed tombs, fools, hypocrites and said not to be like them. The Bible is real and names false *religion.)*

Dr. Peale further said not to bother finishing the book if the reader (me) wasn't serious about making God first in my life. Living for others is what makes life worthwhile, he said, and he gave countless examples, especially in prayers for others that we meet along life's pathway. And that "If God be for us, who can be against us?"

One very positive scripture he talked about throughout was, "I can do all things through Christ who strengthens me." Phil. 4:13. I immediately thought of the upcoming real estate exam.

He also said, it would only work for those who made a commitment. I wondered,

What did I have to lose?

I had thought of a 'believer' as someone who was emotional and thus unstable. But the truth was, I now realized that *I was emotionless and unfeeling.* It no longer mattered to me what I thought of Christians.

I prayed the prayer.

The following day, I walked alone in the back pasture, thinking about the decision I'd made. I couldn't define it, but something was different now. My outlook had changed. I felt strangely optimistic. I'd never noticed the vividness of the colors in nature. Had they always been this brilliant? Birds' songs around me seemed *new.* All of this somehow made something inside of me bubble up - l ike *joy*!

On the day of the exam, I boldly told Larry that I knew I would pass, and that Jesus would be at my right hand.

Hundreds of people crowded that hotel ballroom where we took the test. People came from all over the state. The room was packed with tables and chairs. Most every chair was filled. Except the one *on my right hand side.* I didn't have to wait until I was contacted to know I passed. I knew it. I was relieved and joyous over it. I had experienced a God of power and I didn't even know there was One! God has a purpose for your life too.

Personal Note: Dr. Peale has experienced more than a little criticism for a 'pull yourself up by your own bootstraps' theology and his positivity. (Believe me I was ready for a gospel that wasn't *'suffrin' for Jesus!'* I didn't even know God was FOR me and not against me!)

I met the real Jesus through his writing! And I can only say that this is *my story* and *this is what happened* to ME!

More, if his critics had anywhere near the fruit of changed lives that Dr. Peale had, this would be a better world. He taught me how to live and how to initiate angelic activity in the lives of others by caring and *praying* for strangers! Much as the woman whose eyes met mine that day in a restaurant years before.

I can't help what his followers did or said. I only know what helped me. Moreover, Dr. Peale and his wife hosted John Sherrill, the author of "They Speak With Other Tongues" in their living room and an entire awakening of God began across the earth through that book, at their behest - they commissioned it.

Can one of his critics say that? No.

"For I know my plans for you, plans for good and not for evil, to give you a future and hope...when you seek me and seek me with all your heart, you shall find me."
Jeremiah 29:11,13

All that matters is that one is created anew.
Gal. 6:15

12

The Hound and Company

The real question here is, would my life have been different had I read that book ten years earlier when A.K. Jones, Jr. first told me of it? Would I have been prepared to see my negative personality in it *then*?

The prayer I prayed at Rhonda's birth seemed to go unanswered two full years. But in reality, God had to prepare me for its answer. I had to come to the end of 'me' else I wouldn't have known I even needed a Savior! I was too full of self-effort and self- sufficiency, thinking I could handle life myself.

That's a laugh, huh?

Therefore, the depression I experienced at this time proved in the end to be positive. It caused me to realize change was needed, driving me to answers that worked for me.

So, *depression is to the soul what pain is to the body - a signal.*

Each bear a message if we will listen, *something is wrong!* Pain often signals infection in the body, and I surely had pain in the soul!

After a while, when our lives seem to keep fouling up, we often realize that the 'road signs' were there all along, and we ignored them.

As it turns out, I still had not learned to read life's road signs. God had to wrestle me to the next phase of what He wanted to do in my life, which was bless me.

And in order to do that, *He had to get me to the blessing place.* This is that story.

Passing the real estate exam became an electric charge to my newfound faith. I had confidence I'd never known and I'd never before experienced supernatural power outside of ourselves, as I did that day.

In a few months, I took the broker's exam as well, which was a far more difficult test. I buzzed through that one, finished early, and went into the hall, filled with men in three piece suits, pretty intimidating to this street urchin *that still felt like one*! There were over five hundred candidates taking the test that day. One hundred forty-seven passed.

I was one of them.

Larry's income had improved somewhat, relieving some of the financial pressure. The broker's test results took about four weeks then.

An opportunity to work in a retail department store opened up. I accepted it, partly because the insurance benefits were excellent.

I decided to stay, and start real estate part time.

Within weeks, I found myself a department head of the toy department. It was more dire need than any real skill I'd demonstrated to them. But I thrived in that position and quickly developed a great friendship with a supplier who taught me the ropes and favored me for top selling items. These he had me set up on end caps, which drew customers and sold like hotcakes!

This job did more for my esteem than anything I'd ever done. I had much older people working for me who really liked me. I learned diplomacy, like if you say to someone "Would you be so kind as to...?" No one ever said 'No.'

Within weeks, our store had risen from fifth in a chain of 13 stores - to first and leading by $20k a month in sales. I was the manager's new favorite who sang my praises. No one was more surprised than me at all this.

Not everyone though, appreciated my success there. A veteran retailer who filled in for the manager in his absence, took to me like the plague. She'd been there twelve years and no young whippersnapper would show her up! She knew this business best, and I was on *her* turf. She saw to it I couldn't ignore her 'authority'.

This introduced me to that green-eyed devil, ***envy***.

I was there about eighteen months. Over two Christmas holidays, my children loved my access to the latest toys, at my discount. My income had done a lot to lift our family out of the hole too.

This job and my newfound success did wonders for my soul. I loved the job. However, I'd begun to have the nagging feeling that I should *quit the job.*

Well I can tell you that thought hit me like pure insanity, particularly since we'd grown accustomed to my income and felt we now needed it. The job was sure income. Plus, the real estate market had stalled with interest rates at 18% or more. I wasn't going to go there then.

Throughout the time I worked there, that thought nagged at me over the last eight months or so. I thought, maybe the children, then four and three, *did* need me to stay home with them rather than going to a sitter daily.

At home, Larry had begun a new habit of coming from the barn at bedtime to say prayers with the children and as a family. I'd begun to realize too, the children were socially backward. If someone came to the door, they just peered out from behind me, and wouldn't greet or speak to people, even at my coaxing. I didn't like that!

So one night, Larry and I asked God in our prayers to lead us to a church home for their sakes.

At that time, we'd floundered around in various churches on Sundays, never finding any we liked. One studied Erich Frohm in Sunday school. I knew he was a contemporary atheist. This dumbfounded me. But who was I to question? We kept going.

Then one Sunday, the pastor pointed to a scripture as outdated. He said even more, that it was now untrue, since *we* were more *educated* now. And education was the panacea *needed* to right the world's wrongs.

That was it for me!

That day, I opened scripture for myself for the first time. I think that was the day I began to think for myself.

The very next Sunday, we were late for church, so Larry suggested we attend a little Presbyterian Church nearby. Neither of us knew much about that faith, but as long as there were no holyrollers there, I felt safe. I did hear they could be a little stuffy, but I preferred that over the other.

We were immediately taken with the friendliness of this church. In a way, we felt like outsiders, because it was so very obvious they loved one another .laughing, greeting, embracing one another (that made me uneasy since our family didn't touch)

We could tell it was genuine and they obviously enjoyed one another. Their laughter rang out. I liked the fact they didn't *look religious*. They were more like a family than a church.

I remember nothing of the sermon. But before we left that Sunday, I knew I wanted to be a part of such interesting, caring people. And 'family.'

Larry was invited to a men's breakfast. He said he might go. A mental image of him attending, carrying his horse magazines underneath his arm passed through my mind. I rejected it. But I couldn't believe anything that wasn't horse-related would interest him.

A crisis loomed at work. My arch rival couldn't bear the success the whole store talked about. She told the manager it was her or me. That put him in a difficult place, but she knew - and he knew - he needed her more than *me*. As a conciliatory gesture, he got me the same job in a brand new store just opening. But it was across town! I worked there and helped get the store opened, got disillusioned and then quit the job.

Company records said the two of us, the veteran retailer and me, had a personality conflict (*hers*). And I know I could have handled her more maturely. But let's face it, I was emotionally immature at that stage of life. No, I was an emotionally arrested pre-adolescent right then.

Still, I really wondered about that persistent, nagging voice I'd rejected that wanted me to quit working. Maybe I could've avoided that whole ugly scene *had I listened.*

The very next Saturday after attending the new church, a car appeared in our driveway. Larry was working. I didn't recognize it. I saw it was Helen, whom the pastor had introduced as the person heading up the weekly Youth Club I'd volunteered to help in.

That was my major objective anyway, to get the children involved in regular attendance to make new friends for them. And I'd volunteered to help in that same service, to be with them. When the knock came at the door, I was hoping she wouldn't come in. I felt the house was a mess with children's toys everywhere. Anyway, I wasn't accustomed to folks stopping by unannounced.

Opening the door, Helen held a lovely carnation. "Hi Sharon," she said, striding past me inside.

"I was just out delivering these to the volunteers so we can all wear them tomorrow." Now that she was already inside, I didn't know what to say. "Thank you," I stumbled. "Would you like something to drink?" hoping she would say no.

"Well, yes. Do you have iced tea?" I said yes.

Helen sat for two hours in my kitchen that day while the children rode tricycles over her feet. She didn't even seem to notice. They too were unaccustomed to guests.

(I soon taught them a few manners!)

Her focus was *me*. She asked questions, and then listened. And I talked to fill the air, because I was uncomfortable with silence. So I filled the air with words.

Whatever I said must have made her feel pathetically sorry for me, because she came back for two years! Each visit like the first, questions, then she listened. I didn't know this was what she did, as ministry in mentoring others like myself. If she didn't come by, she would call.

I soon realized that Helen always let me do the talking. So I began listening to what I was saying! I was appalled at the blame I laid on Mom and my Dad too. I totally surprised myself at the malice I felt for them, and the hatred. Or that I viewed both as utter failures.

Worse, my overall view was to anticipate the worst.

The latter was a question asked of me by Helen. Her answer was, *why was I surprised when I got what I expected...?*

Every visit, Helen brought me books to read. Then she invited me to a women's Bible Study Fellowship that met one morning a week. Children were always welcome. Since I was no longer working weekdays, I thought it would be another opportunity for the children to get out and make friends. I said I'd go.

Inwardly though, since I'd read some of the Bible, I knew a lot of it wasn't for today, so I didn't want to get too serious about it. *Who knew* what was no longer for today? This study might be carrying things a little far.

When I got to the group and found out what they actually did, that made my mind go on tilt! *Homework...!!?*

However, I was favorably surprised at the women in this group too. There were *hundreds* of women who came from all over the city from every denomination. And *they all looked perfectly normal.* (I feared people who were serious about the Bible wore long sleeves, head coverings and hair pinned up in a bun.) Some of these women looked interesting to me... maybe fun to know.

I wanted to go back.

From then on, Helen and I frequently went shopping or to lunch after those studies. Or she took me with her on her errands, just spending time together. She did a great job tolerating the children then.

Before long, Larry and I were both deeply involved in this church. We loved their couples group. Together, he and I won the 'worst dancers' award in square dancing.

But it was hilarious to all in winning it!

Over the course of the next few months, I began to suspect that Helen was a 'do gooder'. After all, we had exactly nothing in common. Husband Harry was a tax attorney, were very affluent and both their children were in their teens. They lived in a very prestigious addition near the church, and owned Stiffel lamps. I didn't even know *what they were.*

I'd made other friends in the church, mostly parents of the children's friends. But Helen stuck like glue to me. Yet, I knew she knew everyone in the church too. I began to wonder if she had an ulterior motive. Maybe she was the church gossip. Then I realized she couldn't be that; she spent too much time with me! Nonetheless, I felt like her charity case.

The truth was, as time revealed, I'd never let anyone get to know me on a level as deep as Helen. I felt threatened and now vulnerable. She could hurt me now - I'd never let that happen in years. Worse, l had let my guard down enough to begin to love her.

I was frightened.

I let these feelings fester. So one day, when I was wrestling with them and with false pride, Helen stopped by as usual. She didn't know about the angst inside of me. If she did, she didn't show it.

I met her at the door. I must have seemed distant. I couldn't deal with her inside my house that day. I stood with the door ajar. She could tell I had something to say.

"Helen, I've been thinking a lot about our relationship. I need to tell you that I've decided I don't want to continue it as it is now. I've realized I've lived my entire life without this friendship, and I can live without it now."

Could she tell I suspected her motives? She didn't indicate it. She turned to leave, then turned back and said the words that would liberate this captive heart, completely freeing me to enjoy others in the future. "Sharon," she began, "I only want you to be happy! If that requires our not being friends, that's okay. But I will tell you one thing. *If we ever are friends, I will fail you.* I promise you that because I am human. But, if you will put your trust in Jesus, He will *never* fail you."

On that, she turned and left.

Suddenly I felt I'd turned away the only friend I'd ever had. I was overwhelmed with regret. Then sorrow, that I could be so callous and cynical at what was apparently one of God's blessings and good gifts. I didn't understand what 'mentoring' was.

I couldn't sleep that night. The family in bed, I lay on the couch in the living room, the stereo on low, the lights off. I wept intermittently at my own unmitigated stupidity.

I wondered if Helen could ever forgive me for being such a total fool and overall jerk.

Not really thinking He would, or could, I asked the Lord to somehow make right the mess I'd made, born out of my insecurities and fears.

A *presence* consoled me that night.

It was as though arms embraced me in my pain, literally. I was a broken person, and the One who came for the broken-hearted came in the form of *The Comforter* – the Holy Spirit - and I didn't even know there *was* such a thing! Or that He was the Promise of the Father for all of us. Acts 2:39.

I didn't hear from Helen the next day, Saturday. I refrained from the urge to call. I didn't know what to say.

Sunday came, and Helen was in the church kitchen. She greeted me as though nothing had ever happened! I was totally amazed at God's power. He'd heard me. And I was amazed at her largess- GRACE. New also to me.

Many other wonderful people attended that church, and I amassed great knowledge and experience through each of them. Personal friends, couples who became friends; leaders and the pastor and his family.

Parents of my children's friends began to stop by the house too. Within months, I found that I'd gone from no friends to more than I knew what to do with. Good friends.

I knew they would ultimately fail me. I fully expected them to. But I knew where to go when they did. I had placed my trust in the One who would never fail me!

Logic would have kept me on course, working the job I loved. I'd grown greatly with that new role and responsibility. Yet God had a better plan to bring fulfillment to me in another way, and bless my children while doing it as they learned to sing songs and Bible stories from their activities at church, rather than just wasting time at a babysitter.

He *knew* what I needed more than I did!

Convinced *I knew better* is why I stubbornly resisted that nagging voice. Yet, just at the right time, the week that the Youth Club asked for volunteers that would open my front door to Helen, God worked it all out.

And He sent His 'Hound of Heaven' to relentlessly go after me in spite of myself named *Helen*. He used her to push me on to greater growth and joy. She and her 'company' aided in steering me (and others-It's what she did - mentoring was her gift) to the source of *real* happiness. And how to be a far better mother and wife.

I still marvel at the influence of this little church (about 350 members) on our little family, and in the whole of our huge city. They brought Young Life to the area, and the leader rented an apartment from Larry and me. Its sphere of influence spread citywide through their breakfast club and we hosted 600 teens the first year, just at our church on Friday mornings at 6am, seated on the floor and the halls of our fellowship hall.

Their weekly Bible Study Fellowship group was so successful at that time that, many thousands of people are now involved in different groups throughout the city, both men and women's groups, meeting night and day. I took seven years of their thorough courses.

The very effective Youth Club we led met for years, training and feeding 70 a week, making little disciples.

Evangelism Explosion, written and taught by D. James Kennedy was taught and used as a very effective evangelism tool, leading many in the community to Christ, the most effective 'witnessing' tool I've ever found.

A Luthern project named Bethel Bible project (not Bethel Redding) a marvelous overview of the entire Bible, where we were taught for two years to always 'think Hebrew' in studying the scripture.

These were the *ordinary people doing extraordinary things* Norman Vincent Peal wrote about! At last, I knew I'd met them!

"For a Christian to be a Christian, he must first be a sinner. Being a sinner is a prerequisite for being a church member. The Christian church is one of the few organizations in the world that requires a public acknowledgement of sin as a condition for membership."
R.C. Sproul

"There are only two ways that God's justice can be satisfied with respect to your sin. Either you satisfy it or Christ satisfies it. You can satisfy it by being banished from God's presence forever. Or you can accept the satisfaction that Jesus Christ has made."
R.C. Sproul

13

The Mark

The ringing of the telephone seemed insistent. On the other end, Mom's voice was shaking. Charles had died. Could I come over?

Of course, I said.

On the way over, I was grateful I'd been able to forgive Charles before he died. Not to his face, though I did send him a sweet note, but in my heart.

Mom had never made any attempt to apologize for anything that had ever happened where Charles was concerned, or in her relationship with me. She didn't feel there was anything that needed an apology. She even said so. But she *did* tell me that one time Charles confessed, in a flash of anger, his hatred for me. That was only half of it, he'd said *he always would.* I could tell that was somewhat startling to her.

The coroner pulled into the driveway just as I did. David, then sixteen, led him to the back bedroom. I walked in behind him as though to verify in my own mind that Charles was actually dead. My worst nightmare had come to an end, at last.

I found Mom sitting at her usual post, at the breakfast bar in the kitchen. This was one time she didn't appear to be herself - she wasn't in *control.* The only thing I'd ever seen her acquiesce to was Sis. She appeared terribly fragile that moment. When I looked at her that night, I saw my mother for the first time as the captive she was. And I realized she herself hadn't really ever learned how to genuinely love. Me, or anyone else!

Though our family never touched, I walked over to her and wrapped my arms around her slumped shoulders. She sobbed when I did.

David aided the coroner with the gurney out the front door. Charles died in bed, his heart giving out after years of illnesses and after countless medications had done their due.

Whatever had happened in that marriage, I knew Mom genuinely cared for Charles, though there was never a love like with James. Charles was lucky to have had her.

She too was relieved that it was all over, at last.

After this, I finally was able to lay aside the resentment and the blame I'd felt for her all those years. It no longer mattered. I saw my mother as a fellow struggler on life's highway. She hadn't had such a great life or childhood either. Let the past lie, I felt.

The mourning period for Mom was short lived. Friends introduced her to ballroom dancing classes she'd always thought she'd like to take. Almost every weekend, that's what she did. That and other activities. For the first time, she could enjoy her house and have friends over anytime she wanted. Charles typically greeted every visitor gruffly, then slithered into the back bedroom slamming the door on the way. Or he might creep out and manufacture a scene of some kind at the refrigerator door.

Now she entertained friends and worked in her yard with her stunning roses. She built a patio out back and adorned it with pots full of flowers too.

Larry and I now had the privilege of coming and going without incident. It was years before I'd gone back and that was only at Christmas. But I stopped even that because Charles always punished her for those visits.

This period of my life had become pivotal. A hunger for knowledge consumed my every waking hour. I read books weekly and couldn't get enough of scripture. I studied constantly and attended any Bible Study I could.

I can only explain this in terms of today's technology - a virtual 'download' occurred in me. I took retreats and conferences, then I began to lead them. I attended courses and seminars wherever I could.

Larry found all this disconcerting. And rightly so. Unconscious to me, even my vocabulary had taken a new turn in both the ability to articulate and communicate. And I'd become, to Larry, *overly* confident. He even said, *he wondered what had happened to the girl he'd married.*

One of the reasons he found all this troubling, was that he knew the truth about me. *I was a flake.* I always was. I honestly couldn't remember where my car keys were from one minute to the next - that hasn't changed much! More, the family despaired at ever hearing me say of something missing "Oh, I put that *up*." They shrieked with terror, knowing it might be lost for months! I once lost a much needed check for six weeks!

Some might have called me *simple*, (they probably *did*- and *will*) because that was true also. I can only say 'the testimony of the Lord is sure, *making wise the simple.*' Psalm 19. That would be *me.*

As a youth, I'd naively believed most everything that I read in the newspaper to be true!

Or anything in black and white. I'd still pondered how there could be so many 'brands' of religion that differed so radically.

What *was* truth? And how could anyone *know* the truth? I reasoned the answer must lie in science, which comes from the Greek word for 'knowledge'. Then, I discovered scientists too often change their minds and couldn't agree either. They weren't sure *what* they knew!

But *who* knew?

That's why, aside from escaping the streets, I'd spent so much time in libraries to find out answers. All I did though, was find where truth *wasn't*!

More questions. Next I looked to education. But, I discovered that some intellectuals, particularly genius types that I really *wanted* to believe - often didn't have the common sense of a flea, and that the man on the street often had more sense than they did!

I recalled what Sally had called 'horse sense' - she had plenty, though uneducated. I'd read Plato and Socrates, but quickly found they were on the same search I was! Plus they often seemed confused!

I did find my answers over time.

A better real estate market came, and sales agreed with me. I was doing pretty well in a nice firm, for me anyway. I found a lot of gratification in helping people find something as significant as a home for their families. It was through my ties to real estate that I stumbled (?) onto an important answer to me.

I somehow got involved in delivering a local Christian newspaper to Christian bookstores. The man who published that paper was from Indiana like me, so perhaps that explains my tie there. In doing so, I struck up a friendship with a particular couple who owned 'The In Store For Christ'. Before long, I'd sold them a house, and then, their partners as well.

I found my success was built upon referrals, and I liked that.

One day, while I broused in their store, my eye caught a tiny book, shiney and taupe in color. "The Mark of a Christian', by a Dr. Francis Schaeffer. I'd never heard of him, but I read a few pages, and decided to buy it.

Meantime, our family had now outgrown our home. I wanted to buy two I'd seen that were available with just my real estate commission - but it would mean boarding the horses. (we couldn't afford a house with land yet).

Nothing doing, Larry said. He wasn't about to be confined to a 'postage stamp lot' in some housing addition.

Then I pleaded to just buy and rent them out. *No*. I can tell you that, if we'd bought those two houses, postage stamp lot or not, in ten years that lot would've looked pretty good! And we wouldn't have been homeless either. Not to mention we'd been $100k richer.

Stupidly, I acquiesced.

Jesus said 'the children of this generation are wiser than the children of light."

Luke 16:8 How I wish that weren't so true! Women couldn't buy houses then without the signature of a spouse – it was state law then. (Thankfully things have changed now!)

Our lives had found no 'balance', so fear prevailed.

This account amazes me however, because *God knows our limitations* and loves His people so much, that He **comes to our rescue** in spite of those limiations and/or weaknesses! He did this for my little family at this time.

Pat stopped by the house as she often did. Her children and ours played well together. I knew she was a woman of prayer. I told her how the house had fallen into disrepair and we needed more room. Rhonda would start kindergarten soon, and I didn't want her to start, then stop and re-enter another school. We needed to move then.

So Pat and I agreed in prayer based on Jesus' words that if any two believers shall agree upon anything, they can have it - Matt.18:19. We agreed on the *impossible*. We asked God for a house big enough for us, to rent; near church, a place for horses, that we could afford.

I love the *Message* translation of that verse, which says, 'if any two shall together make a symphony .' That's because the Greek word 'agree' is sumphono, the same word from which comes the English word *symphony!*

Nothing is too hard for the LORD.

Pat herself called to tell me of a house she saw for rent between my house and where she lived. She didn't know anything about it, except for the 'For Rent' sign. It sat way back off the road.

I immediately drove to see it. It was directly across the street from the new elementary school. The long driveway looped into a circle at the center, surrounded with a hedge of yellow blooming shrubs. I couldn't see the house, but the yard was enormous with several fruit trees planted in rows in the front, giving added privacy. Next door was a huge empty field, except for cattle and sheep grazing there. (In 3 years, it would become 550 new homes).

I pulled up to the front of the three car garage, and a man waved from inside the breezeway which separated the house from the garage. He motioned me inside.

Through the breezeway, I could see that the huge back yard sloped down to a creek and the yard was lined by tall trees all around the edge of the yard where squirrels frolicked. I walked through the kitchen area into the L-shaped formal dining and living area. Enormous picture windows gave a full view of the back yard.

One of the first things that caught my *street urchin eyes* was the crystal chandelier hanging in the center of the dining room. *I wondered if I could ever live in a house this wonderful.* Three bedrooms were upstairs with a fireplace. The downstairs walkout basement was finished and carpeted, also with a fireplace and half bath. *This house must cost a fortune*, I thought.

The owner explained that he and his family lived out West and planned to retire back here. Meantime, they wanted to rent the house to people who would take good care of it. I was surprised at the rent. It wasn't nearly as high as I'd guessed, but still seemed like too much for us.

But I decided to have Larry take a look at it that night.

Of course, he looked at the outdoors first, noting that he would have to build shelter and fence for the horses. He didn't seem to mind though. Inside, he pointed out that the downstairs was completely self-contained with a separate entrance and patio. A few modifications and we could rent it to make up the difference. He decided to ask the owner about renting the downstairs, if he finished it.

The owner said that if Larry did the work, he didn't care if we rented the basement (this was before *codes*). He seemed to like us. Before we left, he offered to lower the monthly rent $25 a month as well.

This house had ten rooms, a 3 acre yard and seven other acres behind for horses. It was across the street from the school Rhonda (and later Craig) would attend, and was a half mile due East of the church plus God worked out the money so we could afford it!

The next week, our new unmarried director of Young Life arrived in town to accept his position at our church. He needed a place to live. Our pastor sent him to us. We even had a third garage for him. He took it.

The amazing thing in retelling this true story, is that Larry and I each had our limitations (emotional and financial), yet *God worked within those to bring His answers to us!* This is truly a demonstration that He meets us where we are.

And He'd helped circumstances converge to work it all out.

The book I'd happened to pick up in the Christian bookstore that day became the first of many by the same author. It was a chapter taken from a greater work of Dr. Schaeffer's, who was to become one of the 20th century's greatest authors, lecturers, and speakers. He and his family gave up a successful pastorate in St. Louis to move by faith to Switzerland, and form a retreat named L'Abri, which means 'shelter.' It truly became a shelter where intellectuals from around the world gathered to find hope, meaning, purpose and understanding from he and Edith.

I read many of his books. And I was fortunate - no blessed - to later meet him and spend time at his feet gaining from his wisdom. He and C. Everett Koop, former Surgeon General, put on conferences to educate people of the true nature of abortion in that era. Then Bill Gaither, who's from Indiana, put on conferences at the Convention Center every year for a time and invited his friend, Dr. Schaeffer, and other noted speakers. I reveled in the time we spent with Dr. Schaeffer, and others, in the smaller workshops.

I'd never had anyone affect my life as he was able, at this point. This little man was truly brilliant.

It was the *message* of The Mark of A Christian book that served to change me. One of the major things that I'd first learned from this man was, *misguided people are not God's fault!* Due to Sis's influence, I'd blamed God for religious people who turned me off (others too!) to God for 25 years of my life.

And I'd blamed Him for people who are just plain ignorant. It happens!

That book's topic was a *New Commandment*, the Third Commandment of the New Testament.

Did you know there is a third one? Most people don't.

As unlikely as it sounds, it has little to do with neighbors or unbelievers, except for its impact on them. Jesus talked about relationships inside the church, of brethren.

That's what is *new*!

Relax. This is not some new theology, because it's as old as the gospel of John. People don't talk about it much because they don't understand it, or they think it's an add-on to commandments that exist. False doctrine sometimes hems us in because people believe Christians should love everyone equally, sinners and saints alike.

Not.

The Commandment Jesus said was 'new' – it's not just **more** of the first *two*. .Jesus taught his disciples "to love one another, as (or in the same measure) I have loved you, that ye also love one another." Next verse. "By this" By *what? By this kind* of love! 'By this shall all men know you are my disciples, *if*" you love one another."

Jesus had good reason for establishing this *new* commandment. He wanted to win the lost that He would die for *the very next day!*

This was His final instruction - and the most effective method to win them!

We're not called to love the masses. We can't. Only God can. We are finite and unable to do so. Leave that job to One who is infinite.

Start where you are – with your world. Begin in the arena of our own lives - love *one another* - that's how love starts! From there, it's shed abroad to those in our *entire* arena.

We are to be a people who are carriers of His presence to others.

Marked by His love and set apart for His use. This happens individually then corporately, reflected visibly as we gather in worship and in love.

The previous chapter is the most ardent illustration of what the local church looks like. It should be appealing (never b-o-r-i-n-g or impotent!) to hungry and confused people, and salt and light to seekers of truth. Not to mention a Biblical gospel!

The people at that little Presbyterian church had *something I wanted.* That difference literally changed me forever! They struck me as a family and I'd never had one (except the one I'd formed with Larry).

The fact that they cared for *one another* was obvious and drew me in. That's the way it's supposed to be!

This was a new kind of love that appealed to me. It is found among *brethren.*

For too long the church has been known more for what they're *against* than what they're *for.* Jesus didn't die for doctrine - He died for people! God was looking for family in Genesis. "Let us create man in *our* image."

Only when we resemble Him, will others be attracted to our *Father.*

Jesus said in Matthew 22:29 that we err because we **know not** the scripture and the power of God. Simply put, *ignorance*!

On my journey seeking to find Truth, I stumbled onto Love.

The most fascinating thing I learned from Dr. Schaeffer was that he, a foremost intellectual, presented Christianity as "*the only reasonable and logical way to live*!"

Our beliefs are not a blind 'leap of faith'. Though it is impossible to know God through wisdom, God gave us a mind and emotions to better enjoy Him and one another!

There's a huge caveat. We all arrive on the same ticket, and through the same Door - *simple childlike faith.* Repentance is required. Saying *Yes* to Jesus means at the same time, saying *No* to sin.

Many may wonder what it was that a street urchin such as myself and a leading intellectual like Dr. Schaeffer had in common. I don't have an answer for them, except to say, Perhaps it *was love of the same Truth.*

The first thing visitors see at your church when they come through the front doors is <u>you.</u>
Author

"Never worry about numbers.
Help one person at a time, and always
start with the person nearest you."
Mother Teresa

14

"Ten Minutes Is Enough"

Larry and I and another couple had observed that while local high schools had various outreaches to teens, none existed for Junior High. Our feeling then was that by high school, those youth had already chosen their peer groups, good or bad. So we began a group that met monthly for volleyball games, or tubing the river, bowling and Bible Study after each meeting. Rhonda and Craig were in it and sometimes 70 others. We had so much fun with those kids, watching them grow and seeing leaders rise among their peers - who then went out and did our job by getting those peers to attend, and going on to mentor them besides!

At one of the World Conventions about then, we heard a man say that if we would invest into the lives of other people's children God would be faithful to send laborers into our own children's lives.

Sounded reasonable to us, and so like God. That thought became the seed inspiring us.

So, we had looked into Campus Crusade, Inter-Varsity, and learned a lot about Young Life with George, the area Director who lived with us. Each ministry was effective in their own right, and we were grateful for the many different groups. But

Youth For Christ seemed more our brand of evangelism to youth.

So we got involved.

One evening about 9:00 pm, the phone rang and Larry answered. One of his buddies on the YFC board wanted to know if we'd join him and some others to meet a celebrity at the airport who was coming into town for their week of fund-raising activities.

Larry promptly said 'Sure.'

Though late, we gathered the children and left right away. I asked Larry who the celebrity was, and he said he didn't know.

We arrived and parked our car in short term parking, then joined the group inside of about a dozen people. The same couple involved in our Jr. Hi Ministries, Florence and Jim were also there. They told us they didn't know who it was we were meeting either.

Within moments, a short full bodied older woman walked in our direction, smiling. Accompanying her was a tall, attractive blond woman whose name I learned was Ellen de Kroon, her aid. I couldn't believe it was Corrie ten Boom we were greeting. I'd read a couple of her books by then. Larry knew of her through me.

That began a week that was a complete blur of activities. She promoted both Youth For Christ and her new movie, just being released by the Billy Graham Evangelistic Association in a few weeks.

Soon, we all trailed from the airport to the hotel and it was after 10pm by then. When we all met in a room reserved for such, someone said Corrie was taking a nap.

NAPPING? That was my reaction to that news! With all of us *waiting*? It seemed....

But about the time I got through thinking that thought, Corrie appeared.

Inside the door Someone asked about her nap. She replied she'd already taken it! She said lightly, "Ten minutes in the Lord is enough!"

Larry seemed instantly infatuated with Corrie. She had that way about her. In fact, it amazed me how much she reminded me of Sally - they did their gray hair similarly, a sort of bun in the back. They both wore the same kind of eyewear and had the same kind of wrinkles. *Smile.*

Corrie kidded with Larry that if he weren't already taken, she might want to marry him! She had a great sense of humor. He was flattered.

The children were also invited to many of the dining events and small groups. They couldn't appreciate her for who she was, but enjoyed all the hoopla and eating out and knew she must be important. These small events and gatherings in the hotel afterward allowed us to truly get to know her during that week. Ellen was always at her side making certain she didn't overtire. Corrie was 83 years old then. She lived to be 91 years old.

Near the end of the week, a large banquet, black tie, was held in her honor, and church leaders around the state were invited. It was amazing and memorable.

Aside from her testimony, she told two stories that stayed with me that evening.

One was how, as we'd already discovered, she had difficulty accepting praise of any kind. She was always careful to give any glory to God! So she said that became terribly awkward with everyone constantly offering her praise.

So she began to pray how to deal with it.

At last, she said she just accepted what people said politely, and pretended their compliments were a beautiful rose.

So in the evening before she retired, she just handed her bouquet to Jesus.

It all belonged to Him.

Another was a troubling event she'd had in ministry with supporters who served on her board some years back. There had been disagreement, and a breach of trust occurred after. Ugly letters then came to Corrie defending their positions. She had a hard time working through it and forgiving the whole mess. But she did.

Sometime later, she was going through her desk and ran across those letters. An inquiry began, God convicting her heart.

Had she forgiven these women? Why, yes she thought. Well, the inquiry went on,

Then, why are you keeping those letters ?

Corrie had thought she'd forgiven everyone, but she realized that she would occasionally pull those letters out and rehearse the circumstances again in her mind. She realized if she truly had forgiven them, God wanted her to burn the letters and get rid of them.

True forgiveness!

It was through Corrie that I first realized how short-sighted Americans are. They don't appreciate what's theirs. Freedom is not free and was purchased at great price. It cost the blood of many (and many we know!), both small and great.

At the Coliseum the following Sunday, the big draw was Corrie. We met as a group to pray prior to that meeting. There Corrie asked God to hide her behind the cross of Christ, and that the people would only see Jesus. I found her humility genuinely humbling.

Ten thousand people came to hear her speak. Corrie disdained believers who felt that one never has to suffer once they become believers. (That belief is most popular among Pre- Tribulation folks. We just hope the matter is that tidy and we won't have to go through suffering! But what if it isn't? Will those who believe this be sorely disappointed when serious trouble flares up on them. Will they turn away, disillusioned and offended in God?)

Corrie wondered where people got such ideas? *It wouldn't be the Bible*!

She wept as she told us more believers were martyred in the 20th century than in any other, some personal friends of hers in an African church she'd established. Members had been rounded up in the middle of the night by officials, never to be seen again. Men, women and children all perceived to be a threat to the new government. All dropped into a public grave. Many of the churches she'd helped establish suffered persecution worldwide, she said.

As she spoke the huge audience sat in silence. No one moved around, nor did a child cry.

Corrie used that silence. Her gaze was fixed upon the crowd.

"Persecution is coming," she said "and maybe even to the United States. Being *distanced* from it in miles doesn't change the fact it exists. The U.S. has no guarantee that it is somehow exempt from such things. *Most* disciples were martyred.

Witness in Greek means *'martyr'*." she explained.

Still complete silence in the crowd. They seemed to hang onto her every word.

She inquired, "*Had we counted the cost of serving God?* More importantly, had we counted the cost in those terms?

If called to do so, would we be willing to die for our faith also?"

This was a different kind of message than I'd ever heard. A needed balance was coming in me. And certainly different from much of the gospel preached in the U.S. then. Or now!

Corrie asked those who were willing to count this cost now, to stand up. No one moved for what seemed like moments. Corrie waited - We sat in the center section near the front of the auditorium. A noise in the balcony to my right caught my eye. Like a virtual wave, people began to quietly stand. The wave swept around the balcony behind us all the way to our left. As though on cue, those seated around us began to stand also. There was such a *tremendous sense of holiness.*

A ***holy hush,*** if you will.

We joined the others in standing, a sobering decision and a very sobering moment. Perhaps two-thirds of the people in attendance that day stood with Corrie, because they knew she'd already made that decision decades ago inside a Nazi prison camp.

I witnessed the answer to her own prayer that day, as she truly was hidden behind the cross.

The best of all the meetings we had with Corrie came in the final one at the hotel again.

She accomplished what I'd never witnessed before. She rebuked the whole group and they *thanked* her for it! She had that way about her. The way of true greatness!

Corrie said it had been a wonderful week with us all. However, there was just one area she saw lacking. That area was prayer!

She explained, ***Prayer breaks down resistance in the heavenlies, and in the human heart...***

Interceding to God before the work, before it happens is essential to effective ministry, she said. *Souls hung in the balance,* captives that they are. It must, *must* precede any mighty work of God.

I've never forgotten this. Yet I too was guilty.

The movie, The Hiding Place, was released within weeks and shown nationwide at many theaters, and in a half dozen local theatres.

Larry and I were in charge of one of the theatres in town, agreeing to host the movie for a week. That meant finding volunteers to work each showing, because at the end of each showing, the gospel was presented and we had specially trained counselors (By Billy Graham Evangelistic Association) there to pray with people. A very successful venture with hundreds who prayed the prayer of salvation.

Getting volunteers was no problem. Sometimes we had too many, all faithful members of our wonderful little church.

This was another full week of saturation for me, of Corrie ten Boom. her life, .her testimony and the truth of her personal suffering.

I don't know how many times I viewed it, in part, or whole.

Before her life ended, Corrie had traveled in well over 100 nations, establishing churches wherever she went.

I have only wished men who criticize women preachers would take notice!

God must have *approved of THIS woman preacher...!*

Much of my own philosophy and theology were shaped by the gentle giant that she was. I am so looking forward to thanking Corrie, and Dr. Schaeffer too, one day. I feel my meeting with her was in large part, to write this book, in order to aid people in preparing for a frightful future and to see Jesus return!

Prophecy must be fulfilled and that future is ominous! Our times are in God's hands, but if we are watching his timepiece, i.e. the *Nation of Israel and current events*, then the wise and prudent understand that prophecy must be fulfilled before Jesus comes. That being so, then terrible times may lie ahead, unlike any ever seen upon the earth, or ever will be again according to Jesus' own words. Who knows the chronology of it all...?

It has only been in recent years that I have realized how dramatic the impact of this saintly woman on my life. Probably every day, one of her quips said in private or during meetings while with her runs through my mind. Her life, her suffering, her transparency, her many books and movie of her life, and her wisdom follow me everywhere.

I thought of Corrie a while ago when I was still in business, as I sat in traffic at construction sites. I'd had an exasperating morning with an appointment that took far too long, and cost too much money. I felt frustrated that the day was far spent, and I hadn't even approached the literal mountain of work that should have already been done.

Then in the midst of that scene, I'd accidentally taken the wrong fork in the road, and construction trapped me from even turning around to go in the right direction. There I sat in traffic at a complete standstill, headed in the wrong direction, and the day was further wasting away.

In a word, I was fuming and fretting.

In pure exasperation, I flipped on the radio on a Christian station, which I rarely listen to. However, I recognized the announcer as the Dr. Dobson show, and he was introducing someone that sounded terribly like it would be a tape of Corrie ten Boom.

It was.

Corrie's father, sister and others were captured after smuggling over 800 Jews, of which 100 were tiny infants, out of Holland to safety and freedom.

On the tape that day in traffic, Corrie told how her sister Betsy (who died there) encouraged her to give thanks for everything. Corrie told her she couldn't.

Betsy said, "Oh, Corrie you must." Eventually though, she did thank Him for the lice.

But not the fleas inside the barracks.

Betsy said, "No, you must thank Him for the fleas, too Corrie." Eventually, she did so.

Sometime after, Corrie learned that the reason guards never came around their barracks were the fleas! Thus Corrie was able to conduct her Bible Study every afternoon unhindered, from the little Bible she'd smuggled in.

Most of their students died, but as Corrie was quick to add, they died with the Name of Jesus on their lips. They had graduated, she said.

As I sat there in traffic that day, I was reminded that none of my problems amounted to fighting fleas and lice, much less Nazi soldiers, and the smells of death or the horrors of a Nazi prison camp. While the problems I faced were real, and I *was* behind in business, I sat in an air conditioned car, in beautiful Florida sunshine, and I had tomorrow to get caught up! And a free country to do it in. (*then*, anyway!)

Nor was I or either of my children confined to even a wheel chair for a single day.

What was my problem?

Answer. *Ingratitude.*

I thanked God for that little lesson in priorities that day via Corrie's message. I'd apparently needed it.

It had been many years since I'd heard that familiar voice of Corrie in her broken English, a swee t remembrance to me. Her voice had become so familiar during that weeklong period decades earlier, when our family had been privileged to get to know her.

At the time, it all seemed pure happenstance to me. Perhaps you will see, as I do, in the writing of this book that happenstance was rather 'destiny' for me, and for *you Dear One!*

Born Cornelia Arnolda Johanna Luitingh ten Boom in 1892 in Holland, and she died in a place called "Placentia" California on April 15, 1983, America's tax day.

I believe this points to a foreboding new message born in her death. For America!

I pray God permits me to bear it here. That there will a day we pay, as nations are judged, for our ingratitude and for our failure to stand up for what is right and true!

I'm certain, just as He established Israel and led people to establish the USA, that God wants to use this nation to bring endtime revival. Why? God is a nation-builder from the Outset! What's more, 90% of all world missions have always been funded by our nation!

That is a lot of souls. He's not done yet, yes-judgment **is** coming as all nations will stand In judgment – and we *are* accountable for 60 million abortion deaths – but first, revival!

God is not willing that any should perish, much less billions, untold. Matthew 24:14.

Perhaps we ought to prepare for a future worse than what she endured. Why? Because the future is coming fast and furiously, and prophecy must be fulfilled for Jesus' return.

Corrie's life experience was, to me, a prototype of the future to come!

Have you read the book of Revelation? Better read it again. If we are in end times, *the future sucks if you aren't a true believer!* At one point there will be no peace on the earth at all (unless its in the hearts of those who've trusted Him). We know that God will spare His people His wrath upon sin. I hope it's as tidy as some believe and teach - where the rapture comes early. But, it's God's timetable. Will you be offended then? Will you turn away?

My message is simple: Hope for the best, but prepare for the worst. PREPARE. People don't want to hear this, but half of preparation is m-e-n-t-a-l. Knowing what to expect is next. Read II Thessalonians. 1:7-10 and see if *you* are one of those people God selects to rescue! You get to choose! Study the end time scriptures then.

What a **difference** she made in the lives of others, bringing light into a dark place for many with her simple faith. I was a simple one for whom it was a great privilege to host Corrie that week, and later host her life story at the theatre for another.

Some honors are *humbling*. Thank YOU, Lord.

Corrie and Betsie were in Ravensbruck when I was born. Betsie died in the fall, and Corrie was released on a clerical error on December 31 of that year. Betsie had told Corrie they would both be released from that place by the end of the year. Both of them *were...* It was *Destiny*. You will be hearing more about this dear woman.

A gift should be received in the same
manner it is given. Graciously.
Unknown

God's love still stands when all else has fallen.
Corrie ten Boom

"I have often heard that Life is Short, you better enjoy it.
But remember Eternity is Long and you better
Prepare For It!" Facebook –June 2019

15

Mamie Dearest

I backed out the garage and headed the Rolls Royce out the driveway. Since the Mercedes was in the shop, we took the Rolls that day. Mamie and I preferred it anyway.

Ted, Mamie's husband, often drove the Rolls to work in the mornings, picking up our son Craig, and dropping him and their daughter, whom I affectionately called *Premium*, off to private school. I had enrolled Craig there after fifth grade in public school, where the current principal seemed inane to me - and unreasonable besides.

Ted and Mamie were our next door neighbors, though the deep ravine between our houses separated us, and we had to go around street side to get to either house.

Premium and Rhonda had been best friends for three years and spent time together, mostly at our house.

Mamie deplored driving and their regular driver was with Ted on Tuesdays. Aware that I didn't work, Mamie had asked me if I would mind driving her to the various schools in the mid-state region, so she could observe her students, who were teachers themselves. They were students of Mamie's at the local hub of our biggest state university who taught special education. She was an associate professor there. A psychologist, she also had her own practice, performing studies for our city.

I'd learned that Mamie was for many years in the Who's Who of America for being the youngest black woman in America to have received her doctorate at age 23. Since then, that record has been broken. Originally from South Carolina, she still had a southern drawl at times, when she chose to.

After giving it some thought, I decided I would drive Mamie on those Tuesdays. We were already friends, but I was the one who gained immense knowledge from those trips with her, and in dining out after.

Two things surfaced out of my relationship with Mamie over the course of ten years or so. One was that she became one of the most fascinating people I'd ever known. And the other was that I learned incredibly important social and academic truths from this *teacher of teachers,* during our very long friendship.

Ted was a well-known criminal defense attorney in town, who once ran unsuccessfully for mayor. Sometimes he had those he defended work off what they owed him by driving or doing maintenance at home. I thought Ted was too soft spoken to be effective in the courtroom. Apparently I was *wrong.*

Not knowing them, I watched their house being built through the ravine, You could see through the trees when the leaves were off. That was shortly after we'd moved to the house on ten acres. Obviously their house was going to be a showplace. When it was finished, I reasoned that their pool and bath house was worth more than our home, or the homes of most blacks! (That was *before* I worked in ***Atlanta!***) It wasn't unusual for Mamie to bring children from her downtown clinic to swim and play.

Mamie was unpretentious, but not always.

Without question, Mamie was unusual. Growing up in South Carolina, where her mother still lived, she got her degree from prestigious Boston University, and attended at the same time as Martin Luther King, Jr. Her mother wanted Mamie to marry him, as she did date him some, I understood. But Mamie felt he was a *dreamer.*

I often marvel at how I met Mamie. I met Premium first who seemed to always be at our house. I wondered why. She was there most every evening meal, but her Mother would call for her to come home late, and then I knew Premium would eat dinner again. Premium was always eating and she always asked for the last banana or the reddest apple.

But we loved her and didn't mind.

After a school year of her visits plus summer months, I *heard* that her mother – that would be Mamie – had cancer and, if true, I began to understand.

Premium too was an enigma. She rode this yellow bicycle to our house daily. Instead of leaning it up against something, she dropped it in the middle of our driveway, right in front of the garage. Please understand I kept our entrance immaculate with a beautiful flower garden besides. The bicycle was bright - YELLOW - but ugly, and falling apart! This grated on me. Newcomers introduction to us was - that total spectacle lying in the middle of our driveway! I couldn't figure out how she could live in a mansion, yet rode this piece of trash over to embarrass *us!*

But I laughed good naturedly and began to tease her about not embarrassing me when we took her with us anywhere. She enjoyed it.

I hadn't yet met Mamie, personally, but I'd talked with her on the phone and seen her at evening school events where Premium and Rhonda met at about the second grade. Premium seemed an ordinary second grader *Her mother wasn't.* One time, Mamie came in late, with a bustle and talking out loud to herself or Ted or someone. I'd hear her introduce herself to people in back of me. It was always the same.

She always introduced herself, her title, and her degrees, about three or four of them.

I learned through one of her students I met downtown one day, that Mamie had an IQ of 165.

Mamie's reputation preceded her everywhere she went. It always did. In fact, *she saw to it.* The first twenty or so times I talked with her on the telephone or in person, she always listed her title and degrees to me. I don't know why. I hardly felt it was insecurity. But it caused me to view her oddly, and truthfully, I thought this woman was absurd.

Unquestionably, Mamie was the driving force behind that marriage. She was brilliant, that is, *once she got through her introductions!*

It is no wonder Premium wanted to be at our house. It was an interesting place for any kid to be. Our children were the envy of the entire school, who leered out the windows of passing school buses at our horses, dogs, cats, rabbits, ripening fruit trees with cherries and apples, plus we had miniature English Auraconda chickens we kept in cages inside the third garage due to predators – these laid blue eggs. True.

We were *country gentleman* farmers because I never wanted to be more than five minutes from Kroger!

Mamie's unique personality and immense intelligence caused her to be lonely, I felt. That, and their money. They were envied by whites and blacks, the latter often referring to them as *white* blacks, she told me. As a result, they lived in sort of a self-imposed isolation as one of two black families in our entire upscale school district.

The single desire Mamie lived for was to see her children become, in her words, 'set' in life. That translated an education with a doctorate like herself, so that they could then 'write their own ticket', also her words.

She lived for them, but she also loved the Lord immensely. So when she found me, she felt she'd found a friend. And I considered my friendship with this delightful woman a kind of 'assignment' from the Lord - one I enjoyed.

A couple of years after moving to our new place, I had made more money in real estate than Larry did at year's end. He wasn't happy about that. The male ego at work there. A further complication was, I was under the impression as a believer that I should bow to his wishes and no longer work. That was before I'd read the story of the Virtuous woman in Proverbs 31, where the man *is known in the gate* (where important people sat) *because of his wife's diligence* in selling her wares, retailing, tailoring, and investing in real estate!

Yes, it's all there ladies. Read it and know that is the woman *God smiles upon! Truth is liberating indeed*!

So after that, I had my involvements and stayed busy outside the home with community projects, church, Bible studies, plus a weekday job on Wednesday where I worked for a local newspaper. That job served as 'mad money' for birthdays and extra needs of our family.

I learned that Mamie, Ted and the children attended a Baptist church nearby, and Ted was on the board. Mamie was a serious believer, I discovered, which is why I thought she seemed drawn to me. She revered me for my Bible knowledge far too much I felt, yet I was flattered.

She often asked me to pray she would stop smoking. I did. *She never quit.* As a result her voice was quite raspy. I'd noted that on the telephone, and had always been a little distant to her until I got to know her. I'd thought she was too much and I was too into the 'socially acceptable' scene then. I got over it though. Trust me. I could care less now.

Mamie had a custom of looking through the woods before 11pm, and if she still saw our lights on, she would call. It was always the same, "Wanna go to coffee?" she'd ask. That meant we went down to the pretty white and yellow waffle house with flowers in front that stayed open 24 hours. Premium, Rhonda and Craig would share a booth and laughed and talked while Mamie and I shared another. (This was never on school nights).

If the children were gone - she'd know that because *they were together* -she would call me then too, to go to lunch. I now treasure those countless hours we spent together, for Mamie became a dear friend.

It was impossible to be with Mamie for very long and not be motivated to fulfill your dreams. And if you didn't have any, *she'd supply those too!*

One day, not long after we'd become acquainted, the phone rang. I was alone at home in the early morning. She wondered if I could come over and help her to her car.

I said, *Sure*, wondering what the problem was. She said she'd left the car outside the garage and was afraid she couldn't get to it. Was she *ill?*

Her voice sounded somewhat urgent, so I drove over. I knocked on her front door and she answered, seemingly in perfect health. She thanked me profusely (she never liked to bother people). Then as she motioned me inside, she explained she was too afraid of their two outdoor dogs to go from the kitchen door through the garage to the car door – their own dogs. I thought *and this woman is a psychologist!*

On the day we were leaving in the Rolls, we were headed for a city about forty miles south of Indy. We must have been a comical sight that day, though it never occurred to me then.

Tooling down the highway in a Rolls formerly owned by the Eli Lilly family... Me- a white woman driver, and Mamie - my black intellectual professor passenger!

A comical sight in my mind's eye in retrospect. *My own version of driving Miss Daisy.* (Which movie I happened to watch being filmed at the Biltmore Hotel in Atlanta when I worked for hotels- That hotel is now a *condominium.*)

On our journeys, Mamie spoke often of her disappointment with her field of education.

I learned more in that one semester from Mamie than I ever did before or since. About what a true intellectual is and about how children learn.

She loved seeing them learn above all else.

At that time, in mid 70's, Mamie stated her belief that teachers no longer taught *students.* They taught *information.* They would post information on the blackboard, and if the students 'got it', fine. If not, they were on their own whether they actually learn it. If they didn't get it, get a tutor. If not, tough luck.

The reason for this was because the focus had changed in academic circles from truly challenging students to be genuinely creative, to the suppression of that very creativity! Instead of being encouraged to love learning, the opposite was occurring since schools only sought to turn out robots who sat in their seat and didn't ask too many ***questions***. Those who did ask questions were regarded as mavericks, *troublemakers interfering with the real teaching agenda.*

Students should conform, and all too often, intelligent students were treated as mavericks.

She said this was a direct result, among other things, of an era where too many average students had been encouraged to enter the teaching profession. A teacher shortage had occurred at the same time a surge in new students cropped up.

This had a consequence of its own. *Average* students who became teachers were confronted with the challenge of teaching *truly bright students!* I figured this was her arena, both in education and observing teaching practices over time- she ought to know.

Moreover, Mamie said actual class teaching time had been curtailed by federal guidelines for testing and extra-curricular events. Meantime, funding for supplies often had to come from teachers' own pockets.

Then, there was the grading curve. Instead of challenging students to *rise to a standard*, the standards themselves were constantly being lowered. Music appreciation, art and great poetry were no longer regarded important by teachers, so **the results were dismal in inspiring youth to aspire to greatness**. Teachers got exactly what they expected: Little!

Those who entered the teaching profession in the seventies eventually became administrators, who then chose the textbooks and developed policy among those who taught. It's these pseudo-intellectuals who have dumbed down America, especially NEA.

Today, it is rarely public education that produces excellence. But private, charter and home schooling produces students with much higher rankings. It is ironic that universities are now seeking students from private academies or homeschooling! Besides, they have a better work ethic accompanied by foreign students.

When Premium first entered our lives, she made C's, or an occasional D. (her mother was sick then)

This was no problem to Mamie. She hired tutors, drove her to learning programs, painfully pushed, prodded and shoved Premium to dream bigger. Sometimes Premium hated it, yet Mamie would have it no other way. As a result Premium took college courses, and graduated early one full year, entering college. Mamie didn't want her to be in public school another year. Her brother attended England's Oxford University getting a law degree.

Today, Premium has her doctorate and is married to her college sweetheart. They live in the Midwest and have six children.

It was Mamie who coached me to get scholarships and grants for my own children. I didn't even realize they existed! Brains Matter.™

Later on, during divorce and before we moved away, Mamie and I sat together over lunch. I expressed my dismay then of phony believers. I told her that it seemed to me that sometimes worldly people were far kinder than believers are!

Leaning back, Mamie looked at me fiercely, then reverting back to her South Carolina drawl, which she did on occasion, She said, *"Honey, deyse good! But good for what? Only what's done for Christ will last! Deyse good for nothing!"*

Later, I was doing a word search on II Chronicles 7:14, where God tells Israel "If My people, who are called by my name, will humble themselves and pray, and seek my face, and turn from their wicked ways" I happened to look up in Strong's Concordance the meaning of 'wicked' in the Hebrew. And there it was! Mamie was right all along. Wicked is defined as 'good for nothing'. How about you?

Regrettably, after a cross country move, I lost contact with Mamie.

I now realize that I was so disappointed with my own life then, that I couldn't bear Mamie's disappointment too. I guess I thought I could just pick up in that friendship in the future. I don't think I ever told Mamie that I loved her.

I wish I had.

A few years after we moved to Florida, Premium contacted Rhonda to be in her wedding, so Rhonda flew to New York for that wonderful event –the dream of Mamie's lifetime. There was a sit down dinner for 500 people. No expense spared. Upon Rhonda's return, she told me Mamie looked ill. But since she always coughed with her smoking, I dismissed it.

Two weeks later, Mamie died quite suddenly, of emphysema. No one knew she was that sick. She'd kept it quiet until after the wedding so as not to ruin it for her daughter. She'd sought medical help too late.

I don't believe there's ever been anyone quite like Mamie. She was the most complex mixture of *difficult and delightful* I've ever known.

An irrepressible genius, yet childlike faith and naïvete.

That naivete got her into trouble at one point though, because she trusted the wrong people - possibly having too many felons in the house - causing great loss and humiliation to her family, *because she accepted the blame for it all.*

That was so like her. Years of problems followed.

I don't know what it was that Mamie felt that I ever had to bring to that relationship. But it was she that taught me so much. I was so humbled that Mamie would consider me her peer in any way. She, who seemed to have everything going for herself. Yet, her love for the Lord and her love of scripture made her look to me for something. Whatever it was, I hope she benefited.

I'm thankful to have my friend in heaven waiting for me, leaning over heaven's balcony, leading the cheers for me, *of that I'm certain*!

I rarely pass a pretty breakfast restaurant that I don't think of Mamie's phone calls, day or night, and if the light was on, in which she would say,

"Sharon, wanna go to coffee?"

You always think you have time to say goodbye. But this life is short.

It's the next one that counts!

Teachers don't teach students anymore.
They teach information.
They put the information up on the board,
and if the student gets it, Great.
If they don't, get a Tutor. If not, they're on their own.
Dr. Mamie Wilson

16

Three Introductions

You will find this chapter incredible. I know I still do!

Perhaps it was my love for beautiful horses or the fact that people knew our family owned Arabians. Or perhaps it was mere happenstance that I was somehow invited to be among those who would meet the queen. But first another introduction.

All three of these became pivotal in my life.

Mom stood in a line at a nearby bank one day about four years after Charles died, in 1974.

In the long line, Mom noticed a woman staring at her. She hesitated to look back. But suddenly, the woman asked, "Aren't you Ovie?" Mom turned to find this was the woman where she and James had spent their wedding night in December, 1941, James' older sister, Olivia.

Mom hadn't seen her, or James, since 1949 when they divorced. The two of them were amazed they'd banked at the same branch and had lived within blocks of one another for 16 years, yet never run into one another.

This renewed acquaintance naturally led to one with James, who now lived in Chattanooga, Mom learned. She didn't know where he was because the last she'd heard, Dad was in prison in Starke, Florida.

Many years earlier, when he and his brother-in-law and another man had burglarized a place, one of the other men shot and killed the night watchman. James wasn't the shooter and had only gotten a three year sentence. But he was always out to make an easy buck. His wife, by whom he'd had about seven children, had died of cancer somewhere along the way.

One time as a young woman, I had looked this man up. I'd found his house on a forlorn and forgotten street, children streaming out the door onto the street, appearing neglected and poverty-stricken. I didn't go in.

For Mom to have found her first love after all these years made her happy. I didn't know what to think but it wasn't'happy'! Soon they'd made contact with one another, and he came to visit her. Then she did likewise.

One weekend, Mom called and said she was coming over, which she did from time to time - mostly holidays. I straightened the house and waited. Larry always worked on Saturdays, his busiest day of the week. When her car pulled into the driveway, I saw she had a passenger in the car. A tall man about her age. I'd already guessed my surprise.

And, I'd already considered that I might not even like this man. I'd recently met his sister, Olivia. I didn't care for her. She feigned familiarity with me. (Remember our family didn't touch, yet she was 'touchy-feely' with me). I didn't enjoy her fawning. It seemed fake, like *her*.

I opened the door and greeted Mom. At fifty-two, Mom was still attractive and young.

"Sharon, this is your Dad," she said. I felt nothing, but politely said hello. They both sat on the sofa, Rhonda and Craig crowding around me shyly. No wonder! *Most kids don't have to be introduced to 'Grandpa'!* Dad looked older than his years, the lines of his smooth skin were drawn a man who had dreamed big dreams. Today, he looked like a broken dreamer. I couldn't help but feel sorry for him.

The awkwardness faded as Dad played with the children while they showed him their pets. Mom and I made small talk - which is all we ever did anyway!

I watched out the kitchen window as they both got into the car. What should I be feeling, I wondered? I felt nothing. He arrived a stranger, and left the same way.

On their next wedding anniversary, they married in Effie's church, Feb. 19, 1974. A gentle snowstorm arrived that afternoon and delayed our arrival, but we got there just in time. Just a few family and friends. Sis was there of course, heading up everything like always. David had gotten married to his high school sweetheart by then. His wedding was the last time Mom had attended any church. She only went for weddings and for funerals.

Mom had initially told me that she and James were going to live together, so she probably only married Dad to keep Sis from saying she was 'shacking up'. Admittedly, I might have said that too.

Mom seemed happy that night, but apprehensive. She didn't take marriage lightly not because of the *vows*, but because of her *assets*. She'd worked hard and invested well. She was very comfortable in life. Quite a catch for a felon.

After they'd been married (happily it seemed) a couple of years, Mom took a rare risk with her money and spent $50,000 setting Dad up into business. He'd learned a trade in prison and worked at it in Chattanooga. He was an excellent body man, repairing and painting wrecked cars. He soon got the business of a top Cadillac dealer in town. He was taking in over $10k a month, she said.

It was during this time that Larry and I began to go over and play cards with the two of them about once a month or so. I am notorious for not even knowing what is trumps in a card game, yet *winning anyway*. Being the competitive players they were, we often laughed until we cried, especially at James. But since we lived on opposite sides of town, Mom and I mostly talked by telephone. We always did, since she worked and I stayed busy.

Then I discovered my mother herself did something one can never do with a former alcoholic, binge drinker around. She began to keep alcohol in the house for entertaining.

A very foolish move on anyone's part.

It wasn't long before I could hear the tension in her voice over the telephone. Mom told me Dad had hired some of his old drinking buddies to work for him. She didn't trust them, feeling they would steal his expensive tools to pawn them for liquor. They did.

Then, Dad didn't fulfill some of his jobs. Soon, he was drinking on the job. He lost the Cadillac dealer as quickly as he got them.

The next call I got was from the hospital where Mom had been taken, from an apparent heart attack. She'd collapsed into her rose bed that day.

I was shocked. Mom had always been the picture of good health, though she'd smoked all her life. There'd never been a hint of a problem though. This was 1980.

The hospital assured me that it wasn't life-threatening because they were able to treat her in time. But there had been damage to a muscle in the back of her heart. She'd have to take life easy. No more mowing the yard. No more stress, or the next one could kill her.

Mom got out of the hospital, and packed Dad's things up (loosely) as well as all the books she'd kept for the business and drove to the body shop. There she didn't even open the gate. She threw his things over the fence! Then she went home and changed the locks.

She had cut her losses. The marriage was over.

One good thing came out of all that though. Her need for a man to make her feel like a complete person had finally ended. Peace in the house superceded that need.

Life had offered James - the broken dreamer - a new chance at respectability. A chance at love. He continued to drink for several more years, popping in for an occasional visit to Mom, even after he'd remarried.

It was 1973 that I met the queen. Queen Elizabeth, that is. She regularly visits Lexington, Kentucky where she keeps some of her excellent broodmares. She has dozens of top thoroughbreds in England, where she races them and wins big purses. On one of those trips she visited Indianapolis to open the Indianapolis "500" Festival parade in May.

I knew nothing about this, or even that she visited Lexington often. But through my ties to some of the gals who *did* know, I received an invitation to be among several women who would attend a tea given for the queen.

First though, it was necessary we take a 'class'.

In this class, we were taught to curtsy upon meeting her. That we were never to touch the queen and only she could touch us, if she so desired. She always wore gloves in public gatherings so as not to touch the skin of anyone. I don't recall what else we had to learn.

I remember meeting her but I what does one say to the queen when you are speechless, anyway?... A rare occasion for me, yet it did happen! I watched others talk easily with her, and listened intently. She seemed well - like a queen is supposed to.

Like royalty. Important .

And I wondered how in God's Name I ever got there!

Oh, wait a minute... *God!* Perhaps it was Him behind that meeting, as I recalled a Proverb that says our gifts will take us before kings (and apparently queens too). Some had said I was 'gifted' .... perhaps, I surmised.

Given my humble beginnings, how *else*, but God ?

Until I began writing the revisions of this book, I had completely forgotten about this event for three or four decades.

It was that insignificant to me, but I share it here now because it's true and it really happened in my life.

It was the third introduction during this time that has mattered the most. It still does, *daily*.

I go back to how voraciously I read books about the church fathers, reformation, revivals, new releases, attended retreats and conferences and studied scripture constantly, either in groups or alone. I simply couldn't get enough!

That lasted for more than fifteen years. And after....

Being a reader, the charismatic movement had not exactly been new to Larry and myself. We both knew many spirit-filled believers at the little Presbyterian church.

Admittedly, the truly dynamic ones were very charismatic, it seemed. They were involved, knowledgeable, passionate. I wondered about that 'passion'. Scripture says all of **creation** *groans* for the revealing of certain kinds of the sons of God! When would that happen?

So it seemed to me that I groaned also, for more understanding. Then one year at those annual Presbyterian women's retreats I attended (and later led), they sang a song from Psalm 19 where it says, 'the testimony of the Lord is sure, *making wise the simple.*' That was *it!* I'd arrived at the salvation's door famished for knowledge, groaning for understanding.

And slowly I was becoming filled and satisfied, like a good meal. I simply tell my story here.

Someone handed me a book, by Catherine Marshall, wife of Peter, the Chaplain of the House of Representatives - now deceased – "Something More." They said I might be interested in her topic, which was the Holy Spirit. I didn't gain much from it other than the Holy Spirit is the third person of the Godhead. And that He is a gentleman, so He must be *acknowledged...*

Next I read John chapters 14-16 where the role of the Holy Spirit in our lives is described in the Bible, as our teacher, guide, leads us into all truth. reveals Jesus to us, brings all things to our remembrance (when we need them), helper (three times), advocate, comforter and is the Spirit of Truth. Better, Acts 2:33 says the Holy Spirit is the promise of the Father "for you, and for your children and for all who are far off, everyone whom the Lord our God calls..."

Finally, I saw that Acts 2:4; 8:12-17; 9:11,17; 19:5 all make the receiving of the Holy Spirit *a secondary experience.* This is *Bible*, Friends. Not denominational thinking! The tense in Ephesians 5:18 says to 'keep on being filled with the Holy Spirit'. *We leak!*

It was at that same Presbyterian women's retreat where I found what I'd been looking for. *More of God...* The effervescence; the overflow!..I was **full. Full at last; full at last! Thank God Almighty, Full at last!** (*Forgive me!*)

One of my closest friends introduced me to the baptism of the Holy Spirit. I'd heard about it but was told by another friend (great leader in town whom I thought should know) that that second experience was for the less 'mature' believer. Then she said, "*We who are mature* don't need those kinds of signs because we have scripture itself."

It hadn't been that long since I'd sat in the same room with Corrie ten Boom when someone asked her about being mature.

What Corrie said then blew some of us away. She said, "Oh no, *I don't consider myself mature.* Not at all. Rather, I regard myself a *teenage lamb.*"

If Corrie wasn't a "mature" Christian after undergoing Hitler's concentration camps and all the years of service that had followed, then I didn't think I knew any! Corrie by the way, was a spirit-filled believer and said so in one of her books. Tramp For The Lord, I *think.* (Maybenot.)

My church friend Gwen knew that I was hungry, and cornered me one night after meetings at the retreat. God must have known Gwen is the only voice I would hear on this topic! I was very closed-minded about it.

She shared with me from scripture. I remained reluctant, so entrenched was I in my 'pet doctrine' that this gift must not be for today.

But finally, she asked me if she could pray for me.

I didn't expect her to pray in tongues! My mind wanted to protest, yet her prayer language was the sweetest thing I'd ever heard...!

It broke me completely because *I knew it was of* ***God***.

I repented and told God I wanted *everything* He had for me.

This is not 'religion' because John the Baptist clearly said "He who comes after me will baptize you with the *Holy Spirit and with Fire.*" <u>It is a secondary experience</u>. When we are born again, it is the Holy Spirit that baptizes us into the body of Christ. But when Jesus baptizes us, it is with the fire of God! Fire is a cleansing agent, an illumination, and the Holy Spirit is available to all who follow Jesus. Luke 11:13 and Acts 5:32.

Yes, it was an emotional experience - one that has never worn off. *I can't figure why anyone would resist the experience that prays the perfect prayer for their children according to Romans 8:26...*

(A prayer *language* is not the gift of tongues described in I Cor. 12, which chapter repeatedly says is used 'in church'! Many confuse the two –*<u>Don't!)</u>*

If you don't want this experience, *don't worry!* You won't be bothered with it *it's only for those who believe!* We don't *have* to speak in tongues, we *get* to - and it is a total privilege! Apostle Paul said he was thankful he spoke in tongues more than all the Corinthians.

So am I.

This second experience will give you access to the miraculous- it is a gateway!

You can do what you wish. *I wish to speak in tongues every day until the day I die*, thus 'building up my most holy faith'! Jude 23. Amen.

While this gift is deeply personal, do not think it is only for our personal benefit!

Not. It is for praying for the winning of the lost in our lives.

He knows circumstances and the minds of others.

And for the redemption of all who seek to be found by the Great Shepherd, *through us.*

I don't pretend to understand why God's gifts operate the way they do. But I want to remain childlike enough to just obey. I do know that if we could understand God or all His ways - which are higher than ours - then He would be no greater!

"A religion that is small enough for our understanding
would not be big enough for our needs.
- Corrie ten Boom

When you are filled with the Holy Spirit,
then the ministry just flows out of you."
- Corrie ten Boom

A Chinese missionary visited American churches.
Near the end, he was asked what he
thought of those churches.
He said, he couldn't believe how much
the churches in America could get done
***without** the Holy Spirit!*
Author

17

The Perils of Passivity

Bob and Jo stood beside our little family at the graveside service for David. Larry's younger brother, was dead at only 33 years old. He'd been murdered, by a shotgun blast to the abdomen one February day in 1979.

David had always lived life on the edge of the law; and on the edge of danger. He didn't sell drugs to our knowledge, but he hung out with those who did, and he smoked pot regularly throughout his adult life.

Most of his friends were either borderline, or criminal.

To this day, I don't know if David was a mellow, easy going guy - or if he was just on marijuana all the time! One thing I *did* know; he had a temper. Other than that temper, I would say David was a truly passive fellow.

After a failed marriage, he'd headed for the Southwest where he worked in construction, living with his girlfriend.

It was there that he'd attempted to collect a $20 debt from an old girlfriend. He paid dearly. Her new boyfriend unloaded a twelve-gauge into his midriff through the closed door. Then the killer had walked out and put his foot on David's chest as though he'd just made a deer kill. This was witnessed by David's pal, *who would not testify* due to an outstanding warrant. David's killer was caught, then released.

It was Larry who flew to Phoenix, identified the body and flew home with the casket.

A Puerto Rican man I know has a prison ministry. He says, "You don't have to do anything bad to go to jail – just hang around with them that does."

Apparently, the same can be said of dying.

I learned this principle of making right choices regarding associates, the hard way as a teen. I'd accepted a ride in a convertible filled with friends. But I only knew the passengers, not the *driver*. He drove too fast, too recklessly. After sideswiping a couple of parked vehicles, then fleeing the scene, I told myself that if I ever got out of that car, I would never place myself in a *subjective position* like that again!

I didn't.

It only takes one wrong decision to ruin a life! Prisons are full of these kinds of stories! Trust me, I've talked to them personally. Too often their *boyfriends*, too!

Our little Presbyterian church had come upon hard times. It lost its beloved pastor, who had taken a larger pastorate in California. The new pastor was immediately a big disappointment to most members. The warmth and fellowship we'd had, began to diminish as this man would often try to prove his (unbiblical) points on a blackboard via the Greek language. Such as *Jesus' was not a virgin birth.* Many felt he didn't know God.

People like Gwen's family and others began to leave. (He was the reason I and others began to take Greek, because he always used Greek to prove his point, thus rendering his critics mute.)

By 1975, Larry and I clearly were aiming to leave as well. We began attending a home church meeting with friends on Saturday evenings. Leaving was a slow motion process however, due to the children's ties to friends and programs there at the old church, but they soon could tell the difference, as program after program ended or moved on, including Wednesday Night Youth Club. Young Life also moved to another church facility.

Jesus told us we could KNOW people by their fruit. And this is the *fruit of folks who are not authentic,* friends – *the death of what was previously alive!*

Aware that Bob pastored the biggest charismatic church in the city, we gradually eased into going there. With an orchestra of sixty or more musicians, we loved the amazing worship. Bob too played a *six* string banjo, and he wrote some of the songs we sang. The three elders took turns giving a message on Sundays. It was lively, and following the pall over our old home church, it was a welcome change to our family.

It meant a lot to Larry and me that Bob and Jo had journeyed sixty miles to be there for David's funeral. We knew they were busy, but not too busy to show their caring concern and love for us.

Robert L. Jones was 6'6" in his hulking, handsome frame. It was difficult not to respect him. He towered over everyone, especially me. I am 5'3", and I always felt like I was about belt buckle high to him. When he saw me, he would usually swallow me up in his long arms with a bear hug, eyes sparkling and smiling all over.

He stood, as he always did, head and shoulders above every man at the funeral. Jo too was tall, and they made a striking couple wherever they went. Bob was the most handsome man I knew who was completely *bald.*

He always said God didn't make that many perfect heads (*He put hair on the rest*). He and Jo were also the happiest couple I'd ever known.

It was his treatment of *me* that utterly changed me.

In Larry's and my minds, God Himself had sent His own family to soothe the hurt we felt that day from Larry's earthly family.

Larry's Dad had made no secret that they *wished it hadn't been their 'favorite' son.*

Though our family had been very close to his family for many years since we married, the events surrounding David's death produced a breach that was never completely healed. Rhonda and Craig were about 12 and 13 years old then.

Ironically, none of us could have known that in little more than two months, we'd be standing over another grave, one of our own...!

It rained that February day as it so often does at funerals. Larry and I sloshed back to the car where Bob and Jo bid us farewell and returned home. We then joined family for a while at Larry's folks.

At the funeral home, David's girlfriend had worn black - as though a grieving *girlfriend?* - joining the reception line with the family at the funeral home. None of us had ever even **met** her before. Larry's aunts and uncles were all upscale and honorable folks, and we all found this awkward.

I felt it was poor taste, but it wasn't my call! *What did I know?*

I wish that was the end of it, but Larry's sister gave out 'souvenirs' in envelopes to people - lock's of David's hair cut on the spot. Larry found this vile and said so to his mother.

I saw a side to her then, I'd never seen, when she got right into Larry's face and said, "You're vile."

Her emotions raw, I tried to understand. *I couldn't.*

I saw his father was over the edge, unable to deal with his own grief. Much less *this* scene. But I knew he had more couth than this.

Relationships were tense and painful when we arrived at the house. I hurt for Larry. He'd known his folk's feelings all along, but to have them surface at such a time was unbearable for him, I felt. We left, but not before his sister - the same one giving out hair souvenirs - had her say, consummating the new breach.

Larry and I no longer made the trip on holidays or weekends to spend time there we both figured the road ran both ways-they'd never used it. His Mom and Dad came for dinner a few times after, but never his sister.

On the long ride home, I thought of David's final weeks of life. He'd seemed genuinely trying to get his life together, for the first time. Though very tight with a dollar, he'd called us *long distance* on two different occasions and talked for over an hour. He said he wanted to begin to live right and maybe get married. For the first time ever, he was open to hearing the good news that Jesus had come that we might have life, and abundantly.

Both of us were on the telephone while talking with him, so we'd encouraged him to make a decision for Christ, Who wanted him to be happy more than he did!

Jesus was the only route to true happiness, we said.

We warned him about a *heaven to gain, and a hell to shun.*

When David was shot, he'd lived for two hours in the hospital. In that time, our hope was, this was an opportunity given by a merciful God, who had heard our prayers for him - to repent and accept Jesus before he actually died.

Because I know God is faithful, I believe He gave David that opportunity.

I looked over at Larry who was driving. I chose not to dwell on the funeral or its circumstances. It was too heavy, but I hoped Larry wasn't dwelling on it either. He looked beaten. I put my hand on his shoulder. His nearly six feet frame seemed somehow diminished. I'd spent years in my marriage thinking that I'd married the wrong man. But now in retrospect, I think instead, he was the ideal man for me. A gentle man early on, who was often considerate and thoughtful to people, but I hadn't met too many of those kinds of men in my lifetime. He was one.

Drowsy now, I laid my head back and thought of the past six years since we'd come to know and love Bob and Jo and their family.

In the summer of 1973, I'd gotten a call from an out of state acquaintance who asked me to come lead a workshop at a women's retreat in Champaign-Urbana, Illinois. She was chairing it. She listed the featured speakers and Jo was one of them. I promptly told her I would love to accept. I'd heard a lot about Jo and wished to meet her.

This would be great.

However, after hanging up, I felt a strange sensation I'd never felt before something akin to *restraint.* I didn't understand.

Alone that day in the house, I took my Bible and walked outdoors to the front lawn.

Sitting down in a lawn chair that summer day, I opened my Bible and began to pray about this.

I read about John the Baptist and the time he said of Jesus "I must decrease, but He (Jesus) must increase."

That passage had been in a recent morning devotion. And now *this!* I felt God was talking to me about Larry.

I only lived to serve God. I was most alive when I was able to speak and do so - it was why I was born, I felt. Now, it seemed God was asking me to take a step back .and allow Larry to grow, as the new believer he was.

I died a huge death that day, to self (*flesh* spelled backward without the 'h').

Now it was no longer a matter of trusting a mere man or even Larry. God was asking me if I trusted *HIM* enough to take a back seat to Larry, trusting God to honor that obedience.

I didn't think I *did* trust Him that much!

However, I understood that God is a God of 'order'. The sun was never meant to fulfill the role of the stars and moon. Everything has a function in the universe. He also desired order for the home. My role in that home was not less than Larry's, just different.

Over time, I'd prayed so often, "Lord, make me your instrument." He was telling me now that I needed to shorten that prayer to "Lord, make me *yours*."

I'd already surrendered my life to God. That day I had to surrender even what I would do for Him. I wept.

It was my birthday.

(Don't miss how God honored that decision by the end of this chapter.).

I went indoors and called my friend in Illinois, and told her what the Lord had shown me.

She understood.

Shortly after that - as the Lord would have it - I attended a conference in Brownsburg where Norvel Hayes was speaking. I was surprised to see that Jo was there. It turned out that she and her husband Bob, were personal friends with Norvel and that he owned a home and other real estate in Indianapolis. (His ministry is based in Cleveland, Tn.)

Norvel is an uneducated man who says he'd rather know the Lord than to have a degree from the best university! He was a millionaire owning restaurants and a publishing company.

I learned a great deal from Norvel over the years. I especially appreciated his boldness.

Lunchtime came and someone suggested we all go to lunch. I didn't know Jo would happen to be one of the diners. We chatted amiably and both seemed to like what we heard from the other.

Jo and I became best friends after meeting in Brownsburg. It was just something we agreed upon one day in her living room. "Let's be best friends", we concurred. There was never a more unlikely pair, but it worked for over 40 years, until she died.

I was impressed that her husband Bob wore many hats in life. He ran a consulting business where he traveled a lot. He was a highly respected and longtime state legislator whose name and picture were in the newspaper regularly. As such, he'd been Chairman of the powerful Criminal Courts committee for over thirteen years.

A third hat he wore, with the assistance of two others, was that he pastored our city's biggest charismatic congregation. He was respected by peers.

A final hat was he wore was as a gifted public speaker. He was often invited to speak at men's groups, most of them FGBMFI (Full Gospel Business Men's Fellowship International, based in California). The charismatic move of God was in full swing, and this particular men's group grew parallel with it at that time.

Our family attended Bob and Jo's church for years.

Most people didn't realize both Bob and Jo had endured their own private suffering. Bob had spinal meningitis as a teen where he lost all his hair and almost died. Their only girl died just after being born. And a serious car wreck in New Jersey had broken Jo's neck so she could neither turn it to the right or left. If she turned, her shoulders and entire body turned also. This was due to the fusion of three discs at the base of her neck.

This made driving a car difficult for her.

It was this condition that set the stage for a miracle in her whole family.

Bob hadn't always been a dynamic believer. Though each were raised in believing homes, both had gravitated away from God during college. They attended a nominal church if they could. Church was anything but a priority.

However, Jo had endured a prolonged sluggishness where she couldn't seem to function.

Though she loved Bob, an aching emptiness told her something was missing.

Bob remained unconcerned.

Some years before our families met, a single event changed the course of that *entire* family.

One evening, an acquaintance Jo regarded as somewhat of a fanatic invited her to a meeting with an out of town speaker. She wasn't sure why, but she said 'Yes' she would go.

The meeting was a healing service. During that meeting, God performed a complete miracle and restored Jo's neck to normal. Totally loosened it.

This was a medical impossibility because doctors had fused her spine in three vertabrae. For over 17 years she and her family felt she'd never move normally again. They were just glad she was healthy.

Now, she could suddenly move her neck freely.

That night, Jo went home where her family watched television, and demonstrated her new mobility to Bob and the boys.

This was no small thing!

It was then apparent to Bob, on a first hand basis, *God was still in the miracle-working business!* There was no other way to explain this event.

This also meant to Bob that he had better take a fresh look at God. From then on, Bob was totally smitten with the One Who cared enough about his wife's unnatural movement to heal her. The boys were awed as well.

Since we attended the same church with Bob and Jo, we began to spend countless hours together. Bob and Jo were so very happy. It encouraged me to discover a marriage so loving. They had four sons, all 6'3 to 6'7" and as Jo would add even the dog was male! They were a family of watusi's, all very tall, including Jo. I got to know them well enough to know they were the real thing. Authentic.

The entrance to their downstairs bore a plaque, "All For One. One For All." They meant it!

Bob was a man given to humor. He often said that God had given him a terrific teaching on humility - *he just hadn't found a crowd large enough to give it to!*

Somehow, Bob had the utmost respect for me. I was always awed by that fact. He often shared matters that troubled him, and asked my opinion. The first time or two, I was floored. He trusted I heard from God.

Because I did operate freely in the gifts of God, that brought me into a place of privilege with Bob. I was amazed at Bob's confidence in my ability to hear from God. He liked for me to be in his meetings, when he spoke, because he knew both Jo and I would discern what was happening in them - good or bad, demonic or inspirational.

Larry and I even flew with them on a private jet once to a speaking engagement.

We were with them often in annual World conventions and also regional conventions that we all attended, at least three or four a year.

As God would have it, Larry grew in an amazing manner during this time. He loved Full Gospel Businessmen's Fellowship International, and wouldn't miss a minute of the testimonies and events. These were just ordinary businessmen doing the Lord's work. Their results were astonishing and we heard exciting reports of it at these conventions.

I was amazed too at the wisdom of God in all this concerning Larry. My stepping back had worked.

Before long, Larry was discussing starting a real chapter in our town. That's because we both found the existing one so boring! We knew that wasn't the norm for other chapters, because we met those leaders at conventions. By 1978 Larry was President of his local men's chapter while I was Vice President of the local Aglow chapter that Jo and I had started.

I always served in a servant's role to this wonderful couple, Bob and Jo, and I did that gladly. In fact, this is where I learned the attribute of servanthood. It was an honor and a privilege!

Bob was not a passive guy. Strong, outspoken, principled and caring. I liked that most about him. That, and the fact he favored me. But I learned something else too. *Passive people are not prepared for the future!* Did you know that scripture says the 'timid' will be first to be cast into hell? See Rev. 21:8.

Other translations say 'fearful' (....it precedes all other sins like murder, adultery!)

Why aren't passive people prepared enough? Because they are often not their own person! In fact, they often belong to someone or something else.

As a rule, they don't think for themselves!

Presently, many passive folks belong to the government, often with their hand outstretched. Or they have adopted a 'victim' mindset, so easy these days! Without change, they may soon belong to the antichrist, with that outstretched hand wearing a mark!

Watch out! It's coming to your neighborhood soon.

The new EHR card will be appealing and seem like something to be desired. (New: EHR, or Electronic Health Records, will be first to market a card that carries all health info as of summer 2014. This card is linked to your bank account and has a RFID chip that locates you wherever you are. In case of emergencies, people will want these cards., but if you opt to, you may get a new FDA approved Verichip, the size of a grain of rice placed under the skin.

Food stamp recipients will be next to receive such a chip).

So *there are two marks to look for*. The mark of genuine believers I wrote about in chapter 13, which is love, (I like to call it *family*) and the mark of the beast which is what's coming to your neighborhood soon. And sooner or later, you will have to make a <u>*choice*</u> about the matter. Trust me on this, Friends!

Perhaps it was his charming wit and love for God that so endeared Bob to me. He was the first truly *righteous* man I'd ever known well.

I will always be grateful for knowing, serving and loving him.

I've tried not to tell their story in this book. However, Bob and Jo's positive impact upon me and the fact that our own lives were so intertwined for several years, theirs has become in some sense, *my story*.

I saw greatness in both of them.

It is not my ability, but my response to
God's ability, that counts.
Corrie ten Boom

Faith sees the invisible, believes the unbelievable,
and receives the impossible.
Corrie Ten Boom

18

Shock Waves In Indy

One year at one of the World Conventions we attended, Larry met a fellow who wanted him to become a factory rep for acrylic sunglasses that were scratch and break resistant. He put custom logos for businesses on them. Larry had never tried to sell anything, but he liked the concept enough that he decided to give it a try.

He actually did quite well, getting several large orders, including a national car race.

This was an avocation; he kept his regular job. We traveled on that extra money.

Meantime, I'd been working in real estate for some time again and really loved it. And I loved being home with the children after school.

At tax time one year however, Larry voiced his concern over how much money I'd made (more than him.) I'd also had this nagging (Hello?) feeling that I should quit.

Well, here we go again! I didn't *want* to quit working. I liked real estate and felt it was a nice 'fit' for me and for the entire family. *God is faithful.* He worked that out.

A disappointing Easter Sunday came where we had guests and I had to dash out and fill in for a co-worker in the office (I owed her). I sold the house, but missed the Easter dinner I'd prepared and guests ate without me. Not even leftovers were there.

Then (what I call) I wet-nursed that deal over weeks through to a mortgage they really didn't qualify for but they wanted the house.

Finally, the morning of the closing, my buyer called to tell me they were moving to Houston, Texas instead. *No thank you, Sorry about that, or anything else.* The handwriting was on the for me through that deal. I should have learned the first time. I quit.

As it was, I began to love not having to work, for a number of years after. I budgeted and scrimped, but these were happy times for our family, and we often took holiday dinners either at Mamie and Ted's, or with Bob and Jo's family. (I don't enjoy cooking!)

It was a remarkable thing when God brought Jo and I together. We each felt neither would have sought the other out, yet God knew our friendship would be a true 'fit'.

(I learned from that to permit God to choose my friends - He knows best and He has made me wealthy in friends.)

We'd recognized early, that part of His purpose for us was in praying for others, which we did faithfully over many years. We believed in the power of the 'agreement' Jesus talked about where, if we as believers do agree, *we can have* what we ask!

Jo and I kept our commitment of praying two hours a week from one end of the Pacific to the Atlantic, and Niagara Falls to New Orleans - because we traveled so often to the same events in FGBMFI and Women's Aglow.

Both Larry's local chapter of FGBMFI and our chapter of Aglow grew. Soon several new chapters of Aglow had opened up around town and nearby. Our monthly meetings were usually fun, exciting and well attended. Jo and I also spoke regularly at other chapters, more her than me, but I counted one time and, over seven years or so, there were about a hundred.

It was on a return trip home from one of those speaking engagements that Jo confided to me that Bob had made a new decision, one that apparently troubled her. One of the elders in our church had stepped down a few weeks earlier, and Bob had asked a certain gentleman in the church to fill the vacancy as one of the three governing elders in the church.

I knew this man and his wife, and found them both likeable. But he was new to the congregation, a Baptist, and new to the faith as far as leading those more experienced in spiritual matters than he. In the words of scripture, he was a 'novice', at least to our assembly.

I knew Jo believed the same.

This information upset me, and it upset me *that it mattered so much.* I couldn't shake the feeling this was not a wise decision on Bob's part!

According to Jo, Bob was going to make the announcement the following Sunday, between church and a pot luck dinner we were having that day.

I felt pensive. I tried to dismiss it. A foreboding came that I didn't understand like a weight hanging over me. *Why did I care?* I didn't even want to!

Finally, I became convinced this was God Himself dealing with me on this matter concerning future leadership of the church.

I could bear the burden no longer, and called Jo prior to Sunday to ask her for permission to reveal that she'd told me this information. She agreed.

Sunday came, and I clearly was not myself in the worship and singing. I listened to his message, but didn't hear a word of it. This was unusual.

I went to Bob after the service ended. He wasn't going to like it.

Yet *The Fear of The Lord* on me was greater and made me know what I had to do. I trembled.

Bob greeted me with his sparkling blue eyes and gave me his customary hug.

Bob emanated warmth. But he could tell I had something on my mind. I told him what I'd learned from Jo, that I felt a huge constraint from the Lord about this decision.

(I just had noooo idea!)

Bob looked at me, stammering, "But Sharon. I've already asked him!"

If Bob had a shortcoming, or 'clay feet', it was manly pride. He didn't want to back down on his word to another man.

I looked into his eyes that peered so questionably back at me. How I loved this man!

But he was a man about to *miss God!*

And I didn't understand why it seemed so serious to me.

This event taught me *we don't have to understand to obey.* God knows the future and we don't! Just follow the promptings of the Lord! Today, I know my hands are clean from the events that followed in the aftermath of that tumulteous decision.

Later, Bob announced his decision, avoiding my eyes.

The following day was Monday, and Bob and Jo had arranged to fly to Louisiana to visit their third son, Richie, who was on a track scholarship in college. Bob came from a long line of track athletes. He himself ran daily and was the picture of health.

That week was one of only a handful of times Jo and I ever missed prayer time together.

Circumstances prevented it.

The telephone rang at 3am. Larry answered. I could tell something was wrong. Bob III, Bob's older son was on the line. He wouldn't be calling then if it wasn't something serious.

There had been a tragedy.

At 50 years old, in seemingly perfect health, the invincible Bob Jones, Jr. was dead of a heart attack in Louisiana.

The newspaper carried the front page story.

Mom saw the story, of course, and called. She knew of our close involvement with Bob and Jo and that we attended their church. But she'd taken her cues from James while they were married who'd called me "high-falooting" - whatever that means. Something to do with uppity, I think. She didn't understand that Larry and I shared a Common Denominator with Bob and Jo that breaks down all social barriers of race, sex and class.

We had chosen to surround ourselves with others who were on the same mission!

But Mom never understood that, nor did she perceive the changes going on in my own life. That wasn't wholly her fault. *I never shared my life with her* - knowing she belittled most decisions I ever made anyway.

We never really *talked*. We just filled the air with words, as so many do.

Bob and Jo had had plans to pick up Richie and a friend for dinner.

Meantime, Bob left the hotel to go for a run. Jo often went with him, but this time lingered in the hotel watching the 700 Club.

A woman named Betty Malz - who was from Southern Indiana –was being interviewed on the show. She spoke of the painful process of being 'molded' by the left hand of God.

The thought went through her mind, *I'll never see Bob again*. She dismissed it, and showered for dinner.

The time to leave came and went. This wasn't like Bob. The front desk hadn't seen him.

She called Richie to ask him to come to the hotel.

Something was wrong.

Waiting for Richie, she called the hospital, then the police. Surely someone had seen Bob. There simply couldn't be that many tall, bald-headed men in shorts and Republican elephant tee shirt in Democrat country!

Richie arrived to the hotel.

Soon two sheriff's deputies appeared at the hotel room door, asking her and Richie to accompany them. They wouldn't say why.

A little relieved, she thought, "Oh, Bob's been hurt."

They arrived at the hospital but didn't go into the main or the ER entrance. They drove to a side entrance and parked, then took them downstairs to a long room with small doors.

She knew it was the morgue. Bob carried no identification.

Any ability to be rational left in that moment. She identified his body, then requested a moment alone. Bob's head lay on the rim of the tray in the morgue, his frame too long. Jo immediately thought, "Oh, that must be uncomfortable."

Married 29 happy years, Jo couldn't remember not being married. Or life without him. She looked down at her dead husband's body and remembered their wedding vows *til death do us part.*

Suddenly, her mind screamed "God, how can I live without this man?"

A certainty that Bob was now in the presence of God brought fleeting comfort. She realized that 'death' had changed their relationship. Then Jo said, "But God, *I'm here!*"

A voice, whether audible or inner, she didn't know, spoke to her and said, "*Then **live** here.*"

The very kind deputies told Jo he'd been found outside the hotel, sitting against a grassy knoll, as though he'd sat down to rest. He was already dead when found.

Completely numb, Jo went through the motions of getting the body returned home, complicated by the parishes in Louisiana. Then she and Richie followed.

Shock waves are an understatement for the impact of this 'larger than life', seemingly healthy man's sudden death.. In the prime of life; only 50 years old; in apparent excellent health.

Believers who felt Bob's was a needed voice in the legislature, community, and church were the most confounded. *Why* did God take him?

That would include Larry and me and the children.

Jo couldn't function while details screamed for her attention. While I busied myself relieving Jo and family of the calls, the visits, the flowers, gifts and food constantly arriving at their door, Larry was left to himself to grieve, still reeling from David's death only weeks before.

He fervently loved Bob and held him in the highest regard as friend and pastor.

And worse, our church family was now left with an unfeeling novice at the helm to guide and comfort the flock. The other elder immediately stepped down after Bob died. We didn't know why.

I was fine while I was inside their house, serving the family. But once I stepped out the back, it seemed that heaven was nearer now, I looked up and wept unashamedly.

My dear, dear friend, brother in Christ, pastor, esteemed leader - now gone.

A lady called long distance (then) from Louisiana. She had found Bob and wanted Jo to know that when she found him, he was smiling. Jo was greatly relieved to know he hadn't suffered pain. *God just took him.*

A private funeral was planned for the family. Only Bob's best friend's family and ours attended. Jo buried Bob simply, as she thought he'd have preferred.

I couldn't believe I'd never see those sparkling blue eyes again!

Later that week, a memorial service was held at a huge downtown church. Over 700 people paid their respects. Bob's four sons each gave a short eulogy. It was powerful and moving. Flowers filled the aisles, some from dignitaries, including the governor.

Given Bob had lived by faith, Jo had no concept of what their economic outlook was. She didn't even know if there was money for the funeral.

After the memorial, the boys emptied out his business office, and Jo and I emptied his legislative office, so that the house and garage became laiden with 'files'. They weren't bad.

But his home office was scandalous. As we went through the piles of files, we found ten and fifteen year old birthday cards -with *money* still in them! Bob wasn't organized and neither was Jo - so it was a good thing that *God sent me!* She'd still be in that office...!

Slowly things seemed to be working out. Jo had *enough money.* He didn't believe in them, but Bob had a small, older 401K. Then, the death of Bob's mother months before aided the family when her estate came through. Social Security also stepped in until the youngest son, Doug, who was beginning college, was 21. (He is a Hollywood actor now)

I'm not certain when it struck me as to *why* I'd felt so burdened about Bob's decision on church leadership. It wasn't right away. *God knew Bob would die* - virtually within hours of that announcement! I was sobered as I thanked God I'd obeyed Him.

Whatever happened, I was certain it wasn't going to be *good* given my 'quaking' before I'd spoken to Bob about it.

I could say a lot of things here, but I will skip the middle and say that within six months, church attendance had dropped from 400 weekly to less that 75 people, some of them the new elder's extended family. Most all of the musicians went elsewhere.

The entire church later disintegrated. This was largely due to mismanagement, and the interference of a woman - who called herself a prophet - and who moved in with the novice pastor and his wife.

More death.

She counseled people whose marriages ended. Jobs were lost and businesses failed.

That pastor wouldn't listen to protests by those who cared, and he shielded her from criticism.

Because a man followed people, the sheep knew the voice wasn't that of the Shepherd.

God had wanted to save that very effective and large church family, so it would continue to bless people and draw them to Himself in praise, training in righteousness and good works!

Didn't happen. The devil pre-empted it. This time, God's hands were tied.

"I am not a trained theologian.
I am a student of holy scripture over 50 years.
What I can tell you is that if you are doing anything at all,
for the cause of Christ, you will be the target of the same
legalists and Pharisees who also criticized and eventually
killed Our Lord- and most *of those who followed Him.*
Truth has never been popular!
Yet we have a heritage in Isaiah 54:17+"
Sharon Jackson, Author

PART III

Sidewalk to Nowhere

- -

"If God has shown us bad times ahead,
it's enough for me that He knows about them.
That's why He sometimes shows us things,
you know - to tell us that this too is in His hands."
Corrie ten Boom, the Hiding Place

19

Come Season's End

Larry and I had already made reservations for that year's FGBMFI World Convention in New Orleans, which came two months after Bob died. Jo felt that Bob would have wanted her to go for the refreshing she direly needed after his death. But she didn't think she dare spend the money until monetary issues were more resolved. Larry and I modified the room we'd reserved to a bigger one, and told her she could stay in our accommodations to save money, and we provided banquet meals.

Oddly, we had the largest room we'd ever had at those affairs, in the grand Le Pavillon off Canal Street. I've hadn't seen so many glorious chandeliers inside one facility!

Many friends at the convention offered Jo condolences. She was glad she came, and felt many of them needed the opportunity for closure as well.

(Bob was well loved and often spoke there).

During one particularly moving evening meeting, Jo lifted her hand in faith in God, as an act of believing for a ridiculous amount of money for a woman who hadn't worked in 25 years. But she needed a job!

Jo had a degree in teaching, but it was outdated and she didn't want to renew it. Nor did she want to work for pennies. Some told her she should take whatever she could get. She said no, she'd trust God and *wait.* Then she began to treat her job search as her real job, dutifully following *every lead that came her way.*

Well, after many months of looking, a miracle happened. Someone in the city knew of her community action history that had created programs and united people in effort. So the city created a brand new position, just for Jo. In the right place at the right time - she became their new Permit Coordinator, soon *at the salary she'd believed God for!*

Meantime, all of this turned the focus upon my own marriage - in my mind. *How many truly happy marriages were there anyway?* Bob and Jo's was one. I regarded ours as nominal then... not truly fitted to each other. *(We were becoming less fitted...)*

We had gravitated together out of weakness. We'd thought two lonely people equaled one happy couple. Our math was wrong! All we got was more loneliness! Our marriage was needy from the start, I thought, comprised of two needy people. I knew God could change that. I felt *He hadn't.*

This is what you get when you listen to the tempter (the devil) who wants to destroy your lives and marriage!

The truth is that Larry had done very well until recent events. He'd formed that FGBMFI chapter with three of his friends under his leadership. They'd had great results with big crowds that came, and people looked to Larry for prayer and help. He thrived in that. He'd flourished for six or seven years and had grown a great deal.

His small business had done well too.

But something was coming that would knock him off his feet.

And me as well.

Gradually, life seemed to settle down for all of us. Larry, Jo and I were asked by a Catholic friend to be a part of a leadership team to affect unity between believers throughout the state. I was glad for Jo's sake as it gave her an arena of ministry.

She'd questioned if God could use her again.

Our annual meetings were held the day after Thanksgiving at the Convention Center, now available since Bill Gaither was no longer doing his conferences there that weekend.

We invited celebrities we'd met at world conventions such as Rosie Greer to speak, and Peter Marshall, Jr. They were the draw to bring people in. It worked. A local group expertly led contemporary worship.

Larry emceed and did a great job. I loved seeing him flourish in doing what he enjoyed (more than horses!).

You can't keep a good woman down, so Jo decided to form the very first lunch hour Brown Bag Aglow meeting downtown Indianapolis. I always laughed at where they met - at the *Power & Light* building on Monument Circle! She crammed a lot into that 55 minute meeting. People loved it.

Five years later though, that tall glass building where she worked had become a 'glass cage', in her words. She was frustrated because her first and truest calling was *beingawife!* She felt trapped in the work force by then. But her first love was always serving God. So she created a late night radio program that she'd succeeded in talking a station into donating time for. That endeavor became her ticket out of that cage!

We all traveled to LA for the world convention that year. I loved going to LA. Jo heard an interesting fellow from England speak, and thought she might interview him for her show. (I didn't meet him). So she arranged an interview. She knew he was a new widower. But he was older than she was so she didn't really consider him as husband material at that time.

Upon returning home, she discovered the tape failed. She wrote to this man, Buzz Dully of Kent, to tell him of it, and asked for a remake in Detroit next year?

He accepted saying, "Oh by the way, can we have lunch?"

I was home the day Jo got that letter. It wasn't like Jo to ever dally on an employer's time.

She was too honest. That day she did. I will never forget this as long as I live.

At one point, she exclaimed, "Sharon, what if God wants me to *marry* this man?" I replied, "Jo, for heaven's sake! The man has only invited you to lunch?

It isn't like it's a marriage proposal!"

It's not the first time I've been wrong! But I have never been soooo wrong in my life. Jo must have sensed something I didn't. *From God.*

In Detroit, she met with Buzz, a widower, on the second day. By the fourth day, he'd said "I can't believe you're available." The next day he proposed to her!

Jo was spontaneous. Yet, I would never call her impulsive. Other people would though, when she and Buzz married in only 18 days (a church wedding at that). She quit her job, put her house on the market, gave the furniture to her sons, and shipped the pieces she wanted plus personal items to England by the end of the month!

Jo was not impulsive. She was *certain*. Certain of the leading of the Lord.

Sometimes he moves *suddenly!*

After that, when they came to the U.S. annually, they'd sometimes visit me in Florida.

One time she mailed me a post card from when they visited China. I sat and stared at it. As I sat there musing over that card, the marvel of all God had done for Jo struck me.

She who only lived to be a good wife - was *there in China!* And I'd found just the ***postage stamp*** *amazing!*

FGBMFI failed when Demos Shakarian, its founder, died. Buzz led the European alternate for some years after.

It is said that life has an **ebb and a flow**. I call it 'seasons' and, thankfully, seasons pass. While *in* the bad seasons however... they seem unending.

As Jo's life turned upward in a new and hopeful season, mine and Larry's seemed to spiral down into a strange and fearful season. A slow spin, out of control.

I've enjoyed revising this book thus far. But I am not looking forward to writing this portion because it is the darkest period of my entire life.

I don't like to dwell there. It's the underbelly, if you will. I must write it because what I gained from those experiences was necessary, because God knew what the end was!

And His objective was to bring me to where He wanted. That doesn't mean I understood it, or even *cared* then.

In the springtime, our beautiful grey Arabian mare gave birth to a chestnut filly. She was sorrel color and had three white stockings, a white star and strip on her face. That mare was pregnant when we got her, and we'd refused very generous offers for the filly before her feet even hit the ground - due to her bloodlines. Her mother was a granddaughter of Raffles, a premier horse from England who helped initiate the Arabian breed into the U.S. Her sire, Ramus, was also a prize-winner.

That little filly surpassed our every expectation, and brought our family - and friends - boundless joy. After her sire, we named her SaraFamus, but called her Sarafae.

Her half brother by the same sire, with identical markings, was in *The Return of the Black Stallion* movie as the rival who raced Black.

It seemed high time for a little 'wonder' in our lives. The rupture of family relationships with Larry's folks was painful (we never had any with mine). It was so difficult for the children too, both teenagers then. That hurt, and coupled with the loss of his brother, was terrible for Larry. We regularly talked with his parents by phone, but felt uncomfortable visiting. However, we often invited *them*.

Added to this, we hadn't really found a church home again, and missed having a church family, both for ourselves and for the children.

A big vacuum in our lives.

After Bob died, Larry told me *he wished it had been him* instead.

It would be years before I realized how circumstances (some yet to be revealed) had converged upon Larry in a brief period of time. Old problems dealt with years before, seemed to surface again.

While he remained faithful to his commitments to FGBMFI and other commitments, he now seemed to derive enjoyment only from his horses.

At home, he was just *angry*.

The veneer of our lives was beginning to crack.

I'd noticed a few blemishes in myself of late too. I found it dismaying. We'd grown accustomed to God using us in the lives of others, and were honored to do so. We were very well known in church circles. God had performed a marvelous work in both Larry and me. But unknown to me, that work had only been superficial for me.

Under the surface lay a bevy of problems. Unrecognized, and undealt with. And even though I'd picked up some social graces, the truth was:

I was still a street kid in nice clothes.

A deeper work had to be done in us. God was going *for the root.*

We'd been faithful in the measure we knew, thus God began to prune us, as John 15 says He does to 'fruitful' vines. Very much as a developer who builds, and a farmer who plants, what exists must be torn down first, and the soil beneath dug deep for a foundation *before the works begins.* See Jeremiah 1...

Much of what I write here about our life and marriage is how I perceived them then. It is what it is, and the past is the past. All is forgiven. And I have even forgiven myself!

Do remember at one point in my youth, I'd wanted someone else to hurt as much as I did.

That was a telling sign. I hadn't learned mercy. A hardness still existed inside me. And until I'd learned and received it, *God couldn't trust me with His lambs.*

This was the primary objective God sought in me, but I wouldn't know or understand that for many years!

If I'd known then what I know now, I would have done things differently, made better decisions rather than no decisions at all sometimes, and perhaps learned a few skills in conflict resolution.

Good decisions come out of good guidance and neither Larry nor I ever had that. I didn't know how to find the help we needed as a family. Oddly, this is one time I *didn't think* of the library then! I have no explanation for the following very difficult chapters other than, good came out of it, ultimately.

At first, the change in Larry was only apparent to us as a family. Our family ties began to fray under Larry's relentless anger, often aimed at one or all of us. He grew terribly negative - about life, our family, and work too. Even the neighbors.

Now I see it was depression. He digressed spiritually, no longer trusting God and said so. He became fixated on problems at work, certain that nothing was being done 'right'.

He'd literally built that business by arriving early, leaving late, paying the guys, keeping the books and even doing the janitorial work.

Yet his job status concerned me.

All of this was enough for me to begin withdrawing from my own involvements and all other public commitments. I had a foreboding of something worse coming, plus I knew leaders should have their house in order. Ours wasn't anymore. I never said anything to anyone though, as I refused to tear my husband down before others.

He kept his commitments though, much to our dismay, because now he'd become a hypocrite to us, our family! One thing in public and another in private.

End of summer came. A teenage boy who lived two doors over had a very bad habit. He would shoot a gun out his bedroom window when his parents weren't home. When we found our grey mare dead, Sarafae's mother, we were convinced he did it.

Of course, she wasn't insured.

I later found out the same boy was charged with wounding a horse a mile away in a pasture. Sarafae was only four months old and still nursing. We did nothing about it, because the father was a local builder who had four sons, and all four had been in and out of juvenile hall and jail. Plus there was a meningitis scare (stemmed from horses) in the news that Labor Day weekend. I liked the boy's mother but she seemed terribly fragile.

It was a holiday weekend, so the wait was long to get a source to recover our mare's bloated body. I took Sarafae to the other side of the house while officials hauled her mother's body onto a flatbed truck. Sarafae couldn't see anything, but she could hear noises.

She knew anyway. She winnied, jerked and cried. I cried too.

After the truck left, our stallion Buddy (the most wonderful horse ever) took that foal to his side in a heart wrenching adoptive ritual of some kind -playing and kicking as though telling her it would be okay. And he finished raising that foal (with the local feed store's help.)

I *did* see Buddy kick her once, when she tried to nurse!

Less than a week later, Larry was fired by the owner of his shop. His was one of the top shops in the region, a supplier had told them.

"*Too negative*". I'd felt it coming.

Naturally I was concerned for our family's future, and for Larry.

But I thought, maybe we could survive on his factory rep job. He could work it full time now. But, being a saleswoman myself, I knew sales was 'mental'.

When he wouldn't pursue it, I asked if he would permit me to work it. Nothing doing.

It would just be more proof of his failure. After looking for a few jobs, he learned his old boss had blackballed him through local supply men. He found nothing. Bills were piling up.

Obviously, that job loss and his prized horse being killed had pushed him *on over* after losing his brother, and then Bob too.

Hindsight is 20/20. I now realize Larry was *fragile.* He'd had an emotional breakdown. I wish I'd understood more then.

God has no problems. Only plans.
Corrie ten Boom

20

Atrophy To Ashes

- -

After losing his job, many of Larry's peers began to take notice and gently tried to intervene in our circumstances and his mental disposition. One of our friends in FGBMFI in the state was head of the psychology department at a well-known university.

Larry wouldn't speak to him. He didn't think he had a problem.

He said maybe if *we* - the family - would straighten up, things would go smoother. If I would just respect him more, and the children obey more. But we knew nothing we did pleased him! He definitely needed counseling of some kind.

I thought it was *pride* that kept him from seeing our friend.

Eventually, he became unable to function. I traveled with him upstate to speak for a FGBMFI chapter meeting. He rambled and was unfocused. It wasn't like him. I didn't know what to think. Or do. Like most wives, I just hoped he would snap out of it, or that someone else could help him see he needed outside help.

The five most deceptive words in the English language, according to Turning Point Ministries in Chattanooga are: *Maybe things will get better.*

Weeks turned into months. He still didn't want me to work. Stupid me. I was still of the mindset to 'submit' to my husband. Larry had never wanted me to work, anyway. He took an occasional job on the side.

We had no fuel for winter cold, but a huge tree fell in the side yard. A man cut it up for half the wood. The two fireplaces and that downed tree were a lifesaver, plus space heaters. (We lived there ten years and a tree never fell before or after that!)

God takes care of the fools and the stupid, according to Sally.

Somehow we always seemed to have enough. There was one time though when I went to bed wondering what I'd give the children for breakfast. I fell asleep praying. Just before dawn, we heard a car in the gravel driveway, then a tap, tap, tap at the kitchen door. Before I could get to the door from the back of the house, all I saw were taillights leaving.

I opened the door to hear a noise at my feet. A big white box slid to the side. I picked it up and saw handwriting on it. I opened the box to find three dozen donuts.

My dear friend Barbara who worked with Young Life Teen Breakfast Club on Fridays had left them. That morning, there were lots of leftover donuts. She didn't know of my prayer, but had thought of us. That also never happened before or after. *God knew* – and heard!

God knew our limitations, misguided thinking, even our ignorance, and worked inside them anyway. He does that, meeting us where we are. He loves us so.

We were no longer able to board horses or use our stallion for stud since the place we'd moved to didn't have a barn to accommodate those, or we could've been making some income from them. We were limited on every side it seemed.

Yet as I look back, those limitations were mostly mental!

One day I summoned the courage to ask Larry if we could sell one of the horses. The look on his face said it wouldn't happen. Part with <u>one of us</u>? Maybe.

The *horses?* Never! They represented a dream Larry held, and forfeiting the horses would mean forfeiting the dream. He did anyway.

I'd held it too at one time, but now I was holding onto *survival.*

(He had them until they died.)

After nine months, it became apparent we were losing our home. But money came in that allowed the children to finish the school year. I was grateful.

At that time, we put our things in storage and rented the barn of a friend and moved the horses there. In order to keep the children in their school district, we rented a furnished apartment in the area.

The apartment was small but seemed okay until something better came along. Rhonda and Craig could swim with friends across the lake at an apartment complex. Craig loved that and learned to swim like a fish. I could see them at the pool from our apartment.

Larry was working across town cutting hair again. But our apartment became one of the worst mistakes we made. Talk about atmosphere! Soldiers from nearby Fort Harrison stayed there. It was party city!

While living there, Rhonda found a morning dove with a broken wing. She brought it home to nurse it until it healed – a real feat with a housecat!

But after a few weeks we stood on our second floor balcony as she let it go.

Astonished, another dove - obviously her mate - immediately swooped down and joined her in mid air.

Sometimes it seems God's creatures have more sense than those made in His image!

He'd waited there all those weeks *and knew where she was!*

At last I found a church. I say "I" because Larry wouldn't go. It was the church of a dear friend and her husband, Ted and Elaine. He was one of the fellows who started the FGBMFI chapter with Larry, and Elaine had served on our Aglow board.

The children had friends from school who attended there too and so Rhonda and Craig heard of their great youth group. But when I showed up without Larry, people guessed rightly that something was not right on the home front.

I'd not said anything except to Elaine and Ted.

Larry's double life was now having an impact on all of us. The children now dreaded to see him come home, and believed him to be a hypocrite. They'd lost respect for him - *they didn't see him as sick!*

I could say nothing to vindicate him to them.

A black cloud of depression seemed to sweep in the front door with Larry when he arrived. I labored on what to do. Something I'd read came to me.

If we fail in the community, God will raise someone else up to replace us. But, if we fail at home, there is no one to replace us!

It was a convincing argument. Submission or not, one of us was getting off this merry-go-round!

One day, after realizing the children would begin a new school year catching the bus at a motel, I made a decision. Actually, it was two decisions. Somehow, we were *moving!*

That motel was no place for kids. Further, *I was going to work!*

The very next day, the children and I were grocery shopping and ran into a former neighbor, Mary, whose daughter used to babysit the children. She asked how we were, and I told her we were house hunting. She then said she and her husband owned a small home they were getting ready to rent. Would we be interested? I said Yes, but I had no money right then. Based on her knowledge of us in the past, she permitted me to move in with a $20 bill. Within two weeks, I somehow got the rest!

Larry was standing above me on the staircase when I told him we were moving. He was dumbfounded. He first tried to talk me out of it, pleading with me that we should just move somewhere and forget God.

I looked at him incredulously. I again told Larry I'd rented a house. I will never forget that moment. I'd had a foreboding Larry was going to die. Right then, I felt he already *had.* (In the Garden of Eden, God told Adam: "In the day you eat of it" -tree of knowledge of good and evil – "you shall surely die!" Yet his body lived on) But Larry said he wasn't leaving. I told him that was his choice, but that we were, and he was welcome to join us if he liked.

Craig and I got our things from storage while he was making up his mind. Then sourly, he decided to join us.

That too, was a terrible mistake.

Once there, Larry would go out the door and hint of suicide, by saying "Did you know that over half of all single car accidents are suicide but they just can't prove it?" Then, every siren, every ring of the phone took my breath away.

When he was around, the children and I couldn't even laugh together, because he became so paranoid, he thought our laughter was about *him!*

At one point, Craig happened to observe that the calf of his father's leg most affected by polio seemed to be atrophying (shrinking in size).

When I had the chance, I looked at it - it *did* seem so!

After this, I discovered that a new phenomena was occurring in the medical world at that time. Former polio victims of the 1950's were experiencing a recurrence of symptoms not unlike polio as they aged. Some were severe, a woman I knew of going into rehab.

I wondered out loud if this could be affecting his brain.

Craig then began to dub his condition *Atrophic Brain Syndrome, or ABS.*

If there is no laughter in a crisis, you can easily go insane.
Author

21

Tony The Twisted

I soon found a real estate firm that proved to be marvelous. I *loved* working with those people. It was an older, medium size firm, whose owner Jerry still worked the business.

Over the door of the main room where our cubicles were, was a sign that read, "The harder I work, the luckier I get." I went to work right away.

I thrived there, but I developed a pattern where I sold houses in threes every six weeks. Things got sparse at times, witherratic closings. But I managed somehow. My peers in the office always knew if I sold one house, there were two more coming in.

When Larry moved in, he immediately lost his job. He found another but it lasted only a few weeks. Another lasted less. He always knew how to run their business 'better.' This was the same man who worked 17 years, only missing one day due to the flu. Now, he'd had 15 jobs inside three years. But he still couldn't see that he had a problem.

Night and day, he sat before the TV with his hands folded on his chest. His vacant stare said he wasn't really watching. He went to care for the horses, but if he wasn't working, he went nowhere, seeing no one.

The kids were just glad he wasn't playing the hypocrite anymore.

At the new house, Craig found a great part-time job in a men's accessories section of a department store. He got big discounts on preppy clothes, so he was delighted. However, I'd grown very concerned for him - he was very affected by his Dad and was taking the decline very hard.

Larry only seemed to notice him to thump him on the head.

I wasn't overly concerned about Rhonda. *I should have been.* She began to have problems with ulcers. That should have told me something was terribly wrong. But she was always taking care of me and the family.

That was an *oldest child* symptom, and a need to cover deeper problems. Wish I'd known then what I know now - she was the sickest one of us!

Into the middle of all this came Tony Twist and crew. He was the Youth Pastor at the huge Christian (denominational) Church we now attended. Rhonda and Craig loved him and the youth group he headed. I called him "Tony the Twisted' because he would tell the group: "You know when you go to the doctor and they want one of those urine tests? Did you ever wanna do what I do? Take a little apple juice with you and when you come out of the rest room, you begin to hand it to the nurse, then take a second look at it and say 'Oh that's a little cloudy, let me run it through again.'

Then turn the cup up, drinking the apple juice!

"The look on that nurse's face is worth it" he declared.

Much of what he did with them was *amusement* just like that. And I loved him. His pure love for Rhonda and Craig during this time lifted us all!

Today, he and his wife head a missionary school in Europe.

Craig was able to go on a medical mission trip to Haiti with Tony and several doctors, dentists and nurses in the church. It was amazing to Craig that they traveled out into the bush and sat people down on a stump and pulled their teeth - with no pain killer or drugs! They got up thanking them profusely! They were the happiest people the team had ever seen.

After their ten day trip, I interviewed Tony for a local newspaper article I was writing. He shared how the Haitian children fished down the street from the hotel by the sea. On their way to sell their fish at the market, they would wash the dirt off them in the open sewage drain that exited the hotel! (This is Haiti!)

Another was the culture shock they all experienced. **Not going over to Haiti, but in arriving back in Miami**. After being in poverty stricken people for so long, they saw the lust and greed and self-absorption of our nation right outside their hotel window.

It was a Playboy Club.

I quickly became friends with one of Tony's youth leaders named Linda. She took a special interest in Rhonda – she saw the sorrow I was blind to! I was thankful for her genuine caring. The youth group went on ski trips and other fascinating places, and Linda and hubby Ron were usually along. I sensed Rhonda's commitment to church and to God fading, but Linda was the spark that kept her attending.

I knew Rhonda was bitter.

Where Rhonda was concerned though, I didn't have the right perspective. I kept thinking that she had it far better than I ever did when I was her age, that she had a family who loved her, so she was lucky **in my mind!**

But that attitude didn't address or validate *her* problems at all. Instead, it ignored them! *She needed validation of what was wrong* instead of just dismissing them .

I learned that later too.

I never wanted my children to experience the pain I did as a child. I tried so hard to be a good mother, and overall, I think I was - except in this painful season of our lives when I suffered *paralysis of analysis* in life.

I was wholly focused on whatever it took to save our failing marriage. I knew we needed serious change. I said to God, then *let it begin with me.*

It began with me. It ended there too. It requires two people actively working to salvage a failing marriage. Without that, the marriage disintegrates.

Hindsight has shown me I lacked the coping skills I needed for the magnitude of our family's problems. Larry did too. I didn't have the parental guidance that could have helped me. Some will no doubt ask, Didn't you *pray?* Yes, incessantly.

Ignorance itself did me in!

What you don't know can and does hurt you - *and I didn't know it!*

I didn't know that conflict is normal in relationships. I thought conflict signified problems too profound to fix. That failure was then eminent for the marriage, or any other relationship that encountered conflict.

I hadn't known mere conflict. Only 'war'.

I didn't know how to resolve conflict, or that such a thing as 'conflict resolution' existed. Or how to work through situations. These are acquired skills. They don't necessarily require a four year degree or expensive counsel.

The local library is a good place to start, free.

No one knew that more than me, yet I was so weighed down in the mire, I never even considered it.

More importantly, I didn't know that there are good fights and bad fights. I only knew street fighting, or fighting to win not to resolve differences.

I went for the jugular first. Those fights added further harm to an already fragile situation, like pouring salt into the wound.

Finally, pride compounds ignorance because it will not say "I was wrong" and I had it.

Street fighting uses generalities that are mostly untrue, such as "You always" and "You never." It assigns blame instead of trying to communicate effectively by sending, "I feel" messages conveying the loneliness or hurt at another's actions, not *their failure.*

Blame causes the other person to be defensive, and to withdraw. The pronoun "You" should never be used in a disagreement!

I didn't know how to set boundaries, nor did Larry. Nor that they are needed in any healthy relationship (of any kind). They are like a contract that creates mutual respect, and better, they prevent future misunderstandings. But you cannot create new, or change boundaries with a person without sitting down and discussing the reasons for it.

Finally, neither one of us knew how to explore options together. Or even that they existed. (*There's always options*)! Like so many, we felt boxed in by life and circumstances, blaming each other.

We hadn't developed enough emotional maturity to *roll with the punches that life threw our way!* We felt defeated at every turn and couldn't stop the downward spiral.

Far worse than these, we didn't realize the power of *cause and effect* - that you get back what you put into marriage just like a business. Go travel or abandon a business and when you get back, you'll have one that is defunct. It's the same with marriage. Sow love, and you'll get love.

Sow warmth; you'll get affection. Sow carelessness; and just know your mate could *care less.*

The truth is, if left to itself, hearts harden in a marriage. The relationship is a wholly 'hands on' matter! Just like a business.

What's more, in my life as a believer I'd never felt my prayers went so unanswered.

The heavens truly were brass.

At this time, I can't say that I felt Larry and I were meant to stay together. I'd changed so much, I doubt many men would have tolerated that change. And I felt Larry hadn't changed enough - .unless it's 'for the worse'.

Our family's problems were apparent to all now. Rhonda and I felt we had to sneak out just to shop for groceries, because we would see people who knew us and who asked questions we weren't prepared to answer. So I isolated. I got an unlisted number, and purposely lost contact with friends, except for Linda and Elaine.

It happened that our Congressman attended our huge church, and both the children had served as Pages for him in the House in their early teens, when he was in the State Legislature. Rhonda and his daughter became friends and each loved horses. She asked her dad if we could move our horses to their barn, so she and Rhonda could ride together. That began a lifelong friendship between the two of them.

I liked both Dan and Barbara, who was from a town near where I grew up in Kentucky.

Soon, Larry began sleeping only two or three hours a night- not with me. Our house was a two bedroom, so I shared a bedroom with Rhonda, and Craig had the other. There was a daybed in the family room he slept on. He just crept around the house all night long.

Something about this was reminiscent to me of living with Charles...

Meantime, Rhonda became alarmed, afraid he might kill me some night. His vitriole towards me made it a possibility, even in my mind.

But my concern was for Craig, who stayed up nights also, pacing the floor. I watched the light beneath his door as I watched him pace. His Dad was suicidal, so I battled with that possibility in my mind. He was profoundly affected by it all. How could I pray against it, when his own Dad invited it into our house?

Rhonda was on medication for ulcers now. Craig continued to battle depression. He says he wasn't suicidal as I thought-perhaps I just embraced a worst case scenario. Both were smoking. Rhonda at least enjoyed the horses with her Dad. As for Craig, Larry hardly seemed to notice him. A deep and personal fog surrounded my life too.

I was disillusioned that my prayers for others seemed answered instantly, but prayers for ourselves went unanswered.

Where *was God?* It all made me more bitter than ever... and disillusioned.

One day I saw it. *Larry was holding us in emotional blackmail.* Craig was convinced that if I ever made his Dad leave, he would kill himself in 24 hours. Larry's illness in my mind, was killing us *all.*

Larry got a call for a new job offer, which was again, sales. I knew he wasn't up to it, because sales is mental, and you have to be 'up' to perform. But he elected to take it anyway. It required two week's training in Kansas City. He packed to go. I drove him to the airport.

The following weeks, we couldn't believe our little home. *There was peace.* I studied I Corinthians 7 about the 'Pauline Privilege' in marriage and found that a home is supposed to be one of 'peace', a sanctuary from the world, not a war field.

Peace is God's objective for us!

One night near the end of his training, Craig came to me while I was sitting in the living room. He sat down next to me on the couch, then Rhonda joined us. He said, "Mom, I've been thinking. We just can't keep on living the way we have." He'd sensed that peace as well!

The power of *that emotional blackmail was broken* at last over us all.

Larry was a big boy, and we couldn't be held accountable for his actions, *whatever* he did.

We'd made the decision to survive - even if he didn't.

I knew what I had to do.

Divorce was not on my mind. Or in my plans. Just *peace.* I was working steadily and paying the bills and I wasn't going to move the children from their schools.

I met Larry at the airport, as expected. I knew he would be 'up' and enthusiastic about the future and the job. It killed me to do so, but I knew I had to do it now.

My own mental stability hung in the balance. On the way home, I told him we had to separate.

I didn't mention *divorce.* I didn't want one and I wasn't even thinking of it.

Yet because Larry and I had never played head games or split even a single night in 22 years in anger, he took it as a final decision.

That was the most difficult day of my entire life. Perhaps I'd never loved Larry in a romantic way, yet I *loved him more than life itself at that moment.* Every bit my husband, he was father of my children and I'm still glad I married him.

Together we had dreamed dreams. Dreams die when marriages do.

That night, I sat in the ashes of those dreams. I mourned for all those whom we'd helped sort through *their* marriage problems through the years.

If Larry and I couldn't make it, how could **they** have hope?

I despaired, for the dishonor we would now bring on the cause of Christ, especially if it came to divorce. I could do nothing but trust those wonderful people to the care of God. But I couldn't see how God could ever be glorified in my life again.

And I ached for Larry. I didn't want him to be alone.

Ironically, God's presence seemed especially real and soothing that night for the first time in a long time. The dense fog I'd walked in for months, even years, was now gone.

No more confusion.

Guidance came when I read Proverbs, which said I should 'look straight ahead, not looking to the right or to the left, and walk on.'

That's what I did.

Larry and I were *captives* to ignorance. It destroys.

Because of something we *didn't know...*

"My people are destroyed for lack of knowledge." God
"My people are taken into captivity
for lack of knowledge." God
Hosea 6:4 and Is. 5:13

"You do err, not knowing *the scriptures,*
nor the power of God.
Jesus in Matthew 22:29

Faith is like radar that sees through the fog -
the reality of things at a distance that
the human eye cannot see.
Corrie ten Boom

22

Hello.........ISLAM? (Sandy Beaches, Stony Heart)

Craig and I threw Rhonda a surprise 18TH birthday party in May. I'd never seen a more unhappy kid. She graduated with her class, but looked like the unhappiest student in the whole assembly.

I felt like a total failure. There was a reason for that. **I was**. Just the facts here. About Larry. About me too.

There's no doubt I failed at this juncture. But God wasn' t surprised when I did! And the Father heart of God was there to comfort me in the midst of that failure.

Of course, I could beat myself to death on this, but I choose not to do that. When we pitch a tent and camp at failure, *only the devil wins*.

I didn't see Larry for four or five months. When the sales job hadn't worked, he'd taken a job on a recreational farm facility of a friend of ours, Barbara and husband Loren. He was able to keep his horses there as part of his salary. His job entailed caring for their many horses and the farm. He could handle that job it seemed, due to love of horses.

One summer day, I drove Rhonda out to see him. I was totally blown away! Larry was suntanned from working outdoors, his hair was sunburnt, and honestly, **he looked like a Greek god!** He was in better shape that I'd ever seen him before.

This was a far cry from *suicide!*

Though tan and bronzed on the outside, the inside was still a mess. Truth was, Larry had reached his apex some years before, and *that* man has never returned.

It was an eventful day for us all. While there, I met his girlfriend. *I was happy for him.*

She meant he wasn't alone. I still loved him that much!

Rhonda had borne news to him too, only after she'd told me. She'd graduated high school, then found she was pregnant! I don't think any mother has ever been more caught off guard than I was on that matter!

I couldn't believe it. I planned for her to go to college in the fall. Again, my perception was misdirected. I thought only of her, and *not a little one* inside.

Misguided people are not God's fault. DO remember that.

After she shared with him her news, he told her that Sarafae had given birth to a stillborn foal. It was supposed to be Rhonda's as he'd promised. She never did get anything out of that horse or relationship, except a saddle she'd used to ride Buddy with all her youth 20 years later. He charged her $250 for it. She paid it. Truth *hurts.*

I buried myself in how to handle the dilemma with Rhonda.

Compounding one sin by a worse one of abortion was not an option to her. Abortion was out of the question. I was grateful. And it never entered my mind either. I just didn't know what the next step was.

It soon became apparent to us that we needed a fresh start, a new beginning. And it would have to be somewhere *else.* We couldn't escape the labels in Indy. It wasn't people's fault so much as it was *just life.*

And now they would look for new labels given the coming baby.

In August, Rhonda's best friends all left for college, one to become an engineer; another to become a psychologist; another a lawyer. Rhonda headed to the Carolinas to a new home for unwed mothers that God had led me to, I felt. She became one of the first thirteen girls there... and one of the girls was thirteen herself! Others were sent there by Christian parents, some pastors, against their will. And some of those pastor parents had pushed for abortion, and settled for coming there instead.

Rhonda planned to place the baby for adoption until we both saw her!

Something happened to the adoptive couple at the last moment that they could not take the baby. When I saw her, she was lying in the bassinet with both hands over her tiny head just like I do. I knew then it was God's plan for us to take Krista home. Rhonda too. There's never been a single regret there, because she's always been a wonder and a thrill to us all!

Linda had begun her third battle with cancer in five years. She'd defeated the others so we remained optimistic. She'd lost all her hair the first two times and it came back curly and black. The chemo-therapy now made Linda violently ill.(Better treatments exist now).

Linda's resilience seemed worn down. Slowly we began to wonder if she would recover this time. I secretly (without telling Rhonda) felt she'd resigned herself to dying just to have the battle end! Resignation is a power of its own in cancer. It's the hardest thing to gain victory over or to pray against! I couldn't bear the thought of her ten year old son losing her.

In my isolation, when I wasn't working, I began to spend long hours on the telephone with Linda. She too didn't have people she could confide in.

Then my friend - and Rhonda's too - Linda lost her battle with cancer while Rhonda was away. I grieved for both... and how to tell Rhonda.

Craig had not been able to come for the birth of the baby due to his job in retail. Larry said he'd come stay with him. Later, I learned his girlfriend came too! More *heart wrenching disappointment for Craig* he only told me of it months later. After I learned of this misadventure in my own bedroom, I filed for divorce. I now had Biblical grounds.

Divorce is permissible, Jesus said, for fornication. Justifies a lot of them, huh?

Craig was due to graduate high school, so we planned where we would move to. We considered Phoenix. We liked it there but no water! Then we considered Houston but, the job market didn't look good there. Finally, we settled on Florida. Rhonda and I both liked the idea, and Craig didn't care for he was going off to college in the fall.

We staged a huge garage sale, aiding us in raising money since we could take no furniture.

We left the day following Craig's graduation.

We must have looked like the Beverly Hillbillies in that old Buick!

When Rhonda told her Dad of our plans, his comment was "She'll be back in six months." Many decades have past.

We landed in Treasure Island, Florida where I'd once visited. It reminded me of Long Beach Island, New Jersey where we'd spent summer vacations. Small and narrow with a bay, it was tourist oriented, only better. *It had palm trees!*

Now I was here ...it was a dream.

But the way I felt about God and the future then, this island paradise might be as close as I get to paradise! I felt ***bitter***.

Everybody else had abandoned me in life...now I felt God had as well.

I was to realize later that the little family I'd always wanted and now had for two decades, had been on a slippery slope for months now. I had no idea to what degree. Nor did I foresee the wild twists and turns that family would still make.

I immediately decided to look up the only person I knew in Florida. I remembered my first encounter with her back in Indy. A few months back, I'd stood at the ironing board in my family room. The 700 Club was on TV. I remembered despairing, so terribly alone in my crisis and that *no one* could possibly understand how I felt. To be so well known and fall so hard and so far totally isolated and with zero chances of a future, I felt that I'd somehow been out-maneuvered in life.

The show host introduced a new guest by the name of Arthelene Rippy. I'd never heard of her, but listened as I ironed. Arthelene was a widow from St. Petersburg, Florida. She explained how she'd married a man with the call of God on his life, named Don. She'd aided him in building a big church there. The church grew and they even started a successful school. Then, it was discovered that Don was having an affair. Naturally he was terminated.

*Un*naturally, Arthelene's children were asked to leave the school she and Don had *built!*

Worse, Don ended up killing himself.

Yet, Arthelene was a committed believer speaking at conferences everywhere. She is host of her own television show as well now.

I liked her immediately because she seemed to have grit, in spite of what life had thrown at her. Tribulation does that to you. Most encouraging was that she not only had been where I was in life, but *she'd come out on the other side!* That interview was light to my tunnel.

I decided to look her phone number up and called to explain why I was contacting her.

She invited me to lunch. As a result of that lunch, Craig immediately got a job installing satellite dishes, which were a big thing then.

Since Craig needed the car for his job, that meant Rhonda and I both had to find a job on the island. That wasn't too hard with the abundant hotels and restaurants.

Rhonda had never waitressed before but got a job at an upscale place on the island that might tip well, she thought. I also had never worked in a service industry (I was too snobby then) but I got a job right on the beach in a nice motel.

That job turned out to be therapeutic, working with a view of the beach from every room, not having someone looking over my shoulder. It was just what I needed. It was hard work though. Great tips too.

Right away, Rhonda had a friend who dropped her off from work. Soon he came in and introduced himself. His name was Aziz, a Muslim from Kuwait going to school in Oklahoma, working in Florida summers.

I asked why. He said Florida's weather was most like his Mideast home.

At that time, 1985, few in America had ever heard of Kuwait, including us. Desert Storm occurred in 1991-92 after Iraq invaded Kuwait.

Aziz seemed nice enough, but I wondered if he had romantic ideas about Rhonda. I dismissed that. He was very handsome. I just had nooo idea...

Every lunch and contact with Arthelene after the first became predictable. She wanted me to press Larry for child support. I wouldn't. He couldn't take care of himself! I was just happy to be rid of the albatross from around my neck - his negative views were a drain on all our dreams and goals! Besides, the divorce wasn't final then.

Of course, she was right. Larry didn't pay the first penny for Craig during college, and *didn't even attend his college graduation*, hurting Craig deeply!

I was a total wimp about that support, and I don't even understand *why*. I was DONE.

We found if we committed to a year-round lease on the island, rents were slashed from the tourists' rates. So we were able to rent a nice duplex. That meant I could walk to work and to the beach every evening to view the sunset. I didn't yet have friends, so I went every day.

Craig went off to school in mid-August. Reflecting back to May, two weeks before we left for Florida, and also two weeks before graduation, he'd made a very serious error in judgment. One that could have had him - *not in college the next four years*! I was astounded when I got the call at work to come get him. Rhonda and I drove over together.

It was only the grace of God on all of us that day, and His favor, that spared him. But he learned! He thrived in the wonderful southern college he attended.

Aziz dropped by all summer. I feebly tried to discourage any kind of relationship, both to Rhonda and to him. At one point, he asked me if he could have permission to date Rhonda.

I responded vehemently, "I don't see why! There's no future there, Aziz! Rhonda set the pace with her friends in high school, and she is not - I repeat -not ever going to conform to any of your dietary or customs of attire! Never mind your religion! (I'd studied world religions and having Arabian horses, I'd learned about Islam). There is just no way the two of you are ever going to agree on anything, culturally or spiritually - even in dating. Ever."

They eloped one weekend following that conversation.

I was so upset, I made Rhonda agree to counseling at the church we'd attended. The young associate pastor said everything he should to dissuade her, and convince her to get it annulled. She wouldn't.

She later told me that she might never find a husband who would love her and Krista, given her circumstances!

Nineteen years old, and defeated. The devil's lies.

That's how I woke up one morning the **mother-in-law to a Muslim!**

He left for school, so they didn't get an apartment, meaning Rhonda and Krista would be alone when he was in school. So she stayed with me on the island. He was gone a lot, at that those mysterious 'training camps' he attended in Texas after each school session.

....they'd get an apt in the summer, they thought.

I didn't feel right about doing that *but I didn't want to be alone either!* Three out of four of us had made terrible decisions. That left me.

Rhonda and I both had cars now. Not an easy feat with impact fees near $500 per car then, plus other fees. She earned her paralegal status right after we first came to Florida, and had a good job.

I'd taken up where Craig left off at the satellite company, in the sales department.

As soon as I made a brochure for my own use, owners saw it and wanted me to head the commercial end of the business that developed and sold cable systems to condos in the area. This is the same woman who'd summoned Craig just to set my digital clock for years! (I'm technologically challenged but I do reasonably well on computers!)

It all worked out though.

Meantime, I learned much about satellites and distribution, and the terminology such as 'footprints' and 'geosyncrynal order', Kansas City's significance, etc. that pertain to today, and *the soon coming of the Lord!*

Two weeks before Christmas, just when the commercial end was taking off, Congress shut down satellite sales due to hotels' theft of cable signals in Orlando.

We were all let go. At Christmas.

Aziz drove home for Christmas and since they didn't yet have an apartment, they stayed with me. I learned he attended Oklahoma University, where their Muslim community was so large, they never had to speak English *except in class.*

No wonder he struggled with English!

They had their own banks, grocery, barbers, and every other retail outlet fitted to their needs and eating halal, which I'd learned while shopping with Rhonda. When he cooked, which he liked to, it was always some hamburger medley (casserole type). It all tasted the same to me. They often eat with their hands, using pita bread. Sigh.

But Aziz was very Americanized, *their* word. That wasn't popular among the strictest ones.

And he dressed well, very conventionally.

I saw that this was very effective to other Americans though.

I learned he loved to talk. Every time he came home, we talked into the night - others were in bed.

Understand that as a maternal figure, Aziz deferred to me with respect - it's a cultural thing. And culture was what I was learning most *about* Muslims. The first and primary one is that, unlike Americans, *there is no separation between their culture and their religion.*

None.

I liked that until I learned how that religion was such a despicable bondage, holding them hostage to fear and worse. Their god is *frightening*. Mention the Love of God and you can see their minds go on "tilt." They also lie a lot.

The Quran actually teaches it is okay to lie... I've read it with my own eyes.

Did I mention they *lie*?

He told me at one point, that I was the only American he'd ever met who knew what I believed! *I wasn't so sure myself those days*, and having him in my immediate life was muddying the waters a lot more!

I didn't know a lot about Islam then, but I did know the bumper sticker on his dashboard, *supporting the PLO*, was a radical group. (Muslim nations 'tithe' to that group because the Palestinians have no imports, no exports - just terrorism.)

It was amazing to me - and a real eye opener how naive our nation was -when Aziz explained to me the things they were taught before coming to America. One was to get two driver's licenses. That was easy due to their complicated names Aziz had five. Since his last name was common like *Smith* is here, immigration added MOHD to his name, short for Mohammad. That way he used his passport to get one license and another ID to get an Oklahoma license.

If he was stopped as he sped back to school, he just used the license his car insurance *wasn't* on, so his rates didn't skyrocket!

I learned there were certain college majors his country sought. He started out in civil engineering, but later switched to computer engineering and design. He loved computers anyway, but he was in school a couple of years longer when he did that.

He always talked a lot about 'peace'.

I learned to love Aziz during this time. Yet neither of us were swayed by the other's views. I, and Rhonda too, found some of their customs revolting about 'cleanliness', such as eating with only one hand, and their views toward sex make it seem filthy, not a gift.

But he was very good with Krista and would get onto the floor and play with her.

But, *they will do anything necessary for a green card.* Easier then, but laws were toughened shortly after that time.

Admittedly, I lost it when I saw a photo where he'd wrapped Krista in a hajib. He never got Rhonda in one. Anything for a tradeoff - a green card.

Somewhere around this time, I heard a Muslim who said, 'If we can't defeat America, we will marry them.' Until laws changed, this worked many years to get into the country and remain here after educational visas ran out.

Eventually Rhonda and Aziz did get an apartment. I moved off the beach and took a place near their house, in order to help Rhonda some with Krista.

Since the guys, Craig and Aziz, were both in college and only came home on breaks, Rhonda and I soon decided to pool our resources to rent a house on Clearwater Beach. It had a fireplace, and a screened in porch. We went out the back door to the beach.

That way, when the guys came home on break, they could enjoy the beach as well.

(They were married three years before the honeymoon wore off, Rhonda discovering he was deceiving her about money. *Lying.* He left his checkbook at home, called to see if he did. We found it buried in the couch.

Yes, we looked at it! Thousands of dollars there! His family were wealthy Kuwaitis. I do think he had genuine feelings for Rhonda, *but* Islam permits Muslims to have four wives. Marriage was over for Rhonda when she discovered he had another wife in Kuwait!)

My divorce from Larry was final end of September the first year we came to Florida. However, it was completely botched by my attorney who didn't even show up.

I didn't go back because *I thought she would handle it.* Right.

I'd spent seven months nightly on the sandy beaches of Treasure Island before moving. I'd looked for friends, but hadn't really found any, except Arthelene. I enjoyed my job on the beach, and the nice tips - I hadn't expected that part - but I was lonely.

The sunset drew me every evening.

Once there, I mourned.

I had loved and enjoyed my role as a wife, as a mother, and in the community. I hadn't wanted it to end. I'd never sought divorce, yet divorce had somehow found *me*. Memories filled my mind on that sandy shore.

One memory loomed large regarding the children. At one of the many conventions we'd attended each year, a leader had commended Rhonda and Craig, having them stand up for recognition as outstanding young people whose example to other young people merited praise. Only the children and I knew the real situation with their Dad. Craig and Rhonda *were* wonderful children, but I would replay that scene in my mind many times in the years ahead wondering whatever happened to my precious little family.

What good was there in being a believer in God ?

The next memory was similar. A few weeks before we left for Florida, (Larry and I separated by then) the children and I attended our annual spring convention downtown, seated in the middle section. At one point, I was aware every eye at the speakers' table was upon me. Then they looked to the rear of the room.

I turned to see Larry standing there holding his newborn. His girlfriend stood behind him against the wall. One of Larry's best friends, a huge hulk of a man, hugged me with tears in his eyes when we exited the room, he felt so sorry for me and that display.

We weren't even divorced then.

This life I'd led 22 years was my entire identity and I mourned the loss of it as though that woman had died. She **did**.

So I wondered, *who was I now?* Nothing. No one, and seemingly going *nowhere*. I felt I had no future. Churches treated me as a pariah, as someone who knew the Bible well - but was now *.divorced?* How could that be? *There had to be something wrong with me!*

Well there was. Yet I never wanted divorce.

(However, this was an era when churches began creating singles groups, and eventually I began to attend a few of those. Arthlene herself became primary in leading them, speaking nationally.)

Nonetheless, I felt it was God with whom my argument laid. *Where was He* when I'd prayed for my marriage to be healed? Never having a father in my life, He now seemed like the rest of the men I'd known, a Flake.

I didn't trust Him. At all.

"Seated next to my father on the train, I suddenly asked, "Father, what is sex?" He turned to look at me, as he always did when answering a question, but to my surprise he said nothing. At last he stood up, lifted his traveling case and set it on the floor. Will you carry it off the train, Corrie?" he said. I stood up and tugged at it. It was crammed with the watches and spare parts he had purchased that morning. It's too heavy," I said. Yes," he said, "and it would be a pretty poor father who would ask his little girl to carry such a load. It's the same way, Corrie, with knowledge. Some knowledge is too heavy for children. When you are older and stronger, you can bear it. For now, you must trust me to carry it for you." Corrie ten Boom

23

Charlie's Fandango

Upon Rhonda's divorce, we decided to move from the beach house to cut spending. And she didn't want to be so easily found by Aziz when he came home from school on break.

Divorced now, *she was afraid of him.* Women don't divorce Muslim men. We took a duplex across town, near where I worked then and got a P.O. Box, leaving no forwarding address. We also got a non-published phone. (The advent of cell phones hadn't occurred). I worked nights in a television studio then in order to have days free while I looked for a real job.

I'd attended real estate school in Florida, in order to get my license there, but found the profession to be a complete joke. It was wholly unprofessional, unlike in the north. Every retiree came here and got licensed, but only one out of nineteen ever made any money.

The money was okay on the night job due to lots of overtime. Rhonda worked as a paralegal.

Craig was in college, Rhonda wouldn't attend church, and so before too long, I too lost my interest in church too. Christians just seemed too predictable to me at that time; their services too. We enjoyed taking Krista to the beach and other activities on Sundays. Fresh from divorce herself, Rhonda found an attentive man across the street from where we now lived.

I was appalled, because he had the whiff of loser on him. He lived with his mommy and wouldn't pay child support! So as that relationship progressed, I grew more and more disillusioned with her choices. When I could bear them no longer, I moved out.

Here I want to say, **this is *my* story**. While I do not wish to tell Rhonda's story, I must tell a portion, to the degree her life impacted mine. She will tell her own odyssey one day. In addition, there will be criticism of me because I write this truth so transparently - in order to help other broken people find the wholeness I did - from the perspective of having been a broken person myself.

The important thing is to see beyond this chapter to what comes out of the pall of failure and the mass confusion we all experienced. I certainly understand why it is God hates divorce - repercussions! However, a miraculous dream would be given me that would change the direction of my entire life!

And remember, it is *my* story!

My critics will just have to write their own!

Rhonda immediately took another apartment near the old one, and advertised for a roommate. She found one. His name was Charlie. He was my age, but had a daughter the same age as Krista. Rhonda thought that was a good thing. Not. I was to learn Charlie was a godless and amoral man. He also suffered from severe panic attacks but initially worked driving a truck.

Charlie immediately ordered cable, making both girls watch violence, terror and filth, such as *Rosemary's Baby*. He thought it was funny when they cried, and called them wussies when they had nightmares. He seemed to value little except he loved his daughter In his warped way.

Everything about Rhonda seemed to change. She clung to every word Charlie said as though there might be some fresh revelation she might miss. It sickened me.

A dagger in the chest would've hurt less!

This man was a godless stranger. Now suddenly, flesh and blood *meant nothing* to her, breaking my heart.

For months on end, I'd grown exceedingly bitter towards the Lord. I then decided I didn't want to ever talk about Him again, and I didn't want to be around anyone who did!

(The mind is an amazing enigma to me, because here I rejected all prior knowledge of scripture I'd ever had. If a verse ever surfaced in my mind, I would immediately reject it, saying "I don't believe that!" Eventually, *they no longer did*)

I refused to believe in a God that had so rejected me, my prayers or any aspirations I'd had for our family.

I felt I'd make it on my own without Him. And I did.

A five year odyssey began here. **I'd somehow survived divorce**, but now I found *I couldn't survive what was happening to my daughter.*

Because of Krista's bond to me, Rhonda tried to make up for it by inviting me over for dinner one night. I was sitting at the table with Krista and her, when Charlie, who was standing behind Rhonda, said to me "When I get through with her (Rhonda), I'll wash her mind completely of all that religious propaganda you filled her with."

That was when I *knew* he was **evil**.

I looked up at him and couldn't resist this response, *"Charlie, you are just one more in a string of many, and there'll be another after you."*

Streetfighter, going for the jugular! *Still.*

Soon I realized that the same child who had **drawn me to God** in the first place, **had now driven me completely away from Him**.

I eventually became introduced to a new word called, *codependency*. A plethora of new books about the topic became available about then. I started attending a weekly Alanon group. I went for Rhonda, but soon found *I needed it more than her!*

And I soon learned what had made Effie reach into that glove box to hand Max a flask..

Over three years, I attended over 200 meetings. Oddly, I considered that those groups (good ones; some are *not*) taught me more practical *life skills* than I'd ever learned inside church! I wondered, *what good was spiritual truth to a person, when there was no training in how to apply it in life?* I benefited from other peoples' experiences - their losses and triumphs.

Eventually, Charlie convinced Rhonda that he knew how she could make a lot of money. After all, his first wife did! It was exotic dancing.

That was when the bottom fell out of my world completely.

If I was bitter before, I now became *bitter because I was bitter!*

I don't know how to tell this story to make it okay. I can only say, we all have our own particular 'brand' of sin, and we all tend to feel ours is somehow superior to other people's.

We justify our own 'brand' that way.

Sanctus Real, a contemporary singing group, says it like this, posting this on Facebook: *"We are all messed up. It might be in different ways and some ways of being 'messed up' are more socially acceptable than others in man's eyes, but the fact is, messed up is messed up. We all need Jesus the same amount as one another. No one needs His mercy and grace a little more or less than someone else. We all need Jesus the same."*

I was alone. I no longer even had Rhonda, for Charley kept her from me. I was allowed to pick Krista up for a night or so, but I didn't want to be there at all.

I'd left behind every friend in the north, to start a new life. Jo was in England then; we wrote. (And it was hers and a few others' persistent prayers and undying love that saved me in the end, I believe.) Linda had died and Mamie too. I didn't want to hear the preaching of any others who might have been available. I hid my life from all the rest too.

On those sandy beaches, since I no longer knew who I was, my mind turned to the only thing familiar to me. As a youth, I also had only friends, no family to turn to. At the darkest times of abuse and neglect from Mom, and from Charles and others, I'd turned to Connie on an emotional level. *Theirs was the only warmth I knew then.*

(This is how the devil works: He takes a *good thing* and ***twists it*** into something perverse, thus robbing people of the best gift - explained later!)

Connie and I had shared a two year gay relationship. After that, I turned away - heeding the call to be decent, not 'deviant', Grandma Sally's word.

(She never knew about me though, that I know of). *This was different era.*

Like Rhonda, I ran an ad. And I found a friend. I still marvel though it was one who 'happened' to be a Christian! I wondered why she'd answered such an ad? But it is what it is, I thought. Only, I wouldn't ever permit her to talk to me about God. At all. **Ever**.

In a few months, two other friends and me began working and traveling for a publishing firm, based in New Jersey. He published directories for nice hotels. I learned the ropes, and soon realized I could do that business myself! Graphic arts was a skill I had, using many years for myself and my interest groups, and occasionally for businesses I got paid for. His non-compete clause in my contract didn't include the South, so I managed to get my first hotel while working one for him.

Somehow, this former street urchin started her own business doing hotels in Atlanta! I still marvel at that! I thrived in it, because I had a knack to do what others couldn't - *get contracts with the hotels!* Not *high end* hotels; but more median types that kept me in business because directories are a required amenity on which hotels are graded.

I did end up doing the Biltmore in Atlanta! I thought I'd arrived when that happened! And I operated as a home-based business

I could do that because I knew that image is *everything* in business and people didn't realize it was operated as a home based business. I rented a business address; made glitzy letterheads, logos, business forms and cards. (I used Kinko's, where offices were available in most every city then; perfect for a business like mine. Lots of others did so too.).

However, my cell phone bills were sometimes sky high - $1200 one month because you paid by the minute back then. I tried having salespeople to do hotels, even my son. But I ended up having to do *my* hotels, and then clean up their messes when they left early, or messed up.

So, I decided to keep my business small, a one woman endeavor. That worked for me for eighteen years. Others I knew in the business made big money, but *money didn't motivate me!* If I wanted to do something or travel, I went out and made the money. The problem that hung me up was making the directory- it took precious time.

Yet I know I could've done better!

I enjoyed the perks of being in control of my life, not bound to an alarm clock, or having to drive in daily rush-hour traffic. I also could travel or take time off if I wanted to.

I reveled in that freedom.

Most of my contracts were in Atlanta. I enjoyed working there and came to love the city itself. I still do.

Working a hotel there one time, I noted across the street was a popular place where people streamed in and out, especially weekends. I usually made ads in the hotel room and worked on gathering regional information during weekends. Or sat by the pool. So I paid little attention. At first.

Upon closer observation, I realized these partiers were all women and the sports bar they were entering was no doubt gay. I didn't know what to make of it. Initially, I was both repulsed and drawn. Working hotels for 3 weeks at a time, I thought about it for a week, until the next weekend.

Then I decided to go over and see what made these women tick perhaps I'd understand myself in doing so. I decided I'd subtly conduct interviews without revealing it. I went over on Friday night, but discovered the real crowd didn't even show up until midnight. That's true at most dance bars.

It was about 9:30pm, so I took a table in the corner and observed. I had taken up casual smoking then, (never could get the habit) so I ordered ginger ale (not much of a drinker either). I sat and smoked, feeling I would blend in more if I did so. I chatted with the waitresses. Soon the music started and people danced. By midnight, the place was thronged. I found I enjoyed the energy and the beat.

I talked to the waitress about the bar. She was easy to talk to. I didn't really try to interview right away. I waited. But this opened the door for me to visit dance bars in Florida where I lived. I went alone and never dated.

Over time, I began to see familiar faces at home, people who attended regularly. On the road, I would visit wherever I was in whatever city I was in, and over time felt freer to talk (interview) to people. I made notes.

Funny thing though. At the dance bar at home where I went, I always sat in the same section and had the same friendly waitress who talked a lot. I was naïve. *Oh, Yes.*

Once when I saw my waitress come out of the men's rest room, I gawked. Then I looked more closely at this waitress her hands had veins across the top. She had an adam's apple! Whoa!... That was strangely masculine.

Yep. A man. What a bizarre world I 'd entered, I mused.

Identity crises now seemed all over the place, in my mind! Even my own.

My interviews began to be revealing. Gay women are often educated and bright, and some earn big money, especially in the medical industry. I learned that while many women in society have been molested by adulthood, the numbers for gay women were even higher. Many had come out of abusive marriages, and said they were looking for tenderness and understanding.

They'd found it most in other women, they said. I thought I understood that part!

Since I went back to the same areas due to annual renewal of my contracts and working in Atlanta a lot, I often saw the same women.

None of them will ever agree with me, but here's what I observed. I would see an attractive, often college age woman, very feminine.

Months later, when I'd see the same woman again, I'd sometimes do a double-take, hardly recognizing that same person because *she had taken on a whole new persona.* Sometimes it was extremely masculine, which I interpreted then as gender confusion, with short butch hair. Sometimes a hardness had come over her face, and harshness in actions. I wondered then and still do, if a lot of the gay lifestyle is not *learned behavior.*

I mean they call **Behavioral Psychology a science, for a reason!**

And too. Certain behaviors are learned! Such as anger, for instance. The Bible says, 'Make no friends with an angry man, lest you learn his evil ways.'

Of course, 'behavioral psychology' focuses on *behavior!*

I loved visiting those dance bars in every city. It was there I learned to dance. I danced alone - and I never went home with anybody! I remained friendly to people, but distant. It is rare that you see men in a women's bar, but the young ones who like to dance, come there. They always seemed to like to dance with me.

I'd never felt free enough to dance, nor could I even catch a beat but I learned. I loved that freedom... and that beat.

Someone has said, *dancing is the soul in motion.*

Some bars stayed open until 5am and I stayed until the end, captured by the beat of the music, especially at one bar in Cleveland. I never went out except weekends. I was a workaholic during weekdays. But that music was all I needed to get drunk on.

Meantime, Rhonda and Charlie bought a house - though she was smart enough to put it into her name. I didn't know she'd done that for several years, when the relationship finally ended. I rarely ever saw the house.

Also, my business took a downturn after five years since a dozen of my hotel contracts were in Atlanta, and the city overbuilt hotel rooms in anticipation of the 1996 Olympics. It made my business lose money, since advertisers would no longer spend money for just one hotel, no matter which one it was. I looked around at what I might do for a living then.

It was then I learned Charlie had a fetish or two.

One time I returned Krista on a Sunday afternoon where we'd been to the beach. Rhonda wasn't there. Krista had dropped ice cream down the front of her new dress. I had her take it off and began to wash the ice cream out of the dress at the kitchen sink. Charlie ran into the kitchen screaming at me at the top of his lungs about dirtying up his sink!

I wondered what in the world he meant?

Then he took me by the shoulders and threw me out the front door, before I even knew what was happening, throwing my purse after me.

Rhonda didn't seem to care, and made it sound like
I should have known about Charlie's peculiar fetish.
Unfortunately, I didn't read minds then, or now.

It was clear it was all my fault, though.

I could no longer bear what this evil man was doing to both Rhonda and to Krista.

Or that *she was letting him!* It was an *Ovie repeat* in my mind, ruining her life on a man who didn't even deserve her!

I moved to the East Coast of Florida and worked at the front desk for a hotel until I decided what else I could do.

However, in the weeks prior to moving, I lay in my bed in an upstairs bedroom with the window open. I'd been doing 'my own thing' for several years now. And don't let stuffy Christians tell you that sinners don't have fun! '**There is pleasure in sin** *for a season.*'

I was having a high old time dancing the weekends away, without any of what I regarded as those restraints of my old life.

But *that season was ending.*

I dreamed that I heard my mother's voice calling me. Hers was an unusual, distinctive voice. She called me, her voice filled with anguish, pleading with me and asking, "Shaaaron, Shaaaron....*why didn't you tell me about this place?*"

I sat up suddenly, recalling the dream. But I thought –

It must have been that spaghetti I had for dinner!

Immediately, I dismissed the dream and laid back down to go to sleep.

Again, the very same dream was repeated but this time more terrifying.

I knew in it Mom was calling me from HELL!

When I sat up this time, fear washed over me and I wondered

Is my mother going to die?

It seemed clear to me that she must be approaching death.

Of course, when I called Mom, she seemed fine. Yet I couldn't shake that dream as anything but r-e-a-l. And I seemed to recall something from scripture that God *does* repeat a dream to confirm it sometimes. (Pharoah).

It happened I'd become so disgusted with my mother's behavior, I'd completely given up she'd ever change, about the same time I'd moved to Florida. She was an *old woman* and that made it all the **more** undignified to me.

(Her mother Sally, was very dignified in my mind).

Mom was *cold and uncouth*. An example was, when Rhonda and Craig were little and we finally started visiting after Charles died, my first move upon arriving was to enter the front bedroom and put two dolls into the top of the closet! She kept them on the bed, and their private parts were *life sized!* She thought it was ***so*** funny, but I knew the children could never respect her if they saw them. I wanted them to do so. And I knew I <u>didn't!</u>

Never had...she always enjoyed filthy jokes, which embarassed me.

Yet the dream. It could only mean that I would have to change my life, get the sin out of it - and warn her about hell! But would God accept me after my complete rebellion?

I'd become vile and perverse myself, as I recalled the filthy floor shows I'd enjoyed at three story bars like were in Atlanta. Worse, I'd rejected God almost violently, willing Him to leave me alone because I was so bitter against Him and against life.

I knew I deserved only judgment - never mercy.

Every scripture in the Bible seemed incredulous to me for years, except one. It was Phill, 1:6 "He who began a good work in you will carry it to completion." When that verse ever surfaced in my mind, I'd shout inside the car or wherever, "Then let Him."

I never really believed it.

At one time, I'd been a part of powerful prayer for others, seeing great answers to prayer (always for *them t*hough). I was a far cry from those days - like another lifetime. Or two. I reasoned I'd better start to pray for Mom.

It seemed clear to me *that God wouldn't have given me that dream if there was no hope for her. Or me.*

I just knew I couldn't bear Mom suffering as I'd heard her anguish in that dream!

Circumstances with Rhonda were far worse. My own personal life hadn't helped, though we never talked about it. That was to be expected, yet I'd blamed her! Charlie completely dominated her.

I now felt Charlie was being abusive to Krista in Rhonda's absence. That proved true.

Rhonda was oblivious to all but Charlie, and her new wealth. Wealth that Proverbs says slips through the fingers.

Don't believe it? Just drive by any exotic dancing bar and look at the cars. The ones that are old, ratty. broken down looking and needing paint? Those belong to the *dancers* making **big** money!

Craig was mostly off to college, and after graduation, he'd settled in where his fraternity brothers and friends were. He'd built a life there. I visited him on weekends when I worked in Atlanta while he was in college, helping him financially. But I never disclosed to him any of my inclinations. I don't know whether he guessed.

I'm certain it was information he didn't want to know, if he did! He and Rhonda weren't close then.

I made my visits all about him. He didn't seem interested anyway, busy pursuing his own goals.

About that time living on the other coast, my romance with my Christian friend ended. She had too much guilt and remorse over being involved in something she'd told God she didn't want any part of anymore.

Of course, I was disappointed. But the big problem was, **I was alone**. Again.

At first we have sin. Then we find sin has us.
Billy Graham

Sin is so natural, it is rarely recognized
for the evil that it is.
A. W. Tozer.

24

Kimberly's Konnection

My car got repossessed one night when I was working the front desk at the hotel.

Someone came in and told me a truck was towing it away. I knew why. I hadn't made *enough payments!* I wasn't accustomed to being broke, but it all worked out anyway, because *I lived on the beach and worked on the beach.* That event caused me to downgrade and begin to live entirely within my means. No more debt! How liberating it was.

I went out and bought a scooter that got 89 miles per gallon. Grocery shopping was nearby. It worked for me.

When Mom heard of this, she became utterly convinced that I had become a complete beach bum! The epitome of responsibility and investments and no tomfoolery such as this, she lambasted me on the phone.

I didn't care.

I had decided to simplify my life anyway, and I liked no car payments and being able to pay my bills. Not having to print expensive hotel directories at the back end of every deal was wonderful. *I was stressless.*

I liked my next door neighbor, but I never knew her by anything other than "Schultzie". She was full German and regaled me with her tales about her homeland and husband, who was deceased. We both lived alone, and she was older, probably retired I figured. She cleaned a house now and then.

She told me how her husband had come to America prior to her, and saved money over three years to bring her here. She said he met her on Riker's Island where he hugged and kissed her. Then he told her that was the last time she'd ever hear him speak to her in German. She must learn English!

He kept his word. So she *did.*

When I first moved there, I did visit a few dance bars but there were none I really liked. My desire for going out had waned. I enjoyed staying home and reading. I sat out on the lawn and read the morning newspaper a lot.

Or I would walk over and sit on the hotel beach chairs to read and watch the waves of the Atlantic, and the huge tankers and cruise ships as they floated by.

It happened I had been on a cruise. The week I'd started my first hotel in 1988, my mother called me and told me her friend had broken her foot and couldn't go with her, *would I go?* I thought, the timing simply could not be worse! It was never good business to interrupt a job because they're built on momentum especially your *first* one! Yet I knew that if I didn't go, Mom would not and she'd never had many travel experiences.

So I left the hotel, left Atlanta and went with Mom and Effie and Marion, her new husband, to Cancun, Cozumel and Playa del Carman. I never regretted it, for Mom and I never had any good memories in life. Those were good ones.

(I didn't have the dream until 1990, a year later).

Some months after I'd moved away from Rhonda and Krista, I had another very jarring dream, involving a cruise ship. Rhonda worked nights and would make the long drive home alone across one of the three huge bridges from Tampa to the Pinellas side in the wee hours.

Living on the beach there, it was the middle of a night after 2am when I dreamed Rhonda, Krista - who was about six years old then - and I were enjoying a cruise together. At one point in the dream, Krista and I began to wonder where Rhonda was, so we went looking for her. When we entered the cabin, I left Krista at the entry and stepped up into the bedroom area where I found Rhonda – cut up into bloody pieces all over the floor!

Immediately I awakened, fully alert and alarmed. I looked at the clock and realized it was when she would be driving home. Panicky at the horror of that dream, I decided to call Charlie on the other side of the state. When he answered, he must have realized something was wrong because he listened intently. I told him of the dream - he said he hadn't heard from her sometimes she called before leaving work. She hadn't. He hung up.

I quickly repented of my sins, because I knew God had provided a promise that, "If you confess your sins, **God is faithful and just**, and will forgive and cleanse you from all unrighteousness." Then I prayed for mercy and forgiveness for my daughter, and asked Him to save her.

Hours later, I heard the story.

Rhonda had been walked to her car by one of the bouncers who'd accompanied her. But when she pulled out of the parking lot, a car followed her. He followed her all the way across the bridge, about 10 miles, and continued to do so on her route home. She panicked, and didn't know what to do. Reaching the other side, she finally saw an all night gas station and hurriedly pulled in. When she ran in, the man pulled in and sat at the edge of the lot, watching. She told the man on duty about what had happened. He stepped out of the station, heading right for the car, but the car plowed out of the station leaving rubber on the pavement.

The man on duty that night at that station was in academy for becoming *a state trooper.*

Only eternity will reveal the truth about that dream and the scenario that accompanied it. But I believe a merciful God intervened to save Rhonda's life. An Ohio woman vacationing with her two teenage daughters were all kidnapped and killed off that same bridge about then.

Their murderer, Oba Chandler, was recently put to death. He is now named for other murders as well.

Though I'd repented that night, I was still under the full sway of choices I'd made. But I was now weary of the bar scene and the broken and fragmented lives I'd found there.

Sitting at a stoplight in traffic around that time, I looked over at the family in the car next to me. It was familiar. *I felt moved by what I saw.* **It was wholeness.** Rightness. And it beckoned me.

I never wanted my offspring to ever walk in the same footsteps I walked in, especially Krista.

Later on, in talking to Rhonda, she was finally weary of Charlie controlling her life, and making such a difference over the two girls. It seemed to her Krista was always slighted in every matter, and was made to feel inferior to his 'perfect' child. His panic attacks were worse, slamming his back against the wall and sliding to the floor, paralyzed in fear.

She wanted him out, but knew it wasn't an easy process to force him out legally. And maybe *dangerous* too. After all, he'd evolved into his role of 'househusband' (though unmarried). His job was to get the girls up and off to school, then he ate breakfast out over his newspaper, then watched TV until the girls came home from school. He straightened the house and got Rhonda up at 4pm to spend time with Krista.

His was a very easy life!

It was May. I sat in the yard one Sunday morning reading the newspaper. I yearned for that same wholeness I'd seen inside that car - which seemed so close to 'holiness' in my mind.

Suddenly, I dropped the paper into my lap and prayed, "Lord, I believe. Help my unbelief - *the man who prayed that* in the Bible got his prayer answered! I only have a mustard seed's worth of faith, but you said that was enough! Lord, **I know I want this sin!** But I don't want ***to want it anymor***e. Will You in Your mercy, take it from me? I surrender my life to you, in the degree I am able today, In Jesus' Name."

I felt then that I could somehow reconcile my **anger and bitterness** toward God.

I realized I needed to forgive Him, for *I'd held deep unforgiveness towards God.* He'd not met my expectations or answered my prayers, and I'd become deeply offended in Him.

And I could eventually reconcile my feeling of abandonment from Him, becoming aware that this issue between He and I surfaced from childhood, and always feeling abandoned!. Issues that I hadn't ever dealt with.

What I hadn't been able to reconcile was the certainty I felt that I could ever be anything other than what I was. *Gay.* It seemed to penetrate every conceivable aspect of my life and thinking. It has a demonic hold on lives!

While I enjoyed men and loved intelligent conversation with them moreso than women, I knew I only bonded with women. I felt I'd always been gay. I believed that during marriage and childrearing years, I'd been in 'remission', fully set on building the 'family' I'd always wanted. *Being gay was in repression and under the surface,* I believed.

I wonder how many people buy that they're gay and there's no way out? I'm guessing MOST...

I knew the problem was deep. It's why gays wear their sexuality as a badge of identity; they can't get away from it because it so penetrates their thinking and relationships. Then to top it off, they feel so isolated from those they love.... who don't understand!

Occasionally however, it would roll through my mind (having studied Greek), that the word for 'salvation' means *wholeness.* (Sozo in Greek)

So *were gays somehow excluded by God from that?* This began to bother me.

No one had to convince me that homosexuality was wrong. Others might think it's okay, and many of them do and I've been to their "charismatic churches" that preach that, while raising their hands in praise ....

But even when I was in those bars, I knew I would have my sin, but I could never *justify* it and call it good!

So if homosexuality was wrong, did it mean God simply left those who struggled with it without remedy, as most people seem to think? That it was somehow beyond God's ability to free people who wanted to be free from that lifestyle...?

(Some don't *struggle. This book isn't for them*. It's for those who want the truth!)

But if a gay accepted the free gift of salvation, (it happens), and since no one can earn it anyway - did they become *partially* whole? .....Because God wasn't able to *finish* the process that other sinners do experience, or that the very word means? I wrestled with all this.

But somehow I didn't think gays were exempt from God's redeeming grace. Nor His ability to restore their lives as others.

I just didn't understand.

One thing I knew. Wholeness means to be ***without*** **fragmentation**.

And fragmentation was the one word which I'd often used to describe the broken lives of the dear people I'd met in those many gay bars. Some do experience long term unions, (they don't barhop!) and I met many of them, but that's not the general rule.

It was in reading the newspaper while lounging in the morning sun, that a monumental change came about in my life. It was the story of Kimberly Mays, whose traumatic life made national headlines in every newspaper in the USA for months on end.

It started with the story of Ernest and Regina Twigg's twelve year old daughter, whose illness provoked them to move their family to a children's hospital in Pennsylvania for treatment.

Once there, tests revealed the daughter they'd raised could not be their own. *This was because her blood type was RH negative, and neither parent had that.* Officials questioned the mother, wondering if another father could be at issue. It wasn't.

Eventually, more steps revealed that their daughter had been *switched at birth,* in the delivery hospital in Wauchula County, Florida. The daughter they had raised was indeed, not their own. Their real daughter was named Kimberly Mays and had been reared by a couple in Sarasota, Florida. That mother had recently died.

Lawsuits prevailed and meantime, the daughter they'd raised also died -if I remember correctly. The Twiggs had about five other children as well.

Ultimately, The Twiggs sued the father of Kimberly Mays for custody, and eventually won when Kimberly was fifteen. But she didn't integrate well with the Twigg family or the other children. Soon, Kimberly wanted her old life back, her dad, and her old friends.

Kimberly sued the Twiggs, and left them completely behind, telling the judge she never wanted to see them again.

The part of the story that had literally transformed me were those blood tests!

She was RH negative. **That was *my* blood type**. She couldn't have been their child.

So I couldn't have been the child of Ovie and James!

Memories flooded my mind, as I recalled having James' dog tags around my neck as an adolescent, which I'd retrieved from Mom's cedar chest. This was the only connection I'd had with my 'dad'.

His name, James Oliver Williams, his ID#...and *his blood type* - O positive were imprinted on it.

Mom's blood type was also O positive as well. (I verified that on the telephone after this, in a seemingly innocent question to Mom).

Then suddenly, I recalled my OB/Gyn's comment to me when I was late term with Craig. I'd dismissed it then, as some kind of misunderstanding on his part, or on mine! He'd said it wasn't possible for me to be RH negative when neither of my parents were.

Now I understood...! Proof had been there all along. A fool, I'd ignored it. Why did I believe her? I knew how she *was* anyway.

This information totally stunned me. Little things you've thought about yourself all your life aren't even true. James was half-Cherokee Indian. Neither I nor my children were part Indian. I didn't even <u>know</u> my medical history! I didn't know what I was. Or *who.*

Did I even have a future? Life had made me too afraid to dream dreams. Now there was even more reason.

The father I'd initially not seen for 25 years, but who'd remarried my mother in 1974, wasn't even related to me! Forty-six years of believing a lie. *Her lie.*

The weight of this unfolding realization upon me was overwhelming. It meant my mother had lied to me all of my life and everyone else too.

It meant all of her self-righteous anger against the men in her life was really a truer statement about herself. It meant her entire life had been a complete charade. No one knew the real Ovie. I certainly knew ***I didn't***.

I struggled with what to do, or whether I should do anything at all. I was indignant with the fact that I'd endeavored my whole life just to win her approval, and it had never happened!

I felt *she hadn't even merited my love. I was* **done**.

I got dressed and went to the library, and dug around in medical books. They seemed to confirm what I already was aware of.

I decided to sit down and write a letter.

Dear Mom:
I want you to know Mom, it isn't my intent to hurt you in writing this letter. But the time has come that we both need to be honest with one another.
All of my life, the two of us have played roles, saying and doing what we each thought the other wanted to hear. In doing that, we have succeeded in skirting the important issues between us.
I realize I've been a source of disappointment to you, and I do regret that. Guess I wasn't cut out to put in 31 years at AT&T as you did.
But I can no longer pretend.
Today, I am laying down any future attempt to gain your approval.
What you see is what you get, and you will just have to accept me the way I am.
Secondly, the Twigg family story in the headlines recently has caused me to realize I couldn't possibly belong to Dad due to the blood types of the two of you.
I feel betrayed and deeply hurt that I've been led to believe one thing all my life only to find it isn't even true.
I had the opportunity to change my name back to Williams when I divorced. I didn't for the children's sake. I'm grateful now.
Apparently, I never was one anyway.
Please know that with this letter., I also forgive you.
But our relationship will never be the same.
Love, Sharon.

Like the time I ran away, a deafening silence followed.

More, she never once mentioned the letter to me as long as she lived.

She *did* call, but I didn't think she'd gotten the letter yet.

Rhonda had now taken to calling me on her dime, which I found amusing, given she'd not had the time of day for me when I lived there before. She usually called after 11pm, when long distance rates were lower.

This move of mine might even be healthy for our very sick relationship, I thought. But it needed a lot more than that like multiple miracles!

In one of those calls however, she told me she'd talked to Mom, and they'd discussed the letter. (She didn't even know I'd written it or what it was even about.) Rhonda said Mom spoke in disbelief that I could believe James wasn't my dad. Rhonda herself didn't understand, and ended up commiserating with Mom, thinking I was misguided. Not!

After this, I came to realize how shocking my letter must have been to Mom, like a demon rising from the dark night long ago.

"*Surely your sins shall find you out.*" Number 32:23

She too had been convinced all those years that I was James'. Already five months pregnant with me when she'd returned home, she'd just assumed I was.

It was ironic to me, when I recalled one of my mother's often used comments. She would bow her head a little and look down, then say with resolve, "*It'll come home to 'em.*"

It was her version of reaping what we sow.

That Thanksgiving weekend in 1943 in Fort Carson, Colorado had *come home to Ovie.*

"Today I know that such memories are the key not to the past, but to the future. I know that the experiences of our lives, when we let God use them, become the mysterious and perfect preparation for the work He will give us to do."

Corrie ten Boom

25

DeFragmentation

Before Corrie was released from Ravensbruck, the Nazi prison camp that they both shared, Betsie told Corrie that they would be released before the end of the year. They must bear their message around the world, *there is no darkness so great that God is not deeper still.*

However, Betsie's health was not well and a guard singled sweet Betsie out as a troublemaker and starved her. In her fragile condition, she suffered. Corrie would sneak out of her barracks to run and sneak a look at her through the window of the barracks used to keep the sick, her heart languishing for her and so little she could do.

Betsie died in that camp.

Corrie always said the brave and the valiant died there. Only she, the weaker one, survived.

It came to pass on December 31 that year, Corrie's name was called and she wondered why or if her time was up. As it happened, she was released that day on what she later discovered was a 'clerical error'. True to Betsie's words, they were both free of that prison camp by the end of the year.

When Corrie rode to the next stop and exited that train, she was totally confounded. Bright colors which she hadn't seen in so long; the decisions she needed to make about the next transfer were too much for her. She sat there in confusion for a long time. She hadn't been permitted to make any decisions of her own, nor seen colors other than gray. She later heard all the women her age in the prison camp were put to death the following week.

The average American's response to that story, including mine, would have been, "Gee God, *thanks a lot!* You could have prevented it in the first place!" But God had a plan. He took that whole mess including her family and Betsie and gave Corrie a message that would affect human lives - from then on until *even now* - unlike any other. Her life was uniquely handcrafted to reach into the human heart and bring redemption.

I witnessed that story in her, and on the screen many times and the resulting hundreds of lives who prayed the prayer of salvation.

Those prison camps were terrible and horror-filled on a daily basis, with the stench of mass humanity, and death from the smokestacks that filled prisoners' nostrils, hinting always that they might be next. Yet Betsie coached Corrie to thank God every day, even for the lice and the fleas in their barracks. Corrie told her she couldn't thank Him for the fleas. Betsie said, "You must!" They then discovered that the guards would not enter their barracks due to the *fleas!*

Corrie always said it was Betsie and her father who triumphed there. Corrie counted herself, the survivor, as the failure among them.

Corrie spent the rest of her life, doing as Betsie had directed, one time leaving on a freighter to countries where she knew no one, and with only $17 in her wallet, speading her story. When she arrived in Australia, there was a man who stood with a sign that had her name written on it. No one even knew she was coming, to her knowledge.

Yet she said, her own mother had shown hospitality to countless people. Corrie reflected she was the recipient of the rewards of that gift, by people who opened their homes to her!

God has a story to tell. It's one of redemption. Sometimes he handcrafts His witnesses through suffering. The deeper the suffering, the greater the testimony, oftentimes.

But he saves sinners to save sinners. Bonnke.

My suffering in life has only been deeply personal, emotional and not akin to Corrie's torture at all - which many don't even know. The prisoners were sometimes dragged from their barracks in early morning, 3 am. in the cold and forced to stand for hours, *naked.*

If someone fell, they were shot. Corrie was extremely modest, so she rarely - if ever - shared this.

But one day, when she couldn't bear or believe the horror and inhumanity to man that unfolded before her eyes, she looked up to see a lark flying and calling in the sky. She then raised her eyes beyond that lark and saw there was indeed a God of goodness, greater than what was there, before her eyes! This makes me weep for her and all who endured it.

Nonetheless, **my** story makes some people sad. ***It made me sad!*** But the light at the end of the tunnel is my testimony of how God protected me on city streets, and brought wholeness to me in the midst of my naivete, ignorance, and the effects of abuse.

He brought liberation to me through His holy Word. The truth still *frees* us! And completely restored relationships....

He waits to do so for you! And in a similar way, God permitted me to suffer from my own wrong choices, so that I could also bring a message of hope to others who feel hopeless, or that they've gone *too far to be forgiven.*

If you want forgiveness, you can have it!

"Can Jesus really forgive someone like me," she asked. The pastor, a stranger to her laughed, and said "Yes, God has a place for you."
"Really, He has a place for me?"
She'd never heard that before, a victim of repeated rape and abuse, now an alcoholic.
She'd never known joy or peace.
Her life changed that day

So I also believe God permitted me to sink to those depths, for **<u>you</u>** perhaps, and then He rescued me, (He can rescue you as well!) to help others in *their understanding of His Great love!* His loving kindness is new every morning; it is His *kindness* that leads us to repentance, Romans 2:4 says!.

The devil has painted God as some arbitrary figure who is without mercy. People believe it too.

Please. See Him as He is - the God of Love with a Merciful Heart!

The most important aspect of my story is though, God caused this great servant of God to cross my path, Corrie, so that eventually at 'an appointed time' I could further her message. Now in this time, because we live in those perilous times that the Apostle Paul warned us would come at the end. One that resembles the times in which Corrie lived.

Friends, if you don't believe that, you need to get informed, first, before you do anything else. Because **half of preparation** for the future **is mental!** We need to be prepared for what it holds. For Jesus to return, endtime prophecy must be fulfilled, and the book of Revelation says there's never been a time so terrifying, so horrible as this.

And never will be again! Not even in Corrie's experience.

Too many believers are sitting on their hands waiting for the rapture, letting neighbors and even loved ones go to a real, fiery hell! Truth matters!

I say, *what's the harm in preparing for the worst, but hoping for the best.* And what if the rapture is delayed from what YOU believe.

You may be lost .because you AREN'T prepared at all.

Deception is your adversary. And it will *prevail* in endtimes – it already is, **even in churches!**

A foreboding accompanied my introduction to Corrie, and subsequent events and the movie. **I believe it is this book!** Read on *please.*

I realize I will have my critics for writing such a life story as this. But it is my story, and others are free to believe what they wish. Especially the things I say about being gay. If you don't *want wholeness*, don't worry. *You won't be bothered by it.* It's just for those who believe! The same is true for miracles as well. Believe it or not, Jesus said He didn't come for everybody - *those who feel 'alright'.* "For I am <u>not</u> come to call the righteous, but sinners." Matt. 9:13. Only childlike faith prevails, because Friend, **you are not in charge**!

I believe that God knew my heart from the outset, and that I would eventually return to Him, even though I felt I'd committed the unpardonable sin in my rebellion! I'd railed against God. Sinners *do* that - Proverbs 19:3 says they make bad decisions and then blame God for them! I did. Have you....?

This chapter is not just about homosexuality! It's about becoming liberated from a *mindset*, whatever mindset it is! It's fascinating that the definition of 'repent' means to *change the mind?* Before freedom comes, we have to *know something.* "You shall *know* the truth, and the truth shall set you free." John 8:32. Jesus defined it by saying, "Herein is eternal life. That you *know* God *and* Him whom He has sent." John 17:3

It's first of all, mental. (Though we can't know God by knowledge only**)**

The principles I share here will work for anyone who will accept its truth. In spite of the prolific lies that thrive in society, *in too many - churches who don't accept Bible Truths!!*

But I ask you to remember one thing. From its inception, *Christianity has been about changed lives.* If you fellowship where there are no changed lives, you need to look for a new church! It means the Word is not being lifted up and freely proclaimed! Then look for God to confirm His Word with signs that follow where the Word is preached, per Mark 16:20. That was normal then. It should be today as well. And it will be soon, I believe!

One final thought here. Cana homosexual change? Some think not. Others *hope not!*

And even if they can, they don't want them in **their** church! It's awkward, if not impossible, for religious types who have lived a pristine life and followed all the rules (man's, not God's) I went through a lot of what I did so I, *a religious prude,* could learn God's mercy.

He wanted to use me, but *He couldn't trust me with His lambs!*

I spent my birthday alone in August. Craig sent a sweet card and called.

About 10pm, I heard a tapping at my front door. Schultzie stood outside. She held a beautiful cranberry goblet with a lovely white silk rose in my favorite color - pink. I collected cranberry items. Of course they were in storage somewhere.

"I remembered it was your birthday. I wanted to bring you this," she said, knowing I was alone. I thanked her profusely. *I thought it was God.*

Rhonda called about midnight and said she'd gotten a card but didn't get it mailed, which she used to be terrible at. She apologized. Krista was sending one too, but they'd be late. Charlie was finally gone, she said. She got a restraining order.

Wow-I sighed. I was glad I wasn't there.

Earlier in the summer, I'd bought a new Bible. My old one had notes in the margin that screamed doubts at me, *of another lifetime,* due to the unanswered prayers concerning them. Then I took up the habit of going over to the beach on my days off and reading it on the hotel beach chairs.

But by midsummer, everything seemed so empty and meaningless. *Where was I going in life?*

Worse, **I sorely missed Krista**. I hadn't seen her in months. She didn't have anyone living a good example before her - *I would be one of them.* My job at the hotel was a 'getting by' situation. After you've worked for yourself a few years, you really aren't into making other people rich, so there's little gratification there.

Krista, now six years old, had mailed me a card, and enclosed a drawing of herself crying big black tears. Written across the bottom "I miss you".

It had broken my heart truly.

I'd also made the observation that the region where I lived was nice, but it wasn't really *family oriented* like the West Coast was. There were giant condos everywhere, so that even if you were on or near the beach, your view was obstructed of the water. It felt like Chicago to me! I missed my real home on the West Coast of Florida, It was family-oriented and, it was where *my* family was.

Labor Day weekend came. *Another holiday weekend alone.*

I didn't have to work that holiday. As usual I sat in the yard reading the newspaper. But that day, **a new realization suddenly washed over me**.

Though imperceptible to me, God had removed any desire for sexual sin, i.e. that lustful attraction to another woman. I hadn't even thought of it in weeks. I sat there *dumbfounded and speechless.*

Smitten with gratefulness!

(For a season, I had fears of falling back into sin. But God showed me that He was not only my Savior, but the Great Shepherd of my soul. He'd given me instructions in II Peter 1, that if I followed them, *l would never fall!*)

I'd sought counsel from a huge well known organization in Miami but God steered me away from them, with the warning that they served as a mere dating service!

All in the name of Jesus, of course! (They closed down recently after decades). I visited more 12 step groups, but became dismayed.

I even attended church at a contemporary Methodist Church. Admittedly, it was so I could tell Craig I'd gone to church! I found nothing for me at any of them, except a couple of nicer people.

But now, and sovereignly, God had touched me. I was free. *And I knew it!*

My first response was to get up and call Rhonda. I told her I was moving back. Could I stay with her a while? She was glad.

I hired Schultizie's son, who owned a pickup truck, to move me. We left on Labor Day, eighteen months since my dream about Mom.

Note: *The causes of homosexuality aren't something I've chosen to deal with in this book. There are many. They are controversial and debatable.* I do *not* believe it's genetic!

My point here is - whatever the cause, wholeness is available, *because God is a Deliverer, and that is my entire focus here. There* ***are*** *no exceptions.*

However, the key does lie in wanting that wholeness. As such, we can only pray for that desire and a hunger in our loved ones for 'righteousness', which is a big word for "RIGHT".

Several factors, I've since realized, played a role in readying me for the miracle God wanted to give me.

1. I changed the way I was facing, via a 'decision'. I knew I wanted to turn my life around for my children's sake. This shaped my conduct.
2. Though spontaneous and unplanned, I took steps to do so. I bought a new Bible to read, thus re-establishing the authority of scripture in my life.
3. Reading that Bible had a cleansing effect on me... That summer, reading it on the beach literally 'washed me in the water of the word'. John 15:3, Ephes. 5:27 I'd repented of my 'stout words' to God also.
4. Scripture doesn't say people turned from idols to God! No –they turned *to God from idols*. God knew the hold of that sin was stronger than me. I acknowledged my inability to let go of it Memorial Day weekend. And He was then able to free me.

Added Note: All sexual sin falls under the category of *fornication*, according to the Bible. (Think of a big box, labeled Fornication with all others inside) God knows best - and will aid us - in how we can live a life that is without hindrances and, of the consequences of sexual sins, such as STD's, unwanted pregnancies resulting in abortions, single parenting, broken homes and families, and an abundance of situations that cost individuals - and societies - dearly. After forgiveness, you don't have to be ashamed! God takes *that away*, so you can focus on making a difference in the lives of others now.

God's attitude about sexual matters can be found in the New Testament in Heb. 13:2-3: "Let marriage be held in honor among all, and let the marriage bed be undefiled, *for God will judge the immoral and the adulterous*." For those who are tempted in this way, the Apostle Paul says, get married! Otherwise, you're bringing a host of repercussions from bad decisions, because 'he that sows to the flesh will reap corruption.' You can't blame a holy God (who warned you) about those poor decisions, or for the consequences you experience from those same decisions. *You* made them!

Some believe sexual problems are demonic. Or that every sickness is demonic. I wish it were that simple, for all demons have to flee in the powerful Name of Jesus!

Habits have to be broken; minds need to be renewed. Rom.12:2

The devil is ultimately in every picture that robs or controls you or hinders your pursuit of God. See John 10:10; Acts 10:38. Warfare signifies struggle, and we're in a war.

But let's lay the blame squarely where it belongs! It's usually with us, when we give the devil '*place*' into our lives by making stupid choices in the first place! We're to blame.

Many times it is simply a matter of the flesh reigning in our lives. Delayed gratification was once a welcome part of growth and maturing, but not in this age!

Whether eating (diet causes diabetes, high blood pressure, strokes and heart disease), or unrestrained sexual behavior, we're dealing with a narcissistic society of - ***it's all about me.***

We want it all, ***now!*** Nothing more destroys goals and futures than this matter - people won't *wait*!

There is no cure for that except for repentance, Dear Friends. And only God can save our society. Period.

And too, misguided believers love to throw around the "A" word as though Abomination only belongs to the sin of homosexuality! Not True! The list of things God hates, and 'abominations' to Him, in Proverbs 6:16 *do not include homosexuality!*

However, I've noted that listed there, are a lot of sins that are found in churches everywhere! Pride, lying, false witness, haughtiness ... **The Abomination tag has been unfairly logged against gays** - in view of this passage naming other sins that make God sick, Dear Friends!

Try luke warmness! Jesus said "I will spew you out of my mouth!" in Rev. 3:16.

The devil is a *liar* and the Father of them. That's the primary attribute of his nature! He persuades us to partake of his temptations, then turns and accuses us because we did! The cure for this is to get out of the inability of the flesh in Romans 7 (The inability of "self") and move into Romans 8 (the spirit-led life), where following the Holy Spirit gives us personal victory. Those two chapters reflect the carnal mind versus the spiritual mind!

If we are to win in the future conflict against our adversary, we've got to find the answer to where the war is conducted. *It is the mind*!

"Be careful with half-truths. You never know which end you're gonna get hold of." Unknown.

Thank You, Lord Jesus, that You lift us out of the vicious circle of sin and failure and that You have brought us into that wonderful blessed circle of forgiveness, redemption, and holiness. Hallelujah, what a Saviour!
Corrie ten Boom.

"It was the precious blood of Christ, the sinless, spotless Lamb of God."
I Peter 1:19

"We know that our old self was crucified with Him in order that the body of sin might be brought to nothing, so that we would no longer be enslaved to sin. For one who has died has been set free from sin. So you must consider yourselves dead to sin and alive to God in Christ Jesus."
Romans 6:6-11 (Paul writing about water baptism)

PART IV

Living The Inheritance

- -

There are no 'ifs' in God's Kingdom. His timing is perfect.
His will is our hiding place.
Lord Jesus, keep me in Your will!
Don't let me go mad by poking about outside it.
Corrie ten Boom

26

Dirty Windows

It rained all month that August. I'd never seen it rain so much in late summer in Indiana. It's usually dry. We only saw the sun about once every four days or so. I'd cleaned Mom's house top to bottom, weeded all her flower beds, cleaned and caulked the bathroom, cleared the gutters, washed the windows, and then painted the outbuilding used as a shed.

Mom had been able to do little of anything, except watch, mostly from an inside window.

My half-brother David now lived at Mom's since he and his second wife split earlier in the year. But he was rarely home. He'd now blossomed into the full blown misogynist he'd aspired to all his life. He'd just divorced his second wife for wanting a baby. He wanted *none*. He hated children. He hated Mom's roses, her flower beds, her beautiful and varied trees she'd raised in her yard over 30 years.

David hated most anything Mom liked or did, including her ballroom dancing and nights out with friends. After sleeping until noon, he and his new live-in girlfriend were usually out in the new car Mom recently bought him. A gift no doubt for moving in with her because she now was afraid to live alone anymore. But it was a BIG tradeoff. David worked evenings.

It was autumn when I returned to stay with Rhonda, so I decided I wanted to go back to school, like all the others my age who want to know what to do when they grow up! But I'd moved in short order back downtown to the area I knew so well, and was closer to school than where Rhonda lived. I loved being able however, to visit her and Krista and have Krista come stay with me on weekends.

Rhonda was still dancing then but looking for other work.

I worked out a deal with a couple of old neighbors to be able to live for free while I attended school, by painting and wallpapering their houses. I was able to get into school on grants that paid for books and classes.

It was the summer following that I'd planned to visit Mom in June. However, at the last minute, I'd had a change of plans. When I told Mom I couldn't come, her reaction was surprising to me. She seemed deeply disappointed for some reason. I'd talked to her regularly on the telephone but all seemed normal, except for the fact she'd been hospitalized with pneumonia in January. But that was nothing new, as she'd had many bouts with it, and always came out of the hospital, okay.

A few weeks later, whether on purpose or not, I'm not sure, she revealed she hadn't been out in her yard all spring and that weeds were hip high in her flower beds. That took my breath away. I knew *something dreadful was wrong to keep Mom out of her flower beds!*

I knew I had go visit her now, and so I planned to drive up the first of August and stay a few weeks.

When I first saw her, I became morbidly aware that Mom was deathly ill. Always the picture of health above and beyond her siblings, she walked on a walker now. It was all she could do to move from the kitchen counter to the coffee bar where she always sat. I tried not to reveal how shocked I was, looking away she faced me.

All my hard work that August around the house must have given David quite a chuckle, since the previous month he'd had Mom put the deed - the mortgage paid off – into his name.

I was unaware of that until later on.

I worked hard because I wanted the house easily accessible to Mom. I'd put in more phones, hand rails in the bath, cleaned closets, and washed the windows.

Ever since our cruise to Cancun, Mom had battled pneumonia a half dozen times, or more. It usually started as bronchitis, then she'd end up in the hospital.

But she'd beaten it every time.

Rhonda and Krista and I had visited one Christmas following that cruise. I remember that, because it was the first time Krista ever saw snow. I'm not sure if I saw Mom another time, but I know Craig and I also visited another time at Christmas. His half-brother was born to Larry that day, another brutal shock to Craig... and to me!

My first day there, Mom wanted to go pick out a lift chair that raises a person to a standing position. In order to do that, she had to stop by her cardiologist to get a prescription for the chair, to obtain insurance coverage.

That prescription told it all. She held it in her hand, staring at it closely. I stood with her at the receptionist's station when she read it. She seemed stupefied.

It read, "Final stages of 3 terminal heart diseases" It named each one. I too was shocked beyond words.

It was like it was news to her as well.

In the car, she explained that the doctor said she might live another 2 years if she took care of herself. Somehow I didn't believe that. But I wanted to believe anything right then, *except the truth!*

No matter how they treat you, or how traumatic the relationship is- ***you only have one mother.*** I'd loved her desperately my entire life! Obsessively, compulsively.

I was to learn that Mom was greatly distressed about David then. She'd cherished his second wife, Karen, who'd often come after their divorce and helped Mom when she needed it, even washing her windows. She'd been very good to her over the years. With David there now, she didn't come around. Mom missed her, often mentioning her name.

After divorcing two women over the issue, David's live-in girlfriend was now *pregnant.*

I met her and she was very pretty, perhaps Hispanic, looking older than her age. This helped her get into bars easily, which is where David met her. At age 18, she'd already been married and lost a baby. She was in the middle of a divorce.

Mom wanted David to live with her but she didn't want *her* there! *Mom didn't like her,* saying she was lazy, and in her words, "not worth killing"... said facetiously, of course. But one had to be reallllllllly low for her to regard them that way.

The second day I was there, David and his girl had an early morning appointment to see the Ob/Gyn. Returning all bubbly afterwards, she told us she was so many weeks pregnant. Then, out the door they went.

Mom got up gingerly, moving to the wall calendar where she counted the number of weeks the Ob/Gyn had said. It made conception a holiday weekend, only 2 weeks after meeting David. Mom knew that on Memorial Day weekend, the gal had visited Texas, where her husband still lived.

Rightly or wrongly, Mom was convinced the baby wasn't David's. And that he'd spend his life - and her money - raising it!

Later that week, we decided to have lunch out. Mom was like that then. Strictly adhering to her doctor's diet one day, and then the next, she didn't seem to care. Her credit union was a long drive. She didn't use ATM cards.

I walked with her into her bedroom where she kept a tin of cash three drawers down in her chest. She looked and then looked again about $60 had disappeared since the last time she'd gotten cash. Shocked, she looked at me incredulously wondering if *I took it.* Because David had never done so.

I assured her I didn't even know that tin with cash was there.

Mom seemed to rally in the early part of my stay. Besides eating out, one day she wanted to go play her favorite game of miniature golf. She played on real courses though, unlike the imitation sites everywhere now. I couldn't believe she wanted to play a second 18 hole game, after beating me at the first. Mom was very competitive. I was tired, but I played a second game. She won again. They would be her last.

I'd planned to stay two weeks. The day before I planned to leave for home, Mom asked Effie, Marion and me to go with her to the cemetery to choose a plot. She wanted one close to Max, her brother. We drove to Effie's house, then Marion drove all of us to the cemetery.

After paying for the lot at the main office, we drove back to see the area. While she still sat in the back seat, Effie and I paced off how far it was from Max's grave, beneath a shade tree. Window down, we could see her face as she wept, viewing her final resting place.

My heart broke into a million pieces!

That ordeal proved to be so painful for both Mom, and for me, that I couldn't bear to leave her the next day. I'd stay another week. That would mean I'd miss a week of school.

The tone of my visit seemed to be *set* the very first day I'd arrived. We both sat at the breakfast bar, drinking coffee. Mom gingerly stood to go to get refills.

I watched as she returned.

Something struck me that I had to speak from my heart. Pot in hand, she began to fill our cups.

"Mom" I began, "I know I don't have the financial stability that you'd like for me, nor material possessions. And I know I've been a big disappointment to you."

"But I can tell you what I **do** have, Mom. I have the only thing that matters. I *know* where I will spend eternity. If I were to die tonight, l know I'd be with Jesus, forever." I looked up at her and caught her gaze.

She looked away as though she had nothing to say.

However, each night when she retired, she'd carry an armload of books to bed with her, where she'd read into the wee hours. I felt she was too afraid to go to sleep, for fear she'd never wake up!

During my stay, I would come into her bedroom and sit down in the blue rocker that sat at the foot of her bed. We talked for hours each night.

During those times, she voiced her fears for David. His last divorce had really upset

Mom. A big mistake, in her mind.

Perhaps that was because she'd finally seen that David wasn't as perfect as she'd hoped.

She now had two children racking up failure at a steady pace.

A reality check for her.

The son she'd raised without morals or principles, now had *none*. She and Charles had been confident he'd make the right choices once grown. But he'd simply followed her example, acquiring *her* values (lack of them?) by osmosis.

"Your actions speak so loudly, I can't hear what you're saying." Unknown

But the difference was that she at least knew right from wrong from her own upbringing.

David had no clue. He was wholly amoral.

This same son had also become like his mother in other ways. *Hard*. He could be cruel sometimes toward *her* and hateful like his dad.

Finally, the daughter she'd always told would never amount to anything, *hadn't.* In her closing hours we were all together, one big *unhappy* family!

While I visited Mom that summer, I marveled at how her own sins had come home to haunt her. David's young girlfriend had literally moved in and taken over Mom's own home. Mom was too sick to object. A stranger, using and abusing what was precious to Mom.

Perhaps all this explains a curious event that often occurred while I stayed there those three weeks.

Each evening as we talked at bedtime, it seemed that Mom would ask me a question about God or scripture, or end time issues. I would try to answer, but it seemed to me I only stumbled, my gift of gab absent.

In futility, I would usually end up saying, "Mom I don't have all your answers." "I only know *how to pray.*"

At that, I'd move over to the edge of her bed, take her frail hand, and begin to pray. As I did, she'd begin to cry, which evolved into heaving sobs. This frightened me. I thought she'd die *then!* Every night it was the same.

One night, I rose to go to my own room, tired. "Sharon," she asked, "how can you *know* you're born again?"

I couldn't believe my ears. Twenty-four years earlier, when I became a believer, I'd prayed for two things: wisdom, and for my mother's salvation!

I quickly asked God for wisdom, again - I surely needed it right then! I told her how I John 5 tells us *five different times* that *we* ***can*** *know,* not wonder, that we are saved.

I told her this was the biggest difference between Christianity and other religions that merely require good works and where followers only hope *to gain heaven.*

Christians have a more sure hope!

I told her of Romans 10:9 where, if we believe in our heart and confess with our mouth that Jesus is Lord, we are saved. Not because we 'feel' saved but because scripture says so!

And the Bible merits our belief.

Then I sat down again on her bed to pray with her. She repeated after me a prayer of salvation, sobbing.

But that prayer did not wholly convince her.

One day near the end of my stay, I watched late afternoon rains pelt the outside of Mom's kitchen windows. So unusual.

Suddenly, I realized the "latter rains" of God were falling on the inside as well!

In the face of my own faithlessness, God was proving His faithfulness! I had given up, and even turned away in defiance for *this* unanswered prayer and those for Rhonda and my failed marriage.

Yet God was pouring His great love onto Mom's cold and stony heart each day I was there. A*nd He'd let me witness it!.*

I'd done everything possible to make life easier for her. David at least slept there, and Mom wasn't alone.

It was time to leave.

Mom sat in her lift chair in the living room. She looked up at me and begged me not to go. Tears were in the corners of her eyes, my last memory of her. I leaned down to the recliner and kissed her on the cheek.

"Mom, I have to go sometime. School has already started.

Anyway, David is here."

It was pouring down rain as I headed south on the interstate that day. I put in a CD Craig had given me.

Hardly even listening, suddenly a song got my attention. I played it over several times because the words were unbelievable to my ears.

Rain beat upon the outside of the windshield as gushing tears streamed down my face on the inside of that car.

"*....tears clean the windows of the soul*". The words rang out.

The windows of Mom's soul had become dingy from the grime of sin over decades. God had used my visit, in part, to '*wash her with the water of the word* 'each night.

I don't' know whether Mom ever came to see the hurt and rejection she'd brought to me in life. I do know that she came to *Love* me! At times while I was there, I saw her out of the corner of my eye watching me, as though wondering about something.

I called Mom to tell her of the song. She didn't answer. I still occasionally wonder why she didn't. I left a message.

God's viewpoint is sometimes different from ours -
so different that we could not even guess at it unless
He had given us a Book which tells us such things...
In the Bible I learn that God values us not for our strength
or our brains but simply because He has made us.
Corrie ten Boom

Remember that there's a difference between having
to say something, and having something to say.
Unknown.

27

A Simple Equation

I left Mom's on Saturday, Labor Day weekend. Effie usually checked on Mom by telephone at least once a day. For some reason, she and Marion took their pastor over to Mom's house on Monday. Mom prayed the prayer of salvation with him.

And **this time it *took***!

From then on, it was unmistakable to everyone there'd been a change! I've seen few salvations that were more dramatic! Mom told everyone who would listen, including two or three times to me on the telephone.

With a hushed breath she would ask, *"Did I did I tell you that I got saved?"*

There was a genuine awe in her voice of some miraculous event! I knew the experience was valid. And I was *grateful.*

One year to the very Labor Day weekend that I'd moved back home, Mom was saved.

Thirty months following the dream where she had called to me from hell.

Four days after my departure, Mom was hospitalized again. She'd been weaker the third week of my visit, and had now grown worse. Pneumonia.

Effie and James both provided me with progress reports. I called the hospital regularly too, and talked with staff or Mom. After 21 days, she'd recovered enough to plan to go home. She was up and walking on a walker when I called and talked with her.

She wanted out of there and complained to me that Sis simply would not leave the hospital. She wanted rest from her, too.

Then, without warning, she picked up an infection inside the hospital. Via telephone, I could tell she was extremely discouraged at that point.

I didn't know what to say. I hadn't done so by phone, but I said, "Mom, let me pray with you."

When I opened my mouth, no words came out. I realized I didn't know what to pray then. I didn't know the Lord's will. I began with what I *knew...*

"Father" I began, "I know you love my mother. I've sensed You **loving her through *me*.** Lord, she needs your encouragement right now. Help her trust David completely to You and Your love. Father, I ask you to make my mother whole..."

A loud noise came from the other end of the line. The nurse picked up the phone and said she'd dropped it. She couldn't talk.

Somehow I knew my mother would be whole soon, but *it wouldn't be in this world.* I think she knew it too.

Those were the last words spoken between Mom and me. Still one holds to the thread of hope a loved one will recover. If I'd truly thought she'd die, then I think I would have returned.

It happened I was working evenings then for extra cash, while in school. A friend had purchased ten units and was renovating them. Both Dad and Effie had my number. I sat eating a late meal. The phone rang.

It was James. He'd just returned from the hospital. Mom was dying. I sat in disbelief. *James too.*

After hanging up, I called the nurses' station hoping to talk to someone, *anyone*, in the room. A nurse I didn't know answered. She told me Mom had been hallucinating all day, *seeing Jesus and begging Him to take her home.*

The nurse couldn't say if she was dying or not. She'd just come on her shift.

Shortly, the phone rang again. It was Effie. She'd just left the hospital. *Mom had died.* She said she and James had been with her in the final minutes. I was grateful because Mom loved both. But James had had to leave. He couldn't endure it.

Effie told me of Mom's final words to James. He stood at her bedside. Mom peered into the eyes of the love of her life, her lover and friend.

Now she spoke, and asked him to take her hand. He did. She asked him, "James, do you see my other hand?"

Dad couldn't speak, but nodded. Her breath was very short. "Jesus has my other hand, James. I'm not afraid to die. He's here right now James - don't wait like I did... *Accept Him now!"* she pleaded.

In agreement, James nodded he would.

Effie hung up the telephone to go look for David. No one knew where he was on Saturday perhaps working overtime. He'd hardly been to see Mom.

It was late. I decided to go on home, though dreading it. I went straight in and sat down on the side of my bed. My pain seemed original, like no one had ever felt it in that degree.

The realization struck me that the relationship I'd sought all my life died with her. Any and all hope of it was now gone. I felt cheated. Again.

Regret seemed almost as great as the loss.

I opened my Bible and looked down. Ever faithful, *God didn't leave me in my grief.*

He spoke to me of the letter I'd written to Mom: Paul's words said:

"Even if I caused you sorrow by my ***letter****, I*
do not regret it, though I did regret it - I see my
letter *hurt you, but only for a little while.*
Yet now I am happy, not because you were
made sorry, but because your sorrow led you to
repentance. For you became sorrowful as
God intended, and were not harmed in any way
by us. Godly sorrow brings repentance that
leads to salvation, and leaves no regret."
II Cor. 7:8 NIV

God had used my letter to answer my own prayer for Mom. She was now with *Him!*

I should have realized before I came home from Mom's what to expect. She'd tried to get me to choose what I wanted then, like jewelry. I couldn't.

My plane arrived mid-afternoon, the first flight I could get the day after Mom died. Rhonda and Krista were driving up. I took a limo to the house.

David and his girlfriend were home. A pot of chili sat on the stove. They offered me some. I accepted. I could see David felt he had everything under control, and he was prepared to talk. I saw no emotion. But the trip and emotional fatigue had worn *me* out.

He promptly went and retrieved a copy of the will and said it was mine. It was the first time I'd seen it before.

The chili burned my mouth preparing me for *the scorching to come.* I abandoned my chili to find my glasses, then went into the living room to read the will. When I started to sit down, the bulb blew out. I got up to look for one.

I couldn't recall where Mom kept them when I'd been there a month ago.

David's girlfriend was anxious to oblige. I regarded her as likeable but young, and like Mom, a stranger in her house. She led the way into Mom's bedroom, and opened the third drawer down and handed me a light bulb.

Hmmm. The same drawer Mom kept her tin with extra cash.

I don't know if David was looking for a reaction from me after reading the will or not.

But I have a pretty good poker face when I don't want to reveal my thoughts.

I walked back into the living room and sat down.

They excused themselves for the evening. David had a suggestion though.

He thought I might want Mom's car. If so, he'd trade it to me for my part of the will. I said I'd think about it.

That offer was tempting as I needed a car. Yet, something made me draw on past wisdom.

I'd wait.

Relieved to have the house to myself for a while, I welcomed time for closure. I was spent from tears.

The phone rang, taking me back to the kitchen. Friends of Mom wanted to know how to help. They were bringing food tomorrow. Sis called. And Effie. She wanted to know if I liked the outfit picked out to bury Mom in. I'd briefly looked at it with David.

I asked Effie if she'd helped choose it. She said, No, she said she couldn't. Marion had had surgery the same day Mom died. But she'd seen it earlier that day. It had been late anyway when Mom died. Effie was pretty broken up. She loved Mom. I let her hang up.

I thought about Effie's comment that it had been 'late'. It had been after 9 pm that Mom died, and Effie hadn't even known where David was when I talked to her last - he had no cell phone. My question was, who all was in Mom's house the night before, and why did they feel it necessary to make choices about what to bury her in when they knew I'd be there soon?

The whiff of a 'Sis attack' floated through my mind. (Yes, I've forgiven her long ago, but *she was what she was*).

The will still lay in my lap, where I'd dropped it in shock. *It left nothing to me except household and personal possessions.* David got the house, cars, insurance, investments, bank accounts. A fortune.

How could Mom do this? Worse, ***how could she*** *do this to her own grand- children, Rhonda and Craig?* I wept.

She was an unfeeling monster.

I got up and walked into Mom's room to look over the dress. I flipped on the light to see it. I liked her in that dress. But. Mom had hundreds of dresses (Yes!)

Oh well… . It was alright. Why make a fuss?

My eyes turned to gaze about the room that would never hold Mom again. My eyes stopped on top of the vanity where her jewelry box sat. Next to it were *two bare necklace trees*, stripped. The jewelry box was *empty too.*

Suddenly, it came to me my first hint of what had happened in that house overnight.

It was me that had organized closets for her before I left., so I was familiar with what was in them.

I opened her two drawer file cabinet she'd had me place next to her bed. I couldn't lift it at the time, so I'd shoved it into place. It was empty now.

Behind Mom's door, stuffed into a rack hanging on the back of the door, I found her most recent bank books, the only legal items left, obviously overlooked.

The **ledgers and bank books told the story** a sale of stock, a new garage. A car.

Thousands paid to David.

The closets were the same. Everything of value was missing, electronics, cameras even the big box of family *photos.* I suspected where those had gone, Sis being the big photo buff in the family. Turned out I was right. I knew her history of taking other family pictures from siblings. Had I not borrowed some before Mom died and taken them home with me, I would have had none of her youth, or mine.

Embarrassed after her mom had died, Sis's daughter returned *many* photos to me years later - at least *she* had a conscience! Sis had placed them all into tiny albums.

Mom's beautiful collection of quilts were missing. I did find *one* on a bed. I can't really say what all had happened there. All I have is 'history'.

The middle bedroom had a closet the length of the room. I'd organized it in August for all her dresses to be in the same closet. I opened the doors, first glancing to my left at the hip high safe belonging to David. He kept his guns in it. He'd shown me a sawed off shotgun and a new M-16 in August. He bought the latter to hunt deer - *against the law in every state but one.*

Was David a white supremacist, I mused? I soon dismissed that because I knew they are very religious among themselves, wishing to preserve the Caucasian race from mongrels (mixed races) and non-whites - *all in the name of God,* of course. I'd read a number of their blogs when Craig had asked me to - one of his co-workers was a big wig in one of their groups.

Besides David was too much of a loner to conform!

The Spanish dress Mom loved that we'd purchased together in Cancun came to mind. I looked for it as it was the only one I really wanted, for memories. (Mom and I didn't share the same taste in clothes) It wasn't there. I wondered if it now had an Hispanic owner. Mentally,

I gave it to her if so. Up to a dozen others were gone too.

In the living room, I was relieved the three photos of Mom she had on display were still in their frames.

David had never had a kind thing to say about Sis in his entire life. He'd ridiculed her for being nosey, phony, religious, and controlling.

Mom too had surprised me in August by a sudden revulsion towards her. I wondered what had happened, and also *what had taken so long?*

Mom was right. She'd told me to take what I wanted. *They might not be there when I got back.* Did she know? Prophetic though.

A dear friend and next door neighbor who managed a big funeral home once told me, "A death in the family does one of two things. It brings out the very best, or the very worst in people. *There is no in-between!"*

I retired in Mom's bedroom, but was unable to sleep. Rhonda and Krista and a friend who came along to help drive arrived about midnight. Craig couldn't get off work as he'd just been off work. I was grateful for the additional forces.

David was in bed. We sat and talked quietly in kitchen.

The next morning, I could tell David didn't like having the house full of strangers (that would be *us*). But he knew there was little he could do about it without looking bad himself. He seemed very tense. He never was good at eye contact anyway.

I liked David, but I *knew he was the son of his father.*

David rose early and showered. Then he informed me he and Sis were meeting at the mortuary at 9am to make final arrangements. I was welcome to come.

I shocked him when I told him I didn't think I'd go. He stared at me in disbelief.

Why? he wondered, would I simply acquiesce and stay out of it? He knew it was unlike me. But I avoid drama, and Sis was all about that. Him too now.

I wanted no part of it and *they hadn't needed me so far!* Hello?

David knew I had little time for petty people, thus I saw little of Sis. As in 'never'.

So .he was stuck with her! A fitting union, I thought to myself. He and the girlfriend left.

Later on, the phone rang and it was Sis wanting to know if I was joining them at the funeral home to make arrangements. I told her, 'No'.

I asked God for grace - and strength to forgive them.

As soon as David and pal went out the door, l found my copy of the will and called the name of the attorney at the top of the letterhead. I wanted to talk directly to him, but I had to call him back for he was in a meeting.

I explained the matter to him as best I could. He explained that Mom had secured a codicil from him, which implied to him she planned to change her will. But she'd never given him a copy of it. That wasn't necessary, just as long as heirs had an original copy of the will and amended codicil too.

Well, that explained a lot! While David was the personal representative, the attorney said he wouldn't represent David in filing for probate without the *original document.*

He didn't.

It occurred to me that, if there was a codicil then it was either destroyed or was inside that hip-high steel safe! And I reasoned that Mom was so hurt over losing the friendship of his second wife, perhaps she'd decided to include her in the will. Had she added *me* as well? I didn't think so!

Eventually, I played the messages on Mom's answering machine. It revealed Sis's frantic call to David, requesting he bring over the 'forms' Mom signed right away.

No wonder Mom wanted to die. Sis was there to the end! I wish I didn't have to tell the story this way-but *it is what it is.*

My morning devotions had been on Abraham and Lot. Lot selfishly insisted on the most fertile region in their division of land due to livestock overcrowding. Abraham LET him yet, *it was Abraham that God blessed!*

I decided after reading that, to defer to others.

Time would reveal that *my* inheritance came from God! **I'd asked for *nations*.**

(Note: I didn't do everything right here. Fresh out of the world, I'd picked up careless attitudes. Yet God knew I'd been cast into spiritual warfare here, I was unprepared, and I was emotionally fragile at that time as well. (Though God loves both Sis and David, they were my adversaries here. And since I belong to Him *He takes care of his own!)*

Friends of Mom began to arrive, bringing in wonderful food and flowers. I'd met two of them the previous month, when we'd played cards. All were very kind to me now, obviously moved by Mom's death. Mom possessed a marvelous circle of close friends.

At least she had been a *good friend...!*

Several of them shared with me their futile attempts to see Mom in the hospital before she died. They went there only to be met in the hall by Sis, who'd said only family could visit her. Effie later said that wasn't so. Mom was in Progressive Care, not ICU, Intensive Care.

No wonder Mom wanted out of there! In the end, she, her friends too, were deprived of even a 'goodbye'.

David looked weary when he returned, but went out after changing clothes.

A death in the family only mildly affected social plans.

Before leaving, he made a point of warning me about Krista being in the house with so many guns.

What David failed to realize because he was young at the time, was that I'd survived city streets as a youth (fleeing his father!) by learning the *art of intimidation.*

And I certainly recognized it when others tried to use it on *me!*

I assured him it wasn't a problem. Krista had already been to gun school and knew to respect guns. (True). Rhonda and I both had guns - she drove late at night, and I renovated homes in a drug area where crack houses existed.

More, her friend Paul who came with her was a *state trooper! Only God could have set up that scenario!*

Not surprisingly, David informed me later they would be staying with friends since the house was so 'crowded'. (Too many guns in the house - *outside* of his safe..? Actually, only Paul had one with him.)

The funeral was set for Wednesday. Mom's siblings planned to travel there only for the day. I was relieved. I too didn't want to entertain.

Mom and Sally were the only family I ever saw as an adult anyway.

I was having enough trouble with the *familiar* family...

Food and flowers continued to arrive. Senders knew Mom loved flowers. I picked a bouquet from the yard - the prettiest one of all - and put it on the breakfast bar where she always sat. The house had such wonderful smells of food and flowers.

Mom would have loved it!

By Tuesday, I'd decided to hire an attorney myself. I wanted to find the original will, though I felt it was probably destroyed. I called Mamie's husband, who agreed to take the case. He said he'd probated Mamie's will and knew the judge. After I hung up, I thought about that last statement *a conflict of interest*? He must have realized it too, for he never even returned my calls in coming weeks.

He was also involved in an out of state romance then, so that probably contributed to the matter.

By this time, I couldn't help but be bitter at Mom. I would repent and forgive her, only for it to resurface again and again. I remembered Corrie who couldn't forgive the guard who played a big role in Betsie's death. I now felt Mom had lived her entire life any old way she'd wanted to, with no regard for anyone or anything, just seeking only her own selfishness.

Then at the last moment, *God swooped in, taking her to heaven,* which is where *I* wanted to BE. And *I was left to clean up her mess.* I felt bound there by her 'things' and personal effects until I could dispose of them.

Of course, ***I wouldn't have it another way!*** But it wasn't easy to accept while I sorted through three different sizes of men's clothes hanging in her closet!

It would be a while before I realized the real truth about this whole painful matter. It was about that equation. Turns out it was simpler than it seemed.

David got everything. I got nothing.

Yet the sheer unadulterated truth is - I won, because ***Mom got heaven after all!*** *That* inheritance is eternal, not temporal money or material things, and I will be with her again someday, soon.

"God offers life, but not an improved old life.
The life He offers is life out of death.
It stands always on the far side of the cross.
Whoever would possess it must pass under the rod.
He must repudiate himself and concur in
God's just sentence against him.
What does this mean to the individual?....
How can this theology be translated into life?
Simply, he must repent and believe.
He must forsake his sins and then go on to forsake himself.
Let him cover nothing, defend nothing, excuse nothing.
The cross that ended the earthly life of
Jesus now puts an end to the sinner;
and the power that raised Christ from the dead
now raises him to a new life along with Christ."
A. W. Tozer

"The idea that God will pardon a rebel who
has not given up his rebellion is contrary both
to the Scriptures and to common sense."
A.W. Tozer,

28

A Blundered Blonde

This particular chapter birthed within me the following poem:

Timely Matters

An Owner's Manual with my stove;
There's also one on cars I drove.
Things so trite just so much chatter.
I want one - *on things that matter!*

Babies, business, and burying my mother,
What school prepares for one or other?
Don't tell me this is the way of life;
How come mine - has so much strife?

Is there not some other way?
A means to guide us day by day?
Yes, a method comes to mind!
God the Father gives us *time.*

Time reveals the proof of things.
It shows us friends-some have wings.

This I've learned, time is my friend,
I wait for it - when trials descend.

Better things come, but you'll see
A green-eyed monster time can be.
It robs us of another year.
Before we ever hold it *dear.*

Yet time proves the truth of things.
Cherish the moment else it take wings!
And should we fall on bended knee?
That's where we find our Warranty.

Some of the men's clothes in the front closet were Dad's - (which is what I called him until his death.) I gave them to him when he came over. I hadn't ever told him of my discovery of Mom's secret though I'd been tempted to on my trip to Mom's that August. That was because he'd expressed to me such guilt about his drinking that had caused him to lose Mom. Twice.

He was correct about his behavior.

But it was different now. I'd honored Mom as long as she'd lived -that was long enough. I didn't want Dad excessively grieving, given her deception of him also.

I told him what I knew. He sat in her kitchen before me leaning forward in his chair, as he often did. I watched his stunned face, his mind reeling back fifty years, trying to recall.

Like me, it made no sense to him. But facts are facts.

David and Sis had set time for friends to call at the mortuary from 2pm until 9pm that day. An open casket affair – too country for me – not *my* call.

That was *too long* in my mind. I said I'd go later.

Dad said he'd come back and ride with me. I knew he felt out of place, particularly since he'd remarried. He and Mom were divorced 13 years then.

I walked into the huge room lined with chairs, large enough to hold several hundred people. When my eyes fell on the casket at front, my heart leaped into my throat. I saw Sis, busy arranging flowers to the side. There were a lot of them. Mom would have liked that.

David and a group of people I learned were from his work stood at the rear of the room. They stared as we came in. His girlfriend wore a maternity top, though she wasn't showing. I supposed it was an attempt at trying to 'fit in' since they weren't married. My mind ignored this peculiar scene, given two previous divorces over the pregnancy issue. I only hoped Karen, his second wife, hadn't seen them if she'd come.

She had.

Dad had already walked to the front and was standing before the casket.

I walked to where he stood and placed my arm around his waist. He too put his arm around my shoulder. Dad and I had never truly *bonded*. In that moment, we did.

Both victims of the one we loved.

He didn't stay long, yet returned later with his wife Jenny, and several of his children, all grown. They'd known Mom through the years, working with Dad, and others knew her during their marriage. They all left soon.

The evening wore on as people came and went. Effie seemed to stay near me, but many of Mom's friends were also her friends since she and Mom worked together at AT&T. She sat with them in the rear, her eyes following me. I felt bolstered by her emotional support.

David's bunch left not long after I arrived.

I'd acknowledged Sis when I came in, and then quickly moved to join Mom's friends.

This was my first real encounter with Sis since Sally died seven years prior. I'd seen her briefly in August when I'd visited her daughter, and she came by (barged in, Mom's words). Mom had shuddered when she'd seen her through the window, in the front yard.

I was amazed...

I couldn't believe the number of people who knew Mom, and came to pay their respects.

I have no idea how many there were. Hundreds perhaps. Most waited to speak with me, each wanting to say something about her.

A pretty blonde woman about my age waited to speak with me as I spoke with several others.

It was late. Finally, she approached me, extending her hand in sympathy to me on my loss of Mom.

Hours of being in the same room where Mom lay in an open casket was exceedingly hard for me, each glance painful. A traumatic relationship with a traumatic end.

I loved her. I hated her. I missed her. All at once.

The blonde still had her hand in mine, when she said "I just wanted to tell you how much I appreciated your Mom. She was like a mother to me."

I must have looked like an alien from another planet when I said, "That's funny. She never was to *me*", the sting of Mom's rejection in those words.

I watched as horror filled her face. Slowly, she slipped her hand and backed away, excusing herself as graciously as possible.

I immediately saw what I'd done.

She too was grieved, seeking comfort! This was one of the worst blunders I have ever made. I can't tell you how much I've prayed for that poor woman!

How I've wished I could take those words back! I can only pray that God takes that moment and turns it into good in her life as only He can do.

He is good, even when we are faithless. And couthless too.

The next day, *it's a good thing Mom was dead for her funeral!* We didn't agree on much, but we agreed on **boring**.

Rhonda and I timed it that we would arrive right on time for the funeral. Sis fussed at us that we were late and had made everyone wait - we arrived ten minutes *before* the funeral started.

She had everything all arranged, saving our family seats on the front row where chairs were placed in an alcove, separate from others.

Some honor, I thought. Too little, too late. David and galpal sat behind us.

Solos were sang in falsetto. Mom *hated* that. I did more. Can't help if that offends those who sang - *it would be true anyway!* And this is *my* story!

Effie's pastor spoke, who led Mom to Christ. I was interested in hearing him, but what he said was too predictable - expected.

If unbelievers were there, it was about as effective as a leg cramp.

Sis did the eulogy, mostly historical childhood memories. I *did* find that amusing, some of it funny.

Rhonda heaved uncontrollably next to me. I wept silently.

I wanted to run out of that alcove and sit in the main room with Mom's friends - the ones who really knew and loved her.

And with Dad. He sat alone.

A large number of cars streamed to the cemetery. As the procession pulled up to the tent, Effie and I in separate cars, we both realized immediately that we were pulling up to the wrong grave site, about 400 feet from where Mom had purchased a grave. They'd tried to sell her that site the day she went there.

She'd refused -too near the road; no trees; not close to Max.

All I could see in that moment was my mother's face that day, sitting in the back seat of Marion's car, broken and weeping. It infuriated me that a cemetery would callously take advantage of a family's sorrow, probably hoping we'd just acquiesce.

Not this time.

We had a ceremony under the tent. Then Effie and I went to deal with the office.

Someone else had bought her plot before she did, a 'clerical' error. They buried her near Max though, at the edge of a grassy walkway as close to the one she purchased as possible and under a shade tree.

I noted that another grave was also in that walkway. Hmmm. *Must be their routine*, I thought.

Only Rhonda, me and Krista remained behind for two to three hours to see her new grave dug with a backhoe, and the casket moved to that location.

That was pure torture.

Symbolically for all the others, Mom's friend also stood with us there at dusk in that cold, lonely place.

That was the only time I or Effie took a stand on any issue during Mom's death.

That evening, I had dinner with Mom's best friend. Rhonda was at Mom's when David came home, telling her we had to be out of the house immediately! We stayed three more days. Had I known then that the house was already his, signed over in July that year, I wouldn't have done that. Or, maybe I *would....*

The next day, Rhonda and Krista went horseback riding at her Dad's. Krista fell off and broke her collarbone. Then, Paul had to return to Florida immediately due to Hurricane Andrew hitting the southern part of the state. It was at that time I decided to rent a small van to take back items I wanted of Mom's. That would allow Rhonda and Krista a way home. If I left that house, *nothing at all would be left when I returned.*

Mom's youngest sister, Mary Lou, called me late that night, the same sister I'd stayed with as a high school senior, and whose husband gave me away at my wedding. Her boys, all grown, were there with her, all so handsome and dignified.

I was so proud of them that day, and glad to see them!

On the telephone, Mary Lou was certain the cemetery had come to remove Mom's body and put it where they wanted it! Was I *positive* Mom was really in the casket?

She was drinking.

Did she want me to go check?

David had actually thought I would take the car in exchange for household goods, the only things that were mine. Mom's car was older, so that would have cost me a lot of money if I had.

I placed an ad in the newspaper for a garage sale to sell the things I couldn't take home.

Strangely, Larry and his wife Melinda, came over and helped us load the van. It would've been impossible to have the sale the next day without sorting through things first. It took us until 4am to do so. What they did touched me!

I couldn't have done the sale without their help.

After only three hours of sleep, Mom's friends arrived at 7am like an army in seige to aid me with the sale. They were all so wonderful! I never got a chance to adequately thank them for all their help. They found missing items hidden under things throughout the house.

I sold them.

I sold everything except what was in David's room and his garage where his tools were, and the aquarium in the living room that contained his pet, *a black widow spider.*

Back at home in Florida, I'd missed a lot of school by now, with my August visit and now the funeral. I struggled. As an A+ English literature student, I struggled with math. I could get the answers but professors insisted I must also do the formulas too. My mind just wasn't into learning math right then, or anything else.

I didn't really feel God was calling me to be a Master of Education. I soon dropped out.

My phone calls to Mamie's husband - my attorney - went unreturned. Finally, after many months, a letter arrived. It was hand-delivered by a neighbor, dated two months earlier. I'd kept the same post office box 17 years since moving to Florida, yet this letter came to an address that only one person had. Sis's daughter.

Hmmm. *How* would my attorney ever get that address anyway? I still don't know why I ever gave her that address, when I used a P.O. Box, but it did seem to leave a telltale trail of villainry.

And it demonstrated a "link" of my attorney (Mamie's husband and former dear friend I might add) to Sis and company! They didn't even know him, or him who they were, so it would've had to be HIM who made that contact!

So when I called him, upset, it explained the following conversation.

This time, he called back. He thought I'd dropped the case since he hadn't *heard from* **me** (?) And *he'd been sorely disappointed in me for destroying Mom's house!*

Excuse me?. What was he talking about?

I soon learned this was the picture (literally) that David painted for Sis, even having her husband drive over to take photographs of the damage I'd done. (To be a *witness*?) All Mom's roses were "stolen." (Now I did consider taking one home but didn't have room on the van. However, I'm certain a nearby dumpster would have cleared up that matter).

Holes were made in the walls. David had told me in August he was blending bedrooms and knocking out a kitchen wall to open it with the living room. *Even the carpet was stolen!* Like I'm going to haul used carpet to Florida! David did also tell me he was going to change that carpet. I wondered, *Did insurance paid for damage...?*

It took me years to finally piece together what happened here. After loading the van until 4am the night before, getting up at 7am for the sale and working all day, I was exhausted by

5pm that day. I wanted to get on the road and find a hotel to lie down and rest! So I paid Dad and his wife Jenny to clean Mom's house.

My mistake was that I hadn't thoroughly finished Mom's bedroom throughout the

sale, and Dad bought her bedroom suite, still in there when we left. Dad also knew something about Mom I'd forgotten. She was known to pull up a corner of a carpet and hide cash under there, sometimes $1500 to several thousands of dollars.

This was a huge mistake on my part! I underestimated the skullduggery of this man and his wife.

Dad didn't like David, and never did. He thought he was a little snit. More, for some odd reason he said he expected that Mom should have *left him something in the will!*

Right. He did buy most of her furniture that day.

But I was stunned when Dad told me that! (Well, maybe she did in the *real* will!) Added to this, he didn't like David's treatment of me in this matter. So when I left him in the house to his and Jenny's own devices, was it *they* who stripped the house, looking for money?

Remember Dad was always out for an easy buck, which is what got him sent to prison. If it was they who ripped up the carpet, did David just take advantage of that situation? - adding holes in the wall and ridding the yard of her hated roses?

I'm surprised he waited a while to saw down all of her trees, creating a desert out of her beautiful yard!

Because David knew I loved Mom's roses, he could easily blame me, a win-win situation for him. He probably still laughs about it!

Mom asked me to pray for him before she died. I often start with asking forgiveness for him for this scenario. It took Corrie years to forgive all...

The final point is hilarious because *the devil always overplays his hand.* Sis told the entire family about all the evil I'd done, and told them I was in jail in Florida!

Hearing this, I immediately remembered Revelation 21:8 that says ***all*** *liars will be thrown into hell.* I can only report what the holy scriptures say about this matter...

Sis is now deceased. I've asked God to forgive her and save her, because these aren't the actions of someone who knows and loves God.

Jesus did tell us we would 'know' people by their 'fruit'... what they leave behind them.

I simply leave this matter to God's mercy. He is good! That verse? *All liars. Not some. Not part. Not half.*

"Almost a Christian is not a Christian!" Ray Comfort

Having lost confidence in Mamie's husband altogether after weeks and months, I knew that hiring an attorney across state lines is difficult, near impossible in such matters.

I didn't feel I could deal with this matter any further.

I felt sick.

Reluctantly for Rhonda and Craig's sake, I decided to forfeit it all to David!

I would put my confidence in God! I could trust *His* faithfulness over people anytime, and also trust Him to bless my children who were robbed. By Mom? By David? By Dad?

It just didn't matter anymore.

But I was truly glad my dear friend - and comrade - Mamie was gone when Mom died. In my mind, her husband was a scoundrel, (to me anyway) and I found it unbelievable he believed strangers over me .... his former neighbor and friend.

I knew exactly how King David felt, when he so often spoke in the Psalms of being betrayed by bosom friends!

Mamie's husband had also been involved with Larry and Elaine's husband Ted on opening that successful FGBMFI chapter. He served a short time.

I have no real proof of any of the things in this chapter. I have only *surmised* what appears to be the answer to the puzzling questions surrounding Mom's death.

In June, eight months later, Rhonda drove me to the ER doubled over in excruciating pain. This ordeal had truly made me sick! I had to have surgery; a hysterectomy due to an impacted ovary that convinced my doctor that it was cancer.

He ran four biopsies. All were benign. Then he said the same thing about a breast mammogram.

Another biopsy showed it too was negative.

It was nothing as God had assured me then. Thank YOU, Lord.

Perhaps you are like Mom, uncertain about your own salvation. It's important to note that you aren't saved because you *feel* like it! You're saved because God's Word is *True!*

And for what Jesus did for you that day at Golgotha, on the cross! God cannot lie, and if you have believed in your **heart** and confessed with your **mouth** the Lord Jesus, 'you shall be saved.' Romans 10:9.

Jesus was the 'stand-in' for the penalty of your sins, accepting your penalty so you wouldn't have to. It is by faith, *plus nothing,* that we are saved. No amount of good works or your performance can ever earn you more of God's favor than you already have, because it already belongs to you! Just thank Him.

It is *Jesus plus nothing!*

Salvation is a two-sided coin. The day we say Yes to God, is the day we say 'No' to sin.

Let Him take care of those sinful desires, because it's His job to clean you up.

You can rely on I John 1:9 until then.

I have never been hurt by anything I didn't say.
Calvin Coolidge

29

Miracles From Mayhem

In the mid seventies, when the children were about ten years old, our family drove the five hour return trip to Indiana after visiting Grandma Sally. We'd waited until Sunday evening to drive back, and driving through a town in northern Kentucky, we noticed a Sunday night church service with lots of cars parked outside. On an impulse, we decided to stop and go in.

The service already in progress, we scooted into the first back row that was empty. I slid all the way over next to the wall. I was at the farthest point in the building from where the pastor stood.

When the sermon was over, I considered nudging Larry to see if he thought we ought to get back on the road again when I realized every eye in the place was on *me*. The pastor too was looking at me, making it clear he was addressing me. *The lady who came in late sitting against the wall.*

Surprised, I motioned "Me?" He nodded, "Yes."

"Mam," he began, "I don't know who you are, but ever since you came in, I've seen something supernatural around you. I see questions coming out of the top of your head as far as the eye can see - just endless question marks. I don't know what they mean, but he Lord wants me to tell you ***Answers are on their way."***

I don't recall his name, if I ever knew it, nor that of his church, a small Assembly of God in central Kentucky. Lawrenceburg, I believe.

Ironically, many of the greatest questions in my life hadn't even been asked yet! My marriage seemed good, my children happy, my home in tact, and life seemed good for me *for the first time ever.*

I had what I always wanted. A *home* of my own; some place to *belong*; and *people* to love. But after all, the question marks he saw were endless.

We often talked on the phone but it had been several months since Anita and I had gotten together. We bumped into one another at the printer we both used.

Sitting across from her at lunch, I marveled at how youthful and pretty she still looked. So trim, well-dressed, and *always smiling.* Being a psychiatric nurse who made home health calls, I imagined her patients eagerly anticipating her visits, just for her smile!

Anita and I were old friends. I first met her at Arthelene's church when I came to Florida. She'd just moved to the area too and like myself, was newly divorced I ordered a turkey pita sandwich. Anita ordered a Greek salad. The waitress disappeared.

I looked across the table intently at Anita. Without telling her why, I asked her to describe to me, *not in medical terms,* but the behavior of a patient diagnosed as manic- depressive/ bi-polar. I wrote it down, so she spoke slowly and decisively.

"Well" she began "They go in cycles that include depression but then swing to a euphoric state that is usually acted out in spending money or sexual promiscuity."

"They frequently don't have time for daily living such as eating, sleeping, or housekeeping. Their homes are piled with many 'projects' begun, but rarely completed.

"Their opinion of themselves is often grandiose, and they become greatly perturbed with being confronted.

"They suffer from impaired judgment and have little insight into what is going on with themselves. They will deny their behavior is unacceptable by normal people."

"They also have impaired sleep patterns and don't sleep. They're superb manipulators."

Her words were too familiar, confirming my gut feeling.

Our conversation didn't end there. Anita said new medications can allow patients to live completely normal lives provided they take those medications, another problem for them. I was to learn a lot more about this.

On the up side, bi-polar disorder is associated with creative genius. Therefore it's called the 'fine madness.' That's because gifted individuals are more plagued with the illness than normal folks. That doesn't mean that people who are bi-polar are particularly gifted though. But Hollywood is full of those individuals, along with poets, composers, artists, writers and celebrities. Ernest Hemingway is a prime example.

For more information on this diagnosis, check out Dr. Kay Redfield Jamison's book, *Touched With Fire.* She is a highly functioning Bi-Polar. Her book is excellent.

The down side is, along with the Jews and homosexuals, bi-polars were herded into ovens by the Nazi's.

Defective genes, they said.

I learned bi-polars are not considered dangerous to others, though they can be to themselves through suicide. (I've read some recent accounts that contradict that however. It could be those were not correctly diagnosed because bi-polars can also be schizophrenic).

Many suicides after the fact, are considered bi-polar disorder conditions that went undiagnosed.

I had two brushes with this illness neighbors, both times when I lived alone, my children grown. One was an apartment building where I lived, and another was a woman who lived across the way from me. The former had to be physically removed from her apartment after threatening a neighbor with a shotgun at 3am when the neighbor asked her to please turn her TV down.

The latter was a much longer duration when a neighbor became somehow fixated upon me, because she knew I prayed to God.

And that God answered.

My first realization of the latter's condition was when I was en route on a long trip to my son's from Florida. She called me on the road, when I was somewhere in Georgia and told me she was driving to Denver because the FBI had come and searched her home and bugged it with hidden microphones.

She was afraid to stay there, she said.

I asked her what was in Denver? She didn't seem to have a real plan there. She just wanted me to pray God would keep her safe from the FBI, her worst adversaries. I asked her 'why' they would be after her? She said they'd been after her for years, but had just found her again. She called me again a couple of times on the trip, to pray.

This neighbor had seemed fine to me over several months of association. Now she seemed mentally ill. I realized the problem - she was off her meds!

When I came home, after some weeks, she too had just arrived back and was unloading her car. I watched her through the window carry a rifle wrapped inside a small blanket into the house.

I began to feel a little crazy myself about then! A couple of neighbors I confided to did consider me the crazy one!

Fortunately, another neighbor had seen the gun before. He reported it.

Aware of her fixation on me I didn't know what to do. *What would Jesus do?*

Really? I withdrew from her which created more problems. She came to my door one night. Reluctantly, I let her in. But I wasn't as warm to her as I'd been before my trip - she knew something had changed.

But I didn't know how I was supposed to act with this woman. After that, I became part of the enemy to her, certain I was reporting to the FBI on her comings and goings. The week following, I learned she was being evicted. I couldn't wait.

In the meantime, I kept the light off at night *so she couldn't see where to shoot*! I lived in the back of the house at night until she was evicted.

If you don't think there isn't a troubled world out there, Dear Friend, your world is far too small! Mental illness is real but it isn't always evident.

Unless they're off their meds! You can learn however, to look for the telltale signs. This woman seemed normal to me before.

This is one major reason why we should permit God to ***send us our friends***. He knows best who they should be. Because when you're in the middle of something like this, it's extremely difficult to extract yourself!

Just ask me! Knowing how to walk in the love of God isn't always easy!

I've seen Christians dragged into the problems of such people in Bible Studies or other things. They become beset on ministering to this hurting person. Meanwhile, the devil wins (usually). Why? Most of us are not equipped or discerning enough to see how the devil uses people like this to offset God's real purpose in small groups, meant to study the scriptures! **Others do** have the training; so let *them* handle these folks!

This chapter is where I write about my daughter Rhonda. But I'm going to tell you the end from the beginning, leaving out the critical mass in the middle.

It's not my story to tell. She will tell it herself one day, perhaps.

She already does that in living a transparent witness to youth and any who listen. She warns them against poor choices that have a high price to pay.

She wishes to save others her pain.

One night, Rhonda called me on the telephone here in Florida. It was with hushed breath.

She'd told me some weeks before that she was going to upgrade her taste in men. I wanted to say, *"Who is this and what have you done with my daughter?"*

But I do remember her saying something like she wanted a yuppie who is a Christian and who owned a Harley Davidson motorcycle. (She loves motorcycles). But that's not what she remembers, which is why she must tell her own story.

In hushed tones, Rhonda told me "Mom, I think I've met him." I knew exactly what she was talking about when she said it. She went on to describe him, and how they talked for hours, that like her, he also collected barns on his living room wall, that he was a Christian and had a Harley!

Something unusual had happened, for sure.

She told me, "Mom, and guess what else?" I hadn't the faintest clue. She said, "His last name is *Williams.*"

Something jerked me to attention. **That was my maiden name.** Was this God telling me this was the man I'd prayed for over fifteen years prior? The *right* man for her.

A good man and a *believer.*

They've now been married for years. During that time, both Randy and Rhonda have served on youth ministries at church and in a youth group that's a part of the Emmaeus Walk. Groups meet over holiday weekends throughout the year to experience the Lord and His great love for them. They are perfect for this ministry. Rhonda pulls no punches and speaks to them the hard truth in a world - and church - that avoids it.

Rhonda's story is a many year odyssey, one that taught me many things how to pray how not to give up hope in the face of hopelessness, how to march into the devil's camp and take back what he'd stolen from me! That there's a time to pray and a time to 'say', calling those things that be not as though they are, praying scripture over loved ones - often in the midnight hour!

But in the middle of that odyssey, I learned something about *me.* (By the way, we owned a white Persian cat during this time over 17 years whose name was Odyssey!)

I learned my entire approach to this wayward child (adult though) was *wrong!* I only saw her as my daughter. I'd taught her better, *so she knew better I felt.*

Then one day I realized Rhonda was a fellow struggler on life's highway, doing the best she could to find her way in life. She needed *mercy.*

The best part of what I learned occurred once when I visited her in cold, wintry Indiana at Christmastime. She took her two dogs, a black lab mix and a smaller brindle dog outdoors to get exercise. She used a long stick on which she attached a rope and at the end was an empty milk jug. She stood and turned in a circle as the dogs chased the jug, barking and leaping for it.

I stood washing dishes at the kitchen sink, watching her through the window. She had on a pretty, long black leather coat she'd found at a yard sale, and a baseball cap where her long hair was pulled through the hole in back. As she turned and played with her beloved dogs, it struck me how very wonderful she was, and that there was really no one else like her. Wholly unique. I fell in holy love with my daughter that day and gave up the idea of ever changing a hair on her head evermore!

The third thing I learned, was not to look **at** her, but to look **in** her and call forth *that which was made in the image* *of God!* Always before, I might tell her "That's a pretty skirt." Or something else trivial.

But I changed my language altogether with her.

Again while there, I heard her talking on the phone to a friend. I was taken with her wisdom in that call. So when I later saw her sitting and putting on her make-up, as I walked by her, I leaned down and kissed her cheek and said, "*Honey, I'm so proud of you.*" How long had it been since I'd said anything with any substance like that?

Far too long was the answer!

The bottomline is, God wanted to answer my prayers for her but **He'd waited on me to finally "get it."** He had to teach this old dog some new tricks!

Funny thing was, when I changed? *It was amazing how quickly she changed too!*

So if your loved ones or offspring are out doing God knows what, with God knows whom, and doing everything a parent would not want them to do - then *run* to your Bible. Read it.

Then when you go to bed at night place it in the middle of the floor, open. If you wake up burdened for them at night, then get up and pace your floor praying scripture, calling out their names before God, speaking what the Word says.

Tell that devil that he's a liar and his designs over them are wholly defeated!

Stop and stand on that Bible and tell God you are **standing on His Word alone**, that the seed of the righteous shall be delivered! Prov 11:21. He said so! That you aren't looking at circumstances, or anything else. That no weapon formed against your children will prosper.

Isaiah 54:17, 18.

Don't worry about talking to the devil! Jesus talked to him too and to fig trees, fevers and storms! Don't be *timid.* You have *authority* according to Luke 10:19, "Behold, I have given you **authority** over ALL the ***power*** of the enemy and nothing shall by any means harm you." Then, after you've prayed this, hold on *until the answer comes!*

Reject every evil circumstance as a lie of the devil! The end result is:

Miracles. Yes! Seize the horns of the altar of mercy and don't let go. God doesn't hear all prayers. You need to know that - so you'll have to get your sin under the blood-stained cross before you approach a holy God with your petitions. See Isaiah 59:2. John tells us in I John 3 that if we 'keep His commandments and do what pleases Him, we can ask what we will and He will answer." **So don't think you can move God** if you're living in sin and selfishness. *It won't happen.* Expect His mercy—but you must ask!.

Miracles are our inheritance. Yes. Rhonda is now a strong believer who, I believe, that if I died today would take up my mantle. She is wonderful to me and to others!

Miracles belong to you too - they're your heritage (see Is. 54:17-19), your inheritance just like mine. So raise your expectation level! I'm not special. I'm a believer just like you!

Changed lives are the result of the true gospel. *I am one.* Rhonda is another. If you don't see any at your church, the true gospel *of the Kingdom* isn't being preached there!

Apostle Paul said, "I am all things to all people that by all means I may save some." You can't save everyone. Even Jesus didn't. Nor Paul. But you win the ones you can 'some'.

Learn to go with the flow of the Holy Spirit according to Romans 8!

Here's what's important: I was ill-equipped to save the neighbor fixated on me. I just had to leave her to God and pray for someone else down the road who was equipped to help her. It wasn't that I didn't care - I lacked the skills to deal with the enormity of her problems! Someone better suited could better help her.

And I trust they did.

If you pitch a tent camp where people won't believe and spin your wheels on trying to save people who aren't ready, then people whom you **can help** go unaided.

Learn to listen to the Holy Spirit in this matter!

God knows. Pray for them. Leave it to Him. *And go on.*

One more thing. There were many times in this many year odyssey concerning Rhonda when I felt things were utterly hopeless. I went through weeks of deep depression to make me realize this one thing - depression was what ***Rhonda walked in constantly then*** *and I had no compassion for her!*

After that, I felt our relationship was so damaged as to be beyond repair. But God!

God *wants* to encourage us and He sometimes uses strange things to do that... He can use anything. (I have little time for narrow folks who think otherwise).

I knew Rhonda liked Fleetwood Mac, so I bought her a CD, and one for me too. I didn't realize how much this was a God thing, due to this particular song. It brought me a great sense of direction and tremendous healing as well, over the months that followed.

And hope for the future! *A secular song.* ***Yes, God...!*** He is greater than we think.

I played this song over and over every day. I would forget the past, press on to the future - looking straight ahead! It is, in part, "Don't Stop."

Don't stop - thinking about tomorrow. Don't stop - it'll soon be here.

It'll be here, better than before. Yesterday's gone. Yesterday's gone.

Why do we think about trials to come?
What might go wrong; things that you've done?
Give your life what you've had to do.
Or, just think what tomorrow will do!

All I want is to see you smile.
If it takes a just a little while.
I know you don't believe that it's true.
I never meant any harm to you.

Don't stop - thinking about tomorrow
Don't stop - It'll soon be here.
It'll be better than before.
Yesterday's gone. Yesterday's gone.
Ooooh . *Don't you look back.*
Ooooh. *Don't you look back.*

"You will understand of course, that Jesus is
not going to wait until everyone is ready.
He is coming and there will be a time when
everyone will bow down before Him,
both those who are ready and those who aren't.
Corrie ten Boom

Two percent of people think; three percent think they think;
95 percent would rather die *before being forced to think.*
Henry Ford

PART V

The Foreboding

Your mind is a garden.
Your thoughts are the seeds. You can grow
flowers, or You can grow weeds.

*"I was not afraid. Following Betsie's death,
God's Presence was even more real.
Even though I was looking into the valley
of the shadow of death, I was not afraid. It
is here that Jesus comes the closest."*
Corrie ten Boom

30

Nature's Cathedral

In revising this book, I decided I didn't want a 'finale' of sorts for my readers. Or a jumping off place. Instead, I want to charge people's minds and hearts with *a new beginning!* To motivate them by inspiring them to realize their own value in the Kingdom's economy, in our culture, and in their own arena of life. *I know just how to do that!*

Is there a single ingredient that could positively impact you, or our negative world? ***Yes! Information.*** No weapon is so powerful as 'information'. More wars have been won or lost in the heat of battle and at the last moment, by a key piece of information than by anything else. Even new weaponry springs from an *idea,* which is information converted. Ideas change the world, i.e. the Model T, the steam locomotive, electricity, the light bulb, satellites, cell phones, Hubble satellite, iPads, eBooks, the space shuttle, computers, social media, etc.

These all started as *someone's* ***idea!*** Someone's *dreams....*

"Dreams are not stupid or impossible to you. Everything can and will change. Dreams give us life, inspiration and motivate us and drive us to the unimaginable. Dreams make us break rules, batter obstructions down, generate paradigms and encourage people. Our will becomes unstoppable. And

the greater it becomes the more we can change the world. For those who desire the most in life, for those who have less for you, for everyone, go out and make your dreams come true. Your wildest dreams are closer than you think!" Facebook. Posted on 3/11/14 by **posibl.**

In these final chapters, I wish to share with you, people who have changed my life, and *my thinking* and pressed me on to dream dreams, in spite of a recent open-heart surgery. They are not the conventional people that others might profile, however. But you too will be amazed at each chapter because each will reveal something you may never have thought about or heard before. I promise.

I hope these things will cause you to rise up, become ignited and excited. To realize you were an *idea* in God's own mind before you were created! And no one, positively no one, can fulfill your mission on earth *except you.*

In the distance, I could hear the bell of the trolley that carried visitors to the pier that ran parallel with the marina I now lived in. The pier was the local tourist attraction in downtown St. Petersburg, Florida.

I had been gone for weeks, working a hotel, and I'd longed to sit once again on the deck of my boat, overlooking the basin where some 600 boats were harbored. It is one of the most beautiful marinas in the entire world. A safe harbor.

Many of those boats were homes to my neighbors. About 160 owners actually resided on them, as I did. Others came simply to while away weekends on their boats, or special events. It was like a small community, people friendly, lovers as we all were of marine life.

It was all new to me because a friend had told me of this houseboat being for sale. I'd marveled at this boat before but never dreamed it would come up for sale! Speaking of 'dreams', the 36' houseboat was a former Disney boat that was used for their parades at Disney World. Originally, there were three of them, but this one was the only one left. It had two decks, fore and aft, and overlooked where members of the local yacht club and visitors from other marinas, came and docked.

Living there was a dream. After buying it, someone said, *'boats are for dreamers'* - so I felt right at home!

Suddenly, life seemed to me to be *too* wonderful. And that I was somehow *too* blessed.

The God of Wonder knows how to make us happy, if we permit Him.

After all, **His very *Name* is Wonderful** - Full. Of. Wonder.

The exterior was painted four different colors, the previous owner not knowing what to paint it, or *what he was doing?* And inside there were 12" horizontal stripes and *one was made of aluminum foil.* A mess. First, I hung a beautiful painting on the wall, and chose the interior colors from it. Boats and convex walls such as it had required pictures screwed tight to keep them secure.

I bought my paint at Home Depot, hunter green, and the man asked me what colors the floor tiles were. I said hunter green. He asked, "You making a *cave*?"

But with the white ceiling and the white chair rail I put all the way around, it turned out beautiful. White French doors to the back facing the water, and a single French door to the front.

I painted the exterior white with peach colored shutters, I ended up naming it the *U.S.S. Showboat.*

And indeed it was. People marveled as they walked by the chain-link fence or the docks, peering inside. I was told I couldn't grow flowers on saltwater. You should've seen my tall twisted ficus tree and other thriving plants on the outside decks!

So seated on my deck in paradise, as it were, living on the water and becoming accustomed to its varying moods, tides, storms, it was *the* magical and mystical time of my life. There were all kinds of activities revolving around the Pier, such as fireworks, reggae bands on Sunday evening whose rhythms bounced off the water and seemed next door.

Downtown parades passed nearby and national band competitions occurred at Al Lang Stadium across the way - I loved the drum and bugle corp competitions. Shakespeare in the Park occurred each fall at my door.

When the water was placid, the frequent fireworks reflected on the water so I saw them twice from my deck -one in the sky and one on the glasslike water.

Watching sea gulls swarm, fish jumping, manatees, and dolphins - and once a shark - were daily treats. One time even a huge alligator came through one of the drain holes right next to my houseboat - which sat under a covered slip - protected from the weather elements. Several men residents thought it cool to jump down into the water and have a photo taken of them with that alligator - after it's mouth was taped shut and ropes controlled it, of course!

Stars of the heavens dazzled at nighttime when I sat on the deck, where I had a beautiful multi-colored candle holder reflected all the way across to the other side of the marina where visitors moored overnight. Friends would tell me they saw its flickering flame from my deck.

I've always loved bling and glitz. So living here was like a front row seat to nature's bling and glitz. It was the happiest I'd ever been, or have been since. Yes, Psalm 19:1-2 says the heavens declare God's handiwork. One translation says, *it never stops speaking!*

Even though I only lived there just under two years, I count it an honor to have had that privilege.

In the center of that marina island sits a public park with access to restrooms and a very long walkway that is bordered with lush grass, picnic shelters and a children's play ground. The result is that it draws a lot of tourists, bike riders and people who love strolling the walkway at seaside, watching the sailboats enter and leave the marina to open waters.

I was in this idyllic setting one September morning in 2001, when that serenity was rudely interrupted. The television screen showed smoke billowing from the World Trade Center and as I watched, a second airplane hurled through the second tower. My own horror was magnified by millions of other Americans who saw the same scene on their televisions, at home or at work, telephone lines jammed as callers urged others to watch.

I've never known such horror, and I doubt that others who watched had either. All the more when those buildings collapsed! It was unimaginable horror we all witnessed together.

It was like an emotional shutdown - trying to realize if what was happening was really real.

It was.

Later another plane struck the Pentagon, and another crashed into a lonely field in Pennsylvania. No one, no broadcaster, no political figure, had an explanation as to what was happening that day or for days after.

Yet it wasn't rocket science. The average joe on the street guessed what it was.

Terrorism.

People were stricken for days as they watched people in New York City scrounging for any information whatsoever about their missing loved ones, flashing pictures on television screens or pinning them onto fencelines. More suffering of families of loved ones on the airplanes that crashed. For an entire week, the nation groaned in a holy, corporate shudder. Even sitcoms ceased their raucous laughter and sexual innuendos.

Churches flooded with people who hadn't been to one for decades.

Flags went up all over the nation, in every city, town and community, with signs saying - *We will not forget*

It had appeared that people were turning back to God in the hour of our need, having Billy Graham come speak in the cathedral in Washington, D.C. where every public figure attended. Talk of God everywhere.

But – Within a week, Wall Street was able to open once again. Then within ten days, the same smutty sitcoms resumed, wholly unabridged, bedhopping and barnyard behavior pumped into every living room.

Life had returned to some element of 'normal' and churches were once again, empty. America had forgotten. Already. Except for those who lost almost 3,000 loved ones.

Except for us who saw this event as *something else.* Those whose strongly held faith in a holy God saw it all through a different prism. One that said He had protected our nation from bloodshed ever occurring on American soil, from lives lost here. Men fought wars on foreign soil in World Wars, Korea and Viet Nam, but blood loss from foreign attack was always elsewhere.

Never in America. And now this horrific scene.

It meant to them, the hedge of protection that had kept America safe, was **let down for the first time ever.**

The attack that day meant other things to other people, a myriad of things. But only true believers saw it as a fearful thing that gave them cause to shudder.

Judgment.

Two items that were newsworthy got shoved off the front pages around the time of this attack. One was a story in Texas a few days prior, of where 100 militant Muslims were arrested in Texas connected with a training camp of some kind.

(Aziz went to that area twice a year).

The other was, that two days after the 9/11 attack, Hurricane Gabrielle took a dramatic right turn out of the Gulf and struck the West Coast of Florida in the middle of the night.

Forecasters had predicted it would hit the Panhandle. But she hit Central Florida.

Swiftly, like 9/11/01.

I was asleep at 3am when I heard vicious pounding on the side of the boat. It was the marina manager and a helper who wanted to tie off my boat better. I got up to help them when we realized my ropes were all nylon, which stretches. So I borrowed better ropes from a neighbor boat resident, also up. Soon we got it done to keep it from banging against the dock. The helper fell into the water that night. I saw in them a total act of valor, waves crashing over his head.

After they left, I had to clean off my decks of lawn furniture. Fortunately I had stackable wrought iron chairs and got them inside the boat. You're required to do that to keep items from blowing and doing damage to other boats. The boat rocked viciously but was safe as long as the ropes held.

I did think about being seasick once the first time.

The next day, after the tide went down, I sat on the deck of my boat at evening. Recovering from the storm, the weather had been gloriously beautiful that day, as though nature knew she'd misbehaved and wanted to make it up to us. The sun setting, city lights shimmered on the water.

The evening news told of a local Muslim claiming that someone had sprayed graffiti on his garage door. Did he think he could win sympathy *this week*, I wondered?

God loves them; and we ought to also. But they do *whine*.

The unspeakable serenity there presented the sharpest of contrasts to the 'horror even beyond our understanding' of the previous week, where thousands had died.

But weaving in and out of my memory that day had been another kind of story *another plane crash*.

For many years, it had been the world's worst air tragedy.

I read the story in a book, authored by Norman Williams, who survived that air tragedy. Perhaps no book I've ever read, outside of the Bible itself, *impacted me more deeply than this book did.* It was a tale of horror. But a tale with a different kind of ending for a man and his mother who would trust God for it!

It was the mid 70's and Norman lived in California, where he'd invited his mother to come and live after his father passed away. He was packing for a sudden trip that his boss had invited him on, a pleasure trip to the Mediterranean. Another friend was prevented from going.

Norman's mother came into his bedroom and sat down to pray a travel prayer, a family custom.

Oddly, during that prayer his mother began to sob.

Norman thought to himself, 'Mom it's only a pleasure trip.' But as they prayed, they agreed together that he would return home safely, based on Jesus' promise in Matt. 18:19 that *'whatever two believers shall agree upon, as touching anything on earth, it shall be given.'*

Flying to the Mideast, and near the end of the flight, the pilot alerted the passengers that they were being rerouted from their original plans to land at a Lebanon airport due to a terrorist bombing, common there in the 70's. So they were being rerouted to land at the airport in the Canary Islands, at Tenerife. Norman and his boss thought little of it a possible delay reaching their hotel.

When they landed on the island, they were in a long stream of passenger jets lined up to refuel. A fellow passenger commented that the mountain overlooking the airport was Devil's Mountain.

That comment made the hair stood up on the back of Norman's neck. He dismissed it.

Hours had passed when passengers heard stories about a KLM Dutch pilot creating delays in the line, and that he'd hogged a huge amount of fuel, filling up his 747 completely when others needed fuel also.

A foreboding began to nag at Norman.

Finally, their plane began progressing toward the line where jets were being permitted to take off. Soon theirs was next in line. When the pilot was finally cleared for take off, Norman breathed a sigh of relief.

The plane turned onto the runway and started to taxi when suddenly from the other end of the runway came the KLM Dutch 747 roaring into the air. There was nothing Norman's pilot could do as his plane was a 'sitting duck', unable to move out of the way. The KLM plane came at them, rearing up into the sky, but the plane was so loaded with fuel he couldn't raise the plane up enough to miss Norman's 747 on the runway. The jet's wheels tore into the fuselage of Norman's plane and fuel began pouring in from above into his cabin on the bottom.

The KLM plane veered sharply to the pilot's left and exploded on impact with the ground, killing everyone.

Norman looked around and saw small fires outside the plane and fuel dripping everywhere inside, drenching people.

Now stopped, he looked to the right where his boss had been sitting. The entire seat was missing along with the one next to it, a gaping hole in the floor.

He then looked around at passengers' frozen faces, some of them burning to death as they sat there.

The hopelessness of it all caused Norman to panic.

But suddenly his mother's prayer came to him - *that he would return safely home to her!*

He stood up in his seat and shouted "No! And shouted that scripture out loud.

Then he heard a voice that said, *"Don't panic! Keep out of the aisles. Stay in the seats and head for the hole over the wing."*

Norman looked to his right and saw a gaping hole 20 feet away, about four feet wide and eight feet tall. He feared an explosion of the leaking fuel at any second, but he stepped over the seats as fast as he could. Metal objects flew through the air at him as big or bigger than he was, but he said he felt like Moses as he deflected them with just his arms!

Once to the opening, he rushed through the hole onto the huge wing, where he saw others jumping off. He went to the end of the wing and jumped down, injuring his ankle. He saw the tower and main building of the airport some distance away and headed in that direction.

This is where the story becomes more amazing because when he arrived there, he couldn't get anyone's attention to look at his foot or anything else, *because he didn't smell like smoke!* No one there thought he'd been inside that plane!

However, as it turned out, he did have a broken ankle from jumping off the wing of the plane.

Norman did return home safely, just as he and his mother had agreed in prayer. About sixty other passengers from his plane also survived, though 604 passengers died altogether from both 747's involved in that crash.

Many months later, Norman wrote his book of survival and in doing so, detailed other surviving passengers' stories many remarkably similar to his own.

His book – Terror At Tenerife - was out of print for many years, but is now available again on Amazon. It's been decades since I read the story but I believe this account to be accurate. It's amazing impact on my faith showed me God can take care of His righteous people, no matter the circumstances. It also shows God responds to faith.

I was later to hear of equally miraculous stories of people who survived the WTC disaster on 9/11/01.

One was of a young couple expecting their first baby. He worked in one tower, she the other. But that morning, she'd been delayed getting to work. The first plane had already struck the tower where her husband worked, so she wasn't permitted to enter her tower. She waited nearby, praying for her husband who worked in the top of the building, "God, if you'll allow my husband to live, we will serve you together as missionaries from now on."

Meantime, when the second plane hit, her husband wasn't aware she didn't make it into her building. He prayed for her too while trying to make his way to an escape. He and others were trapped in a stairwell, fire and jet fuel fumes on every floor where they were. Somehow they managed to get through the smoke and fumes and make their way down to the first floor.

Just then, the building began to rumble and jerk. He told everyone to place their backs against the bank of elevators. As the building started to fall, he encouraged everyone - about 15 people - to speak the name of Jesus as the building fell. He was the only one to survive, but the others died with Jesus (His name means *salvation*) on their lips.

Today this couple are serving God together in Texas on short term mission trips and now have a second son.

What can be drawn from these stories? Many things! Here is what I gain. What others gain is up to them.

1. *That if I belong to God, choosing to love and serve him, I can know His eye is ever upon me.*
2. *That God is faithful and answers when we call.*
3. *That fear and panic shuts out reason and hope - and also the very route to safety! But tha t God responds to our faith!*
4. *That He still speaks to us in that still, small voice as He has since the days of Moses and Elijah.*
5. *That He can be trusted to be with us until our final dying breath and then we will be in Glory!*
6. *That when I am alone in a crisis and God is all I have, he is 'More Than Enough', one of His covenant names to Israel in the Old Testament.*

7. *That God doesn't help everyone, if we are to believe holy scripture. In fact, scripture says He will have the last laugh!*
   Take a look at Proverbs 1:25-32ESV.
   'Because you have **ignored** *all my counsel and would have none of my reproof,* I also will **laugh** at your calamity. *I will* **mock** *when terror strikes you like a storm and your calamity comes like a whirlwind, when distress and anguish come upon you. Then they will call upon me but I will* <u>*not*</u> *answer...vs 31 therefore they shall eat the fruit of their way, and have their fill of their own devices. For* the simple are killed by their turning away, and the complacency of fools destroys them'!
8. *My full assurance of His care for me is in that final verse. Vs. 33. 'But whoso listens to me shall dwell secure; and will be at ease without dread of disaster.'* Why? Because God is there! Disaster may come, but I don't have to live in dread of it. *God is already there.*

The Lord has given me the tongue of those who are taught, That I may know how to sustain with a word, Him who is weary. Morning by morning He awakens; He awakens my ear to hear as those who are taught. The Lord God has opened my ear, and I was not rebellious. *I hid not my face from disgrace.*
Isaiah 50:4-6

We'd better learn to Love the Truth!
If we don't, we have the promise of God
Then He will give us over to the lies we embrace!
One version says 'turn us over" to them.
This is in II Thes. 2:12

What is Truth? "Thy word is Truth." Jesus
John 17:17 -Author

31

The 'Denver Mauling'

I waited on the line, after being prepped by Ken's assistant. Ken had the highlights of my new book before him, to use as a guide in interviewing me on his Denver talk radio show.

This was my second time to be on his show.

Before the program went on air, I overheard Ken tell his assistant to put callers who disagreed with the guest up front in line.

Wow, I thought. *Ken is looking for controversy!* No doubt I could supply that!

I worked my business on the road most of the time, which allowed me to pursue what I really loved doing. That was being a national talk radio commentator on Islam and current events. I could do that from any hotel room where I worked, or home. My connection to a national publication, a magazine directed at radio and television hosts, had drawn attention to my first book *Answered By Fire*, and thus the invitations came to do interviews on talk radio about Islam and contemporary events, especially on 9/11 anniversaries.

Talk show hosts enjoyed the fact I had actual up-close experience with Islam, where many pundits then only knew of Islam *in theory*. This was immediately after the 9/11/01 disaster. Others cropped up later, however.

Ken had told me his talk show had three million listeners, not uncommon in radioland. He seemed nice. I generally held radio talk show hosts in high regard, because they were more informed than average, and politically minded like myself. A couple of them happened to be some of my favorite people. I had now been on several dozen such shows, so I was feeling somewhat like a veteran by now. I wasn't selling a lot of books due to its limited availability then, but the reviews were good.

I was aware that time constraints prevented opportunity for elaboration during interviews. Talk show guests must learn to speak in 'sound bytes', thus the format restricts elaboration.

Then once a question was asked, a commercial break often came after the answer.

I made no claims of being an 'expert', but I'd found that people who heard my interviews, often thought the opposite was true. I couldn't help what people thought, realizing such assumptions came with the territory of writing books and talk radio.

The talk show host's assistant came on the line to alert me I'd be on after commercials. I could hear them, but they had to flip a switch to hear me.

Ken opened on air with, "Sharon, welcome! I see from your material that you used to *live* with a Muslim. Tell listeners how that came about."

I described how my daughter married a Muslim with PLO ties when we'd moved to Florida. Since both he and my son attended an out of state college, my daughter had suggested we pool our resources and rent a nice home on the beach. When the guys came home for breaks, they had a nice place to enjoy. That plan had worked.

I knew Ken's next question. They all asked it.

"So, is your daughter still married to this man?" I explained the marriage lasted only three years during the mid-80's, but now my daughter lived in the north, remarried to a wonderful man.

"Well Sharon, *since you endorse 'profiling' Muslims,* and closing America's borders, you must be a pretty controversial figure." Ken inquired.

(Both topics were very hot issues then)

I was ready. I took a deep breath. "I have compassion for law-abiding Muslims, especially here in the U.S. Fact is, they enjoy our religious freedom, since their own countries are mostly tribal.

"But, Americans would be fools to ignore that all **19 hijackers on 9/11/01,** were *both Arab and Muslim,* and 15 were from a single nation, Saudi Arabia. So profiling is a petty inconvenience compared to the Japanese detention camps following Pearl Harbor.

"Besides, **Americans' 'rights' were bought with *American* blood.** Muslims don't belong to any nation other than their own, nor do they ever assimilate when they get inside nations foreign to them.

"Truth is, many are whiners who've come to sack our country, then complain of being denied their rights! I've seen this happen, because they love our technology and our education - but want no part of who we are!

"Multiculturalism and diversity both have cost us - and other nations such as Australia - the sense of citizenship and now patriotism. Historically, those are important to the survival of any nation. I'm speaking of the same kind of loyalty that helps a high school football team triumph over rivals. Everyone needs personal pride and loyalty to what we invest our energies into, else we flounder."

"Even *more* importantly, what terrorists did to America that day - they also did to their own brethren - placing suspicion on them all! They now *merit* our scrutiny!"

"As for our borders, Ronald Reagan said that 'A nation is defined by its borders'. "We no longer *have* any. We are without a defense at home!

How illogical is it to be fighting a war for national security abroad when our back door is left wide open?

With millions of illegals crossing our borders, we're hemorrhaging horrific expense in the social, medical, ecological, educational and judicial arena! The bleeding must stop, Ken! We have a responsibility to drive out those who hate us, not make it comfortable, or to *fund* them!"

Ken stepped in, asking "So then Sharon, tell us what it is you believe America really has to fear?"

"In spite of the history, and recent news stories from the Sudan, Indonesia, Nigeria, Iraq and worldwide, that detail Muslim brutality and butchery beyond belief, such as the maiming of opposite limbs and women's breasts, videotaped beheadings, and women (never men) killed for adultery, these are not what Americans should fear.

"America's epitaph might be written due to our naive ***ignorance* of the enemy** and the resolve of jihadist to ultimately destroy us.

History and today's newspaper says Islam is a militant religion, not a religion of *peace!*

"Islam simply isn't compatible with other cultures, much less democracy. It's eye is set on world domination, and its followers won't be satisfied until their flag with the sickle and crescent moon flies over our White House!

"Worse, they believe this world domination must be ushered into place by violence, in order for their new messiah (caliph) to be revealed."

America's weakness is wanting to believe the best about everyone, but that philosophy denies the existence of the evil like we saw 9/11/01. We have ignored the first law of warfare, which is "Know your enemy."

"Muslims here and abroad have a blind devotion to *a belief system demanding blood.*

History testifies that they subscribe to the world's worst form of bigotry and intolerance, yet we fail to even acknowledge it and cling to the belief that Islam means *peace.* It doesn't.

"Islam means 'submission.' I know. I've read their handbook.

"There's never been a time in history like this, where Islamic leaders have captured the world's stage, leaping into headlines that parallel even an American President by media. This emboldens them, so they're on a roll with perceived importance in world affairs with their eighth-century wisdom.

"Islamo-Marxism is where our non-Muslim foes are joining with the Muslim world to see our demise as a world leader, such as Russia with Iran over 19 years in nuclear development. China with Iran too. It's happening, and the cost is too high to further delude ourselves it isn't.

"Ken, **there's no glory in my being right here**!"

"Consider we have a world leader in Iran (then) who denies the *first* holocaust while planning the *next!* (Ahmadinijab then!). It's pure insanity! Washington is now so consumed with private agendas- getting re-elected -there is a total vacuum of effective leadership in both parties.

Meantime a third party called 'sharia', is being instituted in Western nations such as the Netherlands, EU, Canada, France, and England. Now 300 finance corporations in the U.S. have already instituted sharia finance! Probably your bank is listed in there! Google it. It's a done deal.

*This is **ALL glorified ignorance!***

"I learned from my Muslim son-in-law that ***strength** is the only thing Muslims respect.*

He and his peers truly believe our nation is stupid and weak! I heard them laugh at us in my own living room! I had to bite my tongue from saying I agreed! This was the mid 80's.

"Even after brutal attacks on 9/11, we fail to stand solidified in demanding a 'civilized response' from them, not even from those Muslims inside the U.S.

"Adlai Stevenson, a democrat, said to the Russian ambassador during the 1962 Cuban Missile crisis, "I'm prepared to stand here until hell freezes over, or you give me an answer!"

Where is that kind of leadership today?

"Wow!" Ken inquired, "Sharon, if what you say is true, and Islam is not the peaceful religion American leaders try to convey, (Like GWB, president then, who first propagated this lie, plus he hosted Muslims at the White House during Ramadan) then why is it they hate us so?"

"The Quran says anyone not a Muslim is an 'infidel'. Muslims hate every Judeo- Christian ethic ye t they envy our prosperity. Our freedom however, is hated due to what they perceive as our *baggage* of moral decay, vulgar conduct, women's rights - thanks largely to Hollywood! In most Muslim cultures, women can't drive, travel without permission from a male relative, see a doctor, or even *beg.*

"But here, our women are a sex object and often showing skin."

During a commercial break, I overheard Ken telling his assistant that callers would be next. I felt ready but *nothing* could prepare me for what I would later dub 'The Denver Mauling'.

Unlike other show hosts, Ken was more interested in ratings than truth. Though I liked talking to callers, I felt these might be belligerent.

A man caller said he'd been in the military in the first Gulf War, and hadn't seen any of the hostility I'd described. I thought - but didn't say - *'Well you should've seen our newspaper reports here then! Saudis didn't even want you soldiers in their cities because you ate 'bacon'. Or defiling their holy sites, Mecca and Medina, where no infidels had walked! (Osama declared war on us for that aspect alone!) Not to mention women dressed in uniform, as men.'*

The second man was a frequent caller in my mind, a misguided Christian who just thought *everybody ought to get along,* and that people like me should be more *loving.*

He hadn't read recent news articles which gave vivid detail about thousands of Sudanese or Nigerian ***Christians*** being slaughtered just for claiming Christ! He certainly hadn't read the same Bible I had, that says – ***there is a time for war so principles matter!***

Or that it was *Jesus* who called phony religious leaders of His day 'sons of hell, whitewashed tombs, fools, hypocrites, and brood of vipers!' Matthew 23. Among other things. The Jesus of the Bible loved righteousness but hated iniquity! Hebrews One.

So much for *this naïve* man's shallow concept of the 'love of God' I was expecting the next caller.

He always said, "One of my best friends/roommates / neighbors/co-workers / brothers-in-law is Muslim, and he's just the *nicest guy!* I'm just glad he didn't hear *this* interview."

I explained most Muslims in the U.S. are what other Muslims call 'Americanized', a term of disdain. Many are indeed warm, and love our country largely because they have greater freedom, *especially of worship*! Their homelands are often 'tribal', that aspect inhibits liberty."

(Americans aren't permitted a manger scene during Christmas. *Nor is it now called Christmas!* Turns out all views are tolerated in the U.S. - except Christian! But I always say God has the final say).

So far, I could've written this script, but then, The next caller was a young gal, a university student who spoke in a shrill voice, while crying, **"I just can't *believe* you!** How could *anyone* with your credentials" (Hold on! I thought. *When* did I purport to have any?) Convinced I hated Muslims, she shrieked that 'Nowhere today did Muslims do beheadings. *That just doesn't happen anywhere!'*

Ignorance, I thought this young woman is in training at a huge American university, where according to David Horowitz who heads Students for Academic Freedom, leftist professors outnumber conservatives seven to one.

Worse, her parents are ***paying for her brainwashing!***

I explained that beheadings do occur, for example, in Saudi Arabi on Friday, their holy day. That's why you didn't see Katie Couric there in an interview, on a Friday. *And* that elegant woman professor dressed in black, that she'd interviewed? (This was about 2004) She didn't answer Katie's pointed questions, because she knew *if she did,* her head would be off the next Friday! (*How shallow and frivolous,* this wonderful and brilliant Saudi woman must have thought Katie to be!)

Ken was now elated; jumping in with comments from time-to-time, interjecting valid data he was no dummy! Just **greedy for ratings.**

The fifth caller, about 45 minutes into the interview, was 'Mohammad' himself. Or at least *a code name for Muslims* who stealthily listen to American talk radio, awaiting those who spoke truth about Islam such as myself, or naïve show hosts. Many of the effective callers are women, who often speak impeccable English.

The men are not so skilled with English however.

After the previous callers, he was primed. He began his tirade about how Sharon was ignorant (and *woman*? Did I hear 'woman'? The Quran teaches that women are inferior in intelligence to men. Read it yourself!) He said that the Quran was 'holy', thus no non- Muslim could understand it *or even touch it* 'unclean' (which also means sex without purification rites before touching the Quran. Interestingly, I didn't touch it. I read it on the internet! You can too.)

I responded, "Mohammad, just learning what I have about the author of the Quran is enough for *me*!" I figured it probably *did* sound like deception to him. It's a rare Muslim who knows Mohammad had 15 wives, one was only nine years old, (bretrothed at age six) or that he feared he was visited by demons! Or that he questioned his own salvation before dying. Muslims weren't permitted to say so, even if they *did know these things*-- under a death sentence! It's against their law for them to speak ill of Mohammad.

Besides, 70% of the world's **Muslims don't even read**. They're only as fresh as their local Imam - local *pastor* to us. Usually jihadists, even here in the U.S.

I sat in my comfortable office chair at home, which I commonly did as a talk-radio show guest, shutting out his tirade. I'd heard it all before! Ken reveled, yet my objective of *getting out the real truth* now seemed obscured!

Mohammad ranted on and now had the 'floor.'

I spoke quietly to God Himself. "God, the only reason I do this, is because I believe you sent me! And now this entire interview is out of control!

So what are YOU going to do about it?" I didn't see this as *my* problem, but *His*.

After Mohammad had had his say, the assistant said something to Ken about a woman caller that made me think she also opposed my message. I later realized the assistant had only said the caller had lived in Saudi. A lovely, mature woman's voice came on the line, which said she'd 'served' in Saudi Arabia. I thought that might have been Foreign Service since her English was impeccable.

When she began, I had no idea where she was going.

"While I lived in Saudi," she began, "They *did* have beheadings there, and *hangings* too! I can verify everything your guest is saying. On one occasion, it even made the newspapers. A university professor was hung while I was there. He spoke against Islam, which is against their law."

I sat completely mute! *Stunned*.

Ken and his assistant *thought* that caller opposed my message.... I had too! But instead, she'd verified every word in an irrefutable way.

Plus, *the hour was up!* No time left for anyone to say anything! How utterly *divine.*

Truth had trumped and had the final word, once again! God is good! Ken thanked me off the air. I noted he didn't ask if any caller had drawn blood!

I was exhausted! This had been a grueling battle of wits! America's ultra liberals and the academic elite think any *open declaration of truth* is 'intolerant' .if it differs from theirs! Our nation is captured by the Politically Correct *thought* police. They're fearful of those who speak truth, while totally ignoring blatant evil, hatred, savagery - and even heinous murder.

If this describes mental instability in an *individual . why nota nation?*

It is **glorified ignorance**! It prevails (and has only gotten worse since this interview!) Yet it's more than that. It's calling *evil good* which brings a curse from God! Isaiah

Says, 'Woe' to those who do so.' *I would have no part of it.*

A caveat here. We must be careful not to see the war against terror as a war against 'people'. I hate Islam, but I LOVE Muslims!

Most Americans get confused on this.

Terrorism is an *idea* with no national boundaries.

It can only be replaced with another higher *idea* - freedom. Trust me when I tell you Muslims long for the freedom that Christ gives -"It is for **freedom** that Christ has made you free" Galatians 5:1. Muslims don't have it. All mankind longs for this freedom, and that's why It has enemies! If Muslims follow the Quran at all - they're in total bondage.

Read it for yourself online in Surahs 2, 3, 9, and 47.

At the time I did this interview and others, our ignorance about Islam was, to me, the greatest threat to America. ***Not anymore***. They could never defeat or overtake us ***unless we imploded from the inside***. In a measure, we have!

There are now a myriad of insoluble problems on our homefront, too innumerable to list here. Only God can help us!

Scripture says when people reject God and His ways, He Himself will raise up an enemy against them. Yes, Friends.

Islam stands poised to take over our nation. Other power hungry ogres, in three-piece suits and hijabs, stand poised in that line as well, using Islam and Fascism to manipulate events and circumstances for their own Global agenda.

Yet *none of them* realize endtime prophecy predicts a global economy, global social system, and a global religion so the above will just be mere pawns who are fulfilling God's grand endtime plan!

(Muslims believe their 12th Imam is the antichrist! –And he *does* ride a white horse! (that's after he rises from a sewer in Iran - I didn't make this stuff up! The devil is a counterfeiter). *Of those mentioned above, global religion* will prove to be most insidious to believers than any other. Watch out! It's the great harlot! It's coming to a church near you, and is already in many, all in disguise as **unity**!

Acid test: If they are not "united" around holy scripture, they're not authentic believers, Dear Friends. They're counterfeit ministers of light. Check out Gal. 1:8 and Paul's message to the intellectuals of his day in II Cor. 11:1-4, 16 Lookout!

To unbelievers the future sucks! But believers can dwell in peace then. Ps 46. A great pouring out of His Spirit on all flesh is coming, just like Peter told us in Acts 2:17 with, gifts and miracles accompanying it, because it's time to harvest souls... Get prepared!

Have a 30 day defense according to www.ready.gov- As you should for any emergency emergency such as hurricanes or power outages.

Don't quit reading now! There's more hope than discouragement waiting for *you*. And inspiration.

One man with God is always a majority.
John Knox.

The brave may not live long,
but the cautious don't live at all.
Unknown

He made my mouth like a sharp sword; in
the shadow of his hand he hid me.
Isaiah 49:2

This generation of believers is responsible
for this generation of souls.
Keith Green

32

A New Day Dawning

I was scheduled to renew my best hotel in Alabama, about a five hour drive from Rhonda's home and where I lived in Tennessee then. But when I got up on Monday to make the drive, there was seven inches of snow on the ground! This, where people will look at you with a straight face and say, *"Oh it doesn't get bad here."* They all *lie...*

Besides, if it's under 70°, I'm cold.

And I don't do *snow*! The only way I want to see snow is when I fly over it, or on top of the Rockies. So I delayed leaving for the hotel because, while Tennessee is wonderful, they've never heard of 'salt'.

A bigger problem in this matter is, I've never been able to fully convince Rhonda and Randy that *I'm* not lying that there was that much snow on the ground that week!

They were off in Hawaii.

On Rhonda's way back from the downward spiral that she took over those years 'doing her own thing' like most of us have - Rhonda had proven herself in many ways.

While she worked cleaning houses in Indiana, she organized a man's house and closets so well, he asked her if she'd come to his office and do the same. She organized his files, file cabinets, supply closets and desk drawers. Then he asked her to stay on part time... then full time. John loved the golf course more than he liked sitting in an office! Before long, she was functioning as an administrator, running a fifteen-million dollar corporation!

Moving to Tennessee when her husband got a new job, she wondered what she'd do there. Soon, she was working for the doctor who provided them the *free* trip to Hawaii to help him with a conference. Though she fought health issues and terrible allergies in pollen-rich Middle Tennessee then, she did well for a couple of years. More recently, she's lobbied effectively on matters important to the horse industry and motorcycle safety on a state and national level.

After several years of my living there, Florida kept calling me. But I feared moving back, because I thought I might miss my family terribly, and regret the move. But God assured me Through my sweet pastor that it was He Who was leading, so I moved back.

After all, *I have saltwater for blood*, and the only romance I have is with palm trees! And maybe seabirds. I doubt there's been a day I haven't thanked God for bringing me *home.*

I'm retired now, the happiest I've ever been.

I loved my business but it was stressful with deadlines. Retirement is wonderful! Here I want to focus on a man from whom I've learned most about *love.*

Me – ***a loveless creature.*** Speaking of 'Love', I must add here sadly, that after 17 years Rhonda and Randy have parted ways. It happens because people grow in a marriage... but sometimes they grow in different directions - apart.

I don't know him personally, but I do know he had a tempestuous streak - which is incongruous with what I just said! Nevertheless, *I learned to love through him!* He's no longer with us, but the writing he left behind shows he knew more about love than his peers! He was the youngest of them, and yet left his mark of being one of the most knowledgeable of spiritual matters.

Admittedly, I told a friend I don't feel qualified to write this chapter, yet the deficit in understanding among believers of the *Love of God* is astonishing.

So I want you to see *new things.* A new day is dawning in the church, so I direct this to all true believers. See II Peter 2 and II Cor. 11:1-4. I truly cherish them!

John's gospel proves the things I said above along with his three letters, and the book of Revelation. Yes, I'm speaking of the Apostle John because his words have changed me inside out. *You too will be amazed!*

No doubt our highest calling is *to love.* That comes right after the calling to be holy, without which no man shall see God! We don't really take that first one too seriously....

God took a man whom Jesus dubbed 'son of thunder', and taught him love. So there's hope for us all!

Believers think we should love everyone the same - believer and unbeliever alike! *Not!*

The Bible teaches just the opposite. Love among brethren must be something visible.

Observable. The church is fuzzy here.

The night that Jesus was arrested, He told His disciples He had something 'new' to share with them. But the church treats what he shared that night before being crucified, as *more of the second commandment* to 'love our neighbor as ourselves.'

This is the New Commandment *no one ever talks about!* John 13:34,35

The "***new*** commandment I give you, that you love one another as I have loved you" is a *higher* commandment. Jesus wants us to love, in the same measure He loved us - that He would demonstrate by laying down His very life the next day. Jesus went on to define it. By THIS *kind* of love, "**shall all men know** that YOU are my disciples IF you love one another."

Said backwards, "Few men will know you're my disciples *if you don't love each other with this kind of love!"*

Indeed, scripture - especially John - proclaims Love as God's Agent of Change!

God designed the church to be "family". Jesus is the eldest among many 'brethren' and God is the Father.... "Our Father" Jesus prayed.

Much of the world lacks *real* family these days, so the term strikes a chord in those *looking for one*! Their own families are often split, broken, missing, or dysfunctional, alcoholic - like mine. (CALLING each other 'Brother' is only 'religious'). The love among 'brethren' should woo people, causing them to *want to belong; touching their heartstrings as it did mine in that little Presbyterian church so long ago.* We all need family and all the more as the day draws nigh. So let's look at Biblical *Love* -

John used the word 'love' (or synonyms like loved, loves, etc) 55 times in his gospel. By contrast, Luke uses it only 14 times in his gospel, and not at all in the book of Acts - though it is *implied* there.

In his little letter of I John -only 5 chapters long - John uses 'love' 47 times.

John reveals the ministry of the Holy Spirit in chapters 14-16 of his gospel. Seventeen times in his gospel, he reveals that Jesus is The Great ***I AM***, (ego ami In Greek) which is God's name in the Greek Septuagint when Moses asks God, whom shall I say sent me?

God said, **I AM that I AM.** (Ego Ami).

Before that time, no one knew God's name. They only knew to speak something that Sounded like a whisper, "*Yahh*," and when they spoke it, they fasted until nightfall!

Lately, I have noted that a lot of New Agers are using the I AM in order to obtain Fulfilment, chanting "I am healthy,

I am wise, I am wealthy – or such. You hear this in Texas, South Carolina and especially in California. Seems to be a little dangerous, this.

Saying, I AM in this fashion is sort of like......declaring You. Are. God.

When soldiers came to the garden looking to arrest Him, Jesus said **I AM**, (‘*he*’ is not in the Greek but Ego Ami is), and *the entire company fell backwards*!

Deity was present in John 18:6.

Only John conveys the deity of Christ in John 1:1-14. Jesus is the *object of worship* in John 4:21-26, 20:28; and the Bread of Life; the Door; the True Vine; the Good Shepherd; the Light of the World; the Way, Truth and Life; and the Resurrection and the Life, and Before Abraham was, I am.

“Ego ami” is used in each of these titles! John listened well.

These claims of deity are WHY Pharisees and Jewish leaders wanted to kill Jesus

Jesus accepted worship. Plus the fact He forgave sins, both were *forbidden* in the Old Testament unless you happened to be God!

Only John teaches *our conflict without* is the world, the flesh, and the devil. That *our conflict within* is the pride of life, the lust of the flesh and the lust of the eyes! And it’s the Holy Spirit that convinces us of *sin, righteousness and judgment.*

Only John repeatedly referred to himself as ‘the disciple whom Jesus loved’ in his gospel, seemingly enthralled with knowing Jesus. He didn’t do so later on.

John, Peter and James were given special privileges not given other disciples, at the transfiguration, and the raising of the dead and elsewhere. He details seven miracles, five of which are only in his gospel. He told of Jesus’ humanness in hunger, thirst, weariness, pain and death. It was John who told us our need to be twice born.

John was the only disciple at the cross. It was there Jesus entrusted the care of His beloved mother to John's care, a trustworthy 'son of thunder'.

John had a house in Jerusalem and lived there until 65ad. Then Paul sent him to Ephesus. Paul died about 67AD, Nero in 68AD; the temple in Jerusalem was destroyed in 70AD. It was from Ephesus, in one of the Roman uprisings apparently, John was taken to Rome and boiled in oil, per historian Josephus. Yet John emerged unscathed.

I'm guessing that's why John was exiled to the Isle of Patmos. He wrote it was due to his 'word and for the testimony'. Patmos is where he received Revelation concerning end time events. Where Jesus beckoned, "Come up higher." John lived the longest of all the disciples, to 96AD. Tradition says he too was martyred. It doesn't say *how*.

Journey with me, if you will for a moment, into John's life, realizing he must have experienced and understood the love of God in a special way to write of it as he did. Note he often quoted Jesus on that topic! Too, his understanding was a product of knowing Jesus, as the Express Image of God -Who is *Love*. Heb 1:3.

So John is in his old age, having followed Christ since his youth, having been a 'pillar' in the church at Jerusalem, a leader of the church of Ephesus, having seen his peers die tragically, having suffered persecution for his own faith and work of God, now on the Isle of Patmos. Apparently alone but in the company of God.

Revelation begins with John writing he was 'in the Spirit on the Lord's day' fellowshipping with the Father - Who hadn't abandoned him.

God's eye was upon John that day. He was ready to do something *new*.

John heard a loud voice *like a trumpet* behind him on a deserted island where no trumpets were! And the voice instructed him to *write* to the seven churches of Asia, starting with his home church, Ephesus.

When John turned to see the voice. *What he saw was someone* LIKE the Son of Man (how Jesus always referred to Himself), yet John couldn't believe his eyes! THIS man - his dear Friend, was adorned like a Priest and a Judge, in a white robe with a golden sash.

Was *this Jesus*? It *sort of* looked like Him, but...?

Jesus' hair was white as snow; His eyes were as a flame of fire. Most unfamiliar was His voice - it sounded like the roar of many waters! He held seven stars in His right hand ; a sharp two-edged sword came from His mouth.

His face shone like the sun in full strength! John couldn't fully gaze upon Him!

Do I know this man, he wondered?

The answer to that question is, Yes and No - *for all of us!*

Because we embrace what we perceive Jesus to be - yet are miles apart from the true awareness of His power and magnificence!

Just like John- who unlike us, knew Jesus *in the flesh!*

John said, "When I saw Him, *I fell at his feet* ***as though dead.***"

But Jesus touched him, "Fear not, I am the first and the last, and the living one. I died and behold I am alive forevermore. (and by the way John, I have the keys to Hell and Death." - my paraphrase!)

Friends, what happens when we come face to face with the true and living God?

We fall on our face! What does that mean? Worship!..... translated 'to fall down prostrate before', or 'worthship.' In Hebrew *Shaw Ha*...to bow down.

The first mark of true worship is always *humility.*

The advent of new worship conferences throughout major cities are too often counterfeit. *Why?* Because people are not taught they must **repent!** People are only acceptable to God when we have been washed in Jesus' blood – *without the shedding of blood there is no forgiveness of sin.* (Sorry if that makes you flinch – Remember, you are *not in charge!*) Fear of the Lord is the beginning of knowledge and wisdom. Just the beginning...

People presume they can enter into worship before a Holy God Who sits on a throne from which fire and smoke and lightning flash, a rainbow rises out of it, while seraphim with six wings, each wing 30 feet in diameter circle about that throne, surrounded by 24 Elders who are also seated on thrones. Not to mention countless angels everywhere. We don't have to fear... but His holiness demands our due respect!

He. Is. Not. *Like.* Us! Worship in Greek means *"to fall down prostrate before."* Everyone who saw God in the scripture did this.... You can see ***why!*** His name was too holy to speak until Moses. **He is Holy**...and *without* ***holiness*** *no man shall see God.* The NEW Testament says that in Hebrews 12:14.

People oversimplify the Love of God, often defining it as sappy. No. It is fierce. It is hot. It is passionate. One thing it isn't? Clinical. You can't cut it up and define it.

I have sat in groups where people's concept of 'love' is so shallow, they think all we must do is *love.* That if we *just love* everyone, they'll somehow gravitate their way to God.

Others fear being thought to 'judge'- because it isn't their version of *Love.*

Love necessarily serves as God's *invitation* to enter via the door of repentance to the presence of a holy God! But Jesus said, "unless you repent, you will all likewise perish." Luke 13:5. A 'change of mind' is required!

Friends, this is an anemic gospel, too impotent to make a difference anywhere! Even other believers! Galatians 6 and

Matthew 18 tell us how to restore a brother in sin. Yes, we can and should! If you keep silent so you won't *hurt* someone's feelings, you may be paving the way for them to ***coast into hell!***

Don't be guilty of their blood on your hands because you didn't warn them, Friends!

See Ezekiel 3 and 33; Acts 20:26;27 and 18:6.

Remember Paul's words in Col.1:29, "Him we proclaim, **warning every man**."

Of what? Hell is a real destination to those who reject Christ's penalty paid for each of our sins.

The idea that love is 'enough' is pure fallacy. *Love* is the "Why" of heaven; the gospel message is the "What" Jesus had to die to satisfy the demands of a Holy God.

There simply was no other way!

Else God would be a cruel fool to demand Jesus die after pleading "if there be another way."

Love serves as an unbelievers' introduction to the loving nature of God, whom satan has convinced is hard and cruel! But the "DOOR", Jesus said a holy God demands we see our barrenness - hopelessness so that we repent!

A Eukranian friend recently gave me a publication in English. It said revival is breaking out everywhere, except in America. Why? An interview penned in it with a Chinese missionary may have the answer!

Visiting many American churches, he was asked what he thought after. He answered, "I am amazed at how much the church in America can accomplish **without** *the Holy Spirit.*"

Jesus said in John 15 that we can do nothing of eternal value – without His help!

The path of redemption requires the foolishness of preaching, preaching empowered by the Holy Spirit. The gospel is 'the power of God unto salvation unto those who *believe.*'

Repentance is necessary!

This is why the fiery preaching of Billy Graham, Reinhard Bonnke and others is so effective!

This error is mostly among baby Christians ignorant of scripture, because churches are made up of people who don't know scripture! It leaves the fallen and broken absent instruction, drowning in the sin Jesus died for.

Our job is not to judge. *Our job is* **to lift a standard** and summon people to it, because 'all scripture is inspired, and profitable for teaching, for reproof, for correction, and training in righteousness." II Tim. 3:16.

But don't dismiss I Cor. 5 where Paul says we **must** judge those inside the church!

When there is sin in the house, it must be named! Granted, babies don't like this and will probably call it judging. *Do it anyway, because* **THIS is *Love***! Love that cares about others and realizes *truth* still liberates!

Jesus warned, "Do not think that I have come to bring peace to the earth. I have not come to bring peace, but a sword." A sword divides light from darkness, and the sword is holy scripture. Matt.10:34.

Don't even think it!

I was astonished when I found that the Book of Acts did not the word LOVE in it once. But God didn't want to confuse the issue between 'power' and 'love' so **Acts is a book of *power*.** It requires both love and power to win the Lost.

The first recorded words of John the Baptist in Luke are - "You brood of vipers!" John must have been super harsh to use such language. Oh wait! Jesus said the same and much, much more in Matthew 23. Jesus named sin, and the Apostle Paul named sinners. Also John and Peter. Let us grow up!

Corrie ten Boom knew the fierceness of evil in Ravensbruck. She needed more than a wimpy Jesus (He's the Lion of Judah who hates iniquity!) She daily faced the darkest of the human heart in that concentration camp. If we don't love and counsel *people* with passion against the darkness in their lives, the devil is left to run rampant over them!

Sloppy agape is *impotent!* It's the 'why' without the 'what' or **the power to change**! It's a warm attitude without any content! Betsy said, "There is no pit so deep, that God's love is not deeper still."

Redeeming Love is fierce because the cost of it was so high! And it is too 'principled' to compromise on its mission of holiness.

Don't be a people too empty to be effective witnesses. Broken people need God's power to walk out of bondage!

A final thought about *Love's main objective in our lives..*

John begins Revelation saying, "To Him who loves us and has freed us from our sins by His blood, and made us a kingdom, priests to His God."

Believers are 'made a kingdom' **'priests to His God'** to initiate the presence of God in people's lives! Priests intercede. Priests intervene. They stand between a holy God and sinful man to intervene! It's OUR ROLE. We're a holy priesthood! What a privilege!

If we don't grasp what Biblical love is, HOW can we ever convey it to a lost and dying world to whom we're called? A hungry and hurting world awaits you with outstretched hands.

But, there's another kind of 'love'.

I'm going to say here what others won't. Most churches do not represent the risen Christ today. Instead they feed their flocks with a feel good, junkfood doctrine - a crossless Christianity! Itching ears doctrine!

Too many reject Christ's deity and the grace of God, adding to the scriptures instead!

Apostates' only fruit is death to every life-giving venture of God! They aren't interested in souls **just tithers and converts.** They' re driven by winds *of every doctrine.*

These aren't a legitimate part of the Body of Christ! Cults posing as real churches are prolific, on street corners everywhere! Read Phil. 3:1-3 to find how Paul defines true believers! Then check out www.carm.org. This is a reliable Christian Apologetics Research Ministry. The true gospel is it's Jesus + nothing.

Much of the church today is a ship on the high seas, driven by the wind -absent a rudder for guidance . Thus the ship is tilting to one side. Programs like Purpose Driven Church franchising churches, even changing the 'language' of older churches, have people jumping off, disenfranchised by the very churches they've previously served, funded and loved.

Jude says, false teachers are like wild waves thrashing. Their harvest is destruction.

These are busy building a kingdom unto themselves, not the Kingdom of God! Real believers are left dry and thirsty, confused, disenfranchised. It is to YOU I write!

Here is how to recognize apostate churches and pastors who don't subscribe to scripture.

Words. Empty words. All talk, no walk! "The Kingdom of God does not consist in word, But in POWER," per I Cor. 4:20. It matters not the brand of error - and there are 'many' - there's no power, no changed lives as is seen when the true gospel is preached.

Just words. And new programs or a new edifice as a legacy to their ministry.

These *do* talk a lot about *love* - but it's sappy weakness and intellectual emptiness. Can I tell you that **'nice' is not a fruit of the Spirit**?

Have you ever had a warning about Love...? Well, this is it! And this is why... This counterfeit kind of **love** that tolerates *every*thing will be used, along with **unity**, in the Banner for the One World Order religion portion! It already is, in fact, with books and pastors pushing for meshing Christians with the Catholic faith and Islam. Chrislam. This banner is being prepared for the antichrist and if you embrace this phony **love** and **unity**, you will be deceived. Jesus even says so in Matthew 24:24. And this is that path to deception.

If Paul says he "warns every man," let me say, get off that ship before it sinks! If Apostle Paul warns every man, get off that ship before it sinks!

That's the *organized* church - but the real church is an *organism* and Jesus Christ is the head of that church. That's *us*-ecclesia in Greek meaning *the called out ones!* From WHAT? The world, and in this case - the organized church as it moves closer to endtimes.

You have been warned, Dear Reader.

God will help you find a true church family. Wait on Him.

A new day for the church is dawning. Look for pockets of Glory, bound to the Word in Love, with signs following.

Truth always carries with it, confrontation. Truth demands confrontation; loving confrontation nevertheless.
Dr. Francis Schaeffer

"The chief danger of the 20th century will be: Religion without the Holy Ghost, Christianity without Christ, forgiveness without repentance, salvation without regeneration, heaven without hell."
William Booth, Salvation Army

33

Answers By Fire

In the 20th century, a Purdue University excavation from the prophet Elijah's era, unearthed the remains of infants in jars that were built into the wall. Writings from that period showed these were considered a blessing to the home, to bring 'good luck'.

Babies sacrificed today in our nation's abortion mills are often done, so that older siblings may have 'better luck'.

Seven hundred years B.C. the prophet Elijah felt he stood alone in a decadent society where the sacrifice of infants and nude dancing weren't just accepted - they were part of the worship service! These same excavations revealed Baal images found with exaggerated sex organs. Worship ceremonies were rituals of immoral indulgence that included human sacrifice. These excavations didn't occur *in some pagan culture.* They were made in *Israel*, at Megiddo, in the stratum of King Ahab.

It was God's own people who stooped to such practices, led by the king!

The spiritual climate in Elijah's day was so bad, 850 false prophets daily ate at the table of Jezebel, King Ahab's wife, as the official murderers of children! Scripture says that King

Ahab did more evil to provoke the Lord to anger than all the kings of Israel before him.

Considering there was not one godly king out of 20 in Israel, and only five in 20 of Judah, that's really saying something!

But don't get any ideas that America is off the hook; *we have 60 million aborted babies to account for!!*

How to explain this terrible history of God's people?

It is that **God says He has placed eternity in our hearts**! So if we don't worship Him, we will worship *something!* That 'something' is other gods!

Today, surveys show many people ascribe to being 'spiritual', but not religious. That spirituality is aimed toward New Age, Taoism, Tai Chi, Astrology, Buddhism, Hinduism, superstition, occultism, materialism, technology and science and an entire plethora of other false gods. Which is why God said, 'You shall have no other gods before me.'

It's the first Commandment. There **are** other gods!

Dad died. Jenny was visiting Florida about two months later. Her family thought the trip might lift her spirits as she'd taken Dad's death very hard.

She told me that night of how fearful Dad had always been of dying. Eventually he made her quit her part time job. He would hardly permit her to grocery shop as he feared he would have a coughing spasm and die in her absence (emphysema).

He didn't want to die alone.

However, all that had changed she said, about six weeks before he died.

That statement caused me to catch my breath!

She went on to say he no longer seemed to care where she went or how long she was gone. She couldn't account for what had happened.

Only that, *he'd changed.*

During the previous summer in my visit to see Rhonda and Krista, I'd been in a hurry to get back home. I'm glad I listened to Rhonda, who coaxed me to take the time to go see Dad on a Sunday morning before leaving to drive back. Dad lived a long drive from Rhonda's house and it was out of my way. I didn't want to take the time. I did.

"It might be the last time you ever see him." She said.

Dad sat on the side of a rented hospital bed. I sat down on the other side at the foot of it facing him. Jenny fretted over Dad as usual. He and I played with the little bulldog terrier puppies they were dog sitting.

Though on oxygen, Dad seemed jovial and happy to see me.

My intent was to talk privately with Dad, and perhaps pray with him. But I'm not one to force circumstances, and it didn't work out that way.

Oddly enough though, Dad and I did discuss 'hypocrisy' that day. He seemed to think there were too many of them; some in the family!

I assured him there were genuine believers in spite of it. He nodded and seemed pacified then.

Before leaving, I gave him a hug. I also handed him a couple of tracts I'd made, telling him I'd written them, hoping it would prompt him to read them.

One tract cover had a tiny boy in a yellow raincoat looking up, saying "Looks Like Rain". Dad loved children. It discussed being prepared for the coming storms of life, and that we need a safe harbor before they arrive.

When Jenny said what she did that night, my final memory of Dad immediately came to mind, of the day I'd visited him. Jenny had wanted to show me her flowers. Preparing to leave, I'd walked through the house to the back porch with her. When I returned, I stopped in the middle of the living room to wave farewell to Dad, who still sat on the bed.

He only glanced up, his gaze fixed intently on the tracts he still held in his hand.

Dad's fear of dying apparently brought him to the end of himself. Perhaps the words inside those tracts awakened a memory of Mom's own words to him as she died - that *she wasn't afraid to die,* and *why.*

Jenny's words confirmed what I already believed. Dad had joined Mom in Heaven.

Apparently Dad had prayed the prayer of salvation at the end of those tracts.

That explained why he suddenly had no more *fear of dying! She said this* was six weeks before he died.

I remembered an interview of Billy Graham by Johnny Carson I saw one time. Johnny asked Billy, "What about deathbed salvations? Do you believe in them?" Billy replied, "Well, no one knows the human heart except God. But if a person is sincere according to Romans 10:9, then sure, I believe they can be saved.

He continued, "However, it's not God's best! It's a *soul salvaged.* God would have us live for Him from our youth, and make a difference in our world."

James wasn't my father, but like Mom, I tried to honor him *as that* as long as he lived. His name was on my birth certificate.

One time, **two men dined near me in a restaurant** where I dined alone. I thought they might be professional ball players by their tee shirts, physique, and the new Corvette they drove away in. Their voices could be heard by anyone within earshot. They were discussing children. One lamented he rarely saw his son since the boy was now out of state, a result of divorce.

Rising to leave, the man tossed a tip onto the table.

With feeling, he said, "Here I am, raising a stranger's children!"

I realized the irony of this scene was in light of two parent homes in general. This man was part of a two parent home - highly desired in society -but the real fact of the matter was, he was raising another man's children *while unable to even see his own!* Though a two-parent family, they weren't the original set of parents.

America has virtually abandoned its children, parents in pursuit of personal fulfillment, pleasure and 'happiness'. The result? *Unhappiness in amplified proportions,* especially for the children. Broken people. Broken families. Broken homes. It's more prevalent in society than it isn't! Paul warned us though that in end times people would be 'lovers of pleasure more than lovers of God.'

We're there, Friends. End times, that is!

Question. Given the climate of divorce etc in our world, is there any hope for America's children who feel disenfranchised *from their own families,* fathers missing and live-in boyfriends who often occupy the master bedroom with no real commitment, often abusing the children? *(Been there, Done that).* Or, for the fathers who are shoved to the side, showing their own children father's are totally 'expendable', at the mother's whim?

Well, scripture says things will be put right at the end. Injustices made just. Wrongs made right. Evil punished. But Jesus promised more. *If indeed we DO actually live in endtimes.* Jesus said Elijah will come to restore all things; and 'turn the hearts of the fathers to the children, and the hearts of the children to the fathers.'

I am one among multitudes who grew up the product of divorce, but I'm fortunate because countless others didn't make it past the local abortion mill. I barely did myself! (Back alley abortions were prolific - Mom almost bled to death from one when I was five years old).

Elijah will come and '**restore all things before the Day of the Lord.'**

Jesus said this in Matthew 17 and in Mark 9.... Funny thing about Elijah is, he never died.

He was swept into heaven in a *chariot of fire.* Jesus also told the disciples Elijah had already come in the form of John the

Baptist. That explains why Luke 1:17 says the 'spirit of Elijah' was upon John the Baptist!

Will that same spirit rest upon servants of God before Jesus comes?

Looking for similarities between Elijah and John the Baptist, I discovered a common denominator. Both ministered in relationships. Elijah *may well come* and 'restore all things' but I tend to read it as, 'restore all things *relational*'. Here's why...

The last verse in the Old Testament tells us Elijah comes before the Day of the Lord, 'turning the hearts' that is *relational.* When John the Baptist told Herod he couldn't have his brother's wife, Herodias that is *relational.*

She was the reason that Herod ended up beheading John, tricked by Herodias.

Little is known about Elijah, whose name means *Yahweh is God.* He was profoundly named to turn the hearts of Israel to the only living and true God! Like John The Baptist, he wore skins, ate locusts and honey. His appearance must have been fierce, as his people were sheepherders and outdoorsmen.

Consider when Elijah appeared at the palatial palace of Ahab - on a mission from God - strolling through the courtyards, then appearing before King Ahab on his throne, (unannounced which was a penalty of death then) wearing royal robes.

Elijah must have appeared mad to observers!

What's worse was Elijah's message! A pronouncement of a coming drought.. a judgment from God because of Ahab's own deeds: *He'd abandoned the commandments of the Lord, and followed other Gods.* (This is sobering to me - think of America!)

Some people thought Jesus *was* Elijah! That's because Elijah was known for miracles and prayer. And because his was the last name anybody had heard from God in hundreds of years, at the end of Malachi.

God wasn't talking to an adulterous people who'd turned their back on Him! The result was they had been taken into captivity by foreign nations.

Besides, *they hadn't listened when God last spoke to them* which was **why they were in captivity** to begin with.

Ironically, when God *did* send Jesus? Jesus lamented people didn't recognize their *day of visitation.* Many say that God is going to judge America. Yes, He will! But it's not time for that yet. It's harvest time, and USA has always sponsored 90% of missions worldwide...think how many souls that is to God, Worldwide over 240 years!

Friends, **we have to know what time it is! It's Harvest time...**

Today in the U.S., God is no longer welcome anywhere in the public square; schools, the marketplace, courthouses, public arena and and many churches themselves deny Jesus or that 'God was in Christ reconciling the world unto Himself,' as scripture proclaims. Our nation has chased 'other gods'.

The life-sized bull on Wall Street says we are no different than Israelites worshipping the *golden calf*! (It's bronze color)

I know very intelligent people who argue that America was never founded on Judeo- Christian principles. Apparently they don't travel, because a trip to the U.S. Supreme Court would reveal Moses was once important to some founders because, a lifesize figure hangs over the entrance, holding the Ten Commandments!

The doors themselves are covered with those Ten Commandments themselves. Inside, it's the same. Or they're ignorant of the fact the House of Representatives has had a PAID chaplain since 1877 who opens sessions with prayer. Or with Plymouth Rock.

I know another man who loudly proclaims Ben Franklin was a Nazi! *Hello*? This man calls himself a Marxist and worked for a powerful congressman.

Ignorance is so very rampant these days. Brains Matter.™ This protest in our nation is not just unbelief.

"Their venom is only exceeded by their ignorance." Laurence Leamer. It's complete *rebellion against God!*

Does Elijah's judgment spoken to Ahab belong to the U.S. today?

Is that why Elijah must come and turn hearts, especially concerning our broken homes? Does our prolific divorce rate and our children play a role...?

California, our most liberal state and over the top into New Age, at this writing, 2013 was their driest year in history. Hosts of grasshopper 'clouds' often appear on weather screens. Is this an oncoming plague?

Did I mention that California is also a state where many teachers present the five pillars of Islam in classrooms, endorsing the wearing of birkas by girls, and teaches prayer to Allah? Colorado too. It has spread to the East Coast as well.

But just try mentioning the Name of Jesus, or praying to HIM, or find a manger scene at Christmas in the public square!!

After three years with no rain whatsoever, God told Elijah to come out of hiding and meet with Ahab. Funny thing is that Elijah was hidden in Jezebel's hometown!

That is comical and so like our God!

When Ahab saw him, his greeting was, "Is it you, you troubler of Israel?" But Elijah said, "You are the troubler of Israel, Ahab." (This is like our critics, who blame us for **their** own poor choices).

Then Elijah told him rain was coming, but first to gather all Israel and the 850 prophets of Baal and Asherah (Baal's female counterpart) for him to address the people on Mount Carmel. Ahab did so... *anything for rain at this point!*

Elijah came near to the people and called, "**How long will you halt between two opinions? If the Lord is God, follow Him; if Baal, follow him**."

Then he requested two bulls be chosen, one for the 450 prophets of Baal, and one for him. Place the bull on the altar and then "the God who **answers by fire**, he is God."

All the people answered, "It is well spoken."

Prophets of Baal called upon their god from morning until noon with no results, even though they yelled and cut themselves to blood, petitioning him.

At noon *Elijah mocked them,* (Now is this Christian?) saying their god might be out to lunch or asleep. Then they carried on until 3pm that day. No results.

Elijah then prepared his offering and dug a trench, then filled it all around with wood and twelve barrels of *water* until it ran all around the altar. (Elijah knew it would rain, but everybody else must have thought he was *crazy to use all this water during a drought*).

Then Elijah prayed, "O Lord, God of Israel, let it be known this day that **you are God in Israel, that I am your servant, and that I have done all these things at your bidding.** Answer me, O Lord, answer me, so that this people may know that you, O Lord, are God, and *you have turned their hearts back*.. Then the fire fell, licking up all the wood and water.

When the people saw it, they said, *"The Lord, He is God"* - *"The Lord, He is God."*

Read the story in I Kings 18 for yourself, and see how Elijah later prayed seven times for rain. When it came, *'there was a* ***great*** *rain."*

The story didn't end there. It seems Jezebel had other plans that day, and missed out on this great scene. She put out an edict that Elijah should be dead by sunset the next day.

Elijah ran for his life, literally!

He had called fire down from heaven, but one puny woman's threat pulverized him, which may be why James says in the New Testament that he was a man of 'like passions as we are.' Yet Elijah got the last *word.*

I have met many people over the years who are fascinated by the life of Elijah, as I am.

I believe the reason is: Power. Passion. The Fiery Response! Or perhaps it was **that God answered his prayers**!

"For the eyes of the LORD roam to and fro over the earth, to show Himself strong on behalf of those whose heart is full devoted to Him. 2 Chronicles 16:9

What's more, in endtimes we're told, "those who know their God will be strong and do exploits." Dan. 11:32. If you're not these, you may fit into the first part. Read it.

Today, the whole earth is yearning for restoration a release from death and bondage. In fact, Romans 8 says all of *creation* '**groans**' for the revealing of a certain kind of sons of God. The *Spirit* **groans** within us. And *we also* **groan**.

All travail for a new day and those who bring it to *life!*

Are YOU one of them?

More, people groan to have their prayers answered like Elijah did! And God waits to answer their prayers!

He can't always do that though, because his people have dirty hands, loaded with materialism and unconfessed sin. Others are loaded with self-absorption and worldliness and pride. Idolatry! See Is. 59:2 His arm is not shortened...

But I promise you if you will obey His commandments, repent, and seek to do what pleases Him - **you too will see Answers By Fire in your life**.

God has a plan for your life, and no one can fulfill it but you, Dear One. The world, your world, is diminished without YOUR labors to bring forth new life!

God seeks servants who will *love others more than they hate their sin* the outcasts, the lame, the unlovable, the rejected and socially unacceptable - homeless, pimps, prostitutes, alcoholics, despised and drug addicts.

Like John the Baptist and Elijah, there's a fierceness about these servants that'll speak against unrighteousness, calling for repentance - even if theirs is the only voice!

They 'love not their lives unto death...' Rev. 12:11

These are ordinary people who will carry out His extraordinary plan. It is ***they*** that will call forth the latter rains upon a dry and parched land, because they know *nothing happens until something is spoken.*

They've learned the faith of God, which is to 'call those things that be not as though they are.' They're bold as a lion and worship Him wholly with reckless abandon, aglow with the Spirit. (Worship is best defined by humility! It means to "bow" or "fall prostrate before." Beware of counterfeit, feel good worship out there!!)

Flambeauant.

The banner they bear will tout a *Kingdom principle* - "The Kingdom of God does not consist in *word*, but in power." I Cor. 4:20 and Mark 16:20

They say what Jesus said in John 10:37 "If I don't do the works, then don't believe a word I say!" (My paraphrase). *Can you say that*? I want to.

They are given to prayer, seizing the hem of Jesus' garment, insisting that God bring *His* answers. Much like Elijah, I have prayed, 'Let it be known this day that you are God, *that I am your servant, and that I have done all these things at your bidding.*

Answer me, O Lord, answer me, so that this people may know that you - *You have turned their hearts back'*

Answers by Fire.

Below is a prayer I love because it's the cry of my own heart. It was first prayed by Missionary Jim Elliot, recorded in his journal, just days before he was martyred by the same Auca Indians that he attempted to reach with the gospel. His wife Elizabeth and daughter went back and did so with his murderer as her chief aid. An extraordinary and true story!

> *"I have prayed for new men, fiery, reckless men; these lit by the Spirit of God I have prayed for new words, explosive, direct, simple words I have prayed for new miracles; Explaining old miracles will not do. If God is to be known as the God who does wonders in heaven and earth, then God must produce for this generation. Lord, fill preachers with thy power. How long dare we go on without tears, without* moral passions, hatred and love? *Not long, I pray Lord Jesus, not long"*
> Jim Elliot, 1947 Jim must have loved Elijah.
>
> I am one of them...

Dear Reader:

Please visit www.RainDancing101.com for further information. Sharon's Book in print is available at Amazon, and other fine booksellers.

Also, look for her new site HerestoYOU.org which will be published soon. She is planning HerestoYOU-Image Conferences in the next year.

You can learn all about them at this website...

If you have any questions or comments, please email Sharon at: SharonJackson@www.RainDancing101.com.

Or, you may call 727-824-7740

Thank You.

And Thank You for reading this book.
I am always honored when people do!
I pray it blessed and encouraged you...

Sharon Jackson

"Why... we have people at our church who are
former pimps, prostitutes, addicts, alcoholics,
homosexuals.... and that's just the *staff*!"
Tommy Barnett, Author, Pastor

Printed in Great Britain
by Amazon